PILGRIM WAYS

*To my late mother and father
and to all who have passed this way before;
and for my children, Marianne, Padraig,
Philip and James, as they undertake their own
pilgrim's progress.*

DAVID ALTON

Pilgrim Ways

A Personal Guide to Catholic Pilgrimage Sites in Britain and Ireland

ST PAULS

Also by David Alton

What Kind of Country? (1987)
Whose Choice Anyway? (1989)
Faith in Britain (1991)
Signs of Contradiction (1996)
Life After Death (1997)
Citizen Virtues (1998)
Citizen 21 (2001)

Cover photo: Iona Abbey (Scottish Viewpoint)

ST PAULS Publishing
187 Battersea Bridge Road, London SW11 3AS, UK
www.stpauls.ie

Copyright © ST PAULS UK 2001

ISBN 085439 605 5

Set by Tukan DTP, Fareham, UK
Printed by Interprint Ltd., Marsa, Malta

ST PAULS is an activity of the priests and brothers
of the Society of St Paul who proclaim the Gospel
through the media of social communication

Contents

Stand at the crossroads and look.
Ask for the ancient paths,
Ask where the good way is,
And walk upon it,
And you will find rest for your souls.

Jeremiah 6.16

Introduction

ON the last day of the last year of the last millennium I made a short visit to Glastonbury – where Christianity made its first mark on our islands. As we stood in the ruins of the abbey my daughter, Marianne, asked me what happened to the buildings and to the monks.

As we wandered around Glastonbury's high street, brimming over with shops full of New Age memorabilia and artefacts of the occult, she might also have asked what had happened to Christianity.

Her question prompted the idea of writing something about the holy places of Catholic Britain and Ireland. This is not meant to be a walk down memory lane but an aid in planning our journeys of faith.

Being made whole is the purpose of the Christian journey. The destination is to be brought into harmony and into peace with God.

Pilgrimage often brings the grace to deal with all the things life throws at us and to prepare for death as well.

Pilgrimage is not about processing around broken stones, however ancient and venerable their provenance may be. But the broken stones can become a metaphor for our own broken lives. Being in these holy places reminds us that we are not alone: that others have travelled these highways and byways before; that all pilgrimages have a final destination; and that always on the road with us is the unknown, unrecognised pilgrim who first appeared on the road to

Emmaus. The sacred places exist in every part of these islands. Like the sacred places within each of us, they can become overgrown and neglected and may need to be rediscovered.

At the conclusion of his remarks at his Westminster inauguration, Archbishop Cormac Murphy-O'Connor told his congregation that his uncle, a priest, had always quoted the words of Isaiah at family gatherings: "Remember the rock from which you were hewn." Pilgrimages, for families, individuals and parishes, take us back to the rock from which we were hewn. They also help us to answer the question my daughter put to me at Glastonbury.

That question about the fate of the monks of Glastonbury reminded me of something which a twentieth-century monk, Thomas Merton, wrote in his *Seven Storey Mountain* (SPCK, 1999). He wondered whether any of the picnickers sitting down to their sandwiches and Thermos flasks in the ruin of one of the great monastic houses ever wondered what went on inside these buildings. In writing this book I had the chance to revisit a number of sites and to visit others for the first time. As two of my children and one of their friends enjoyed a picnic against the stunning back-drop of Fountains Abbey I remembered Merton's observation. I hope that this inadequate book will provide a few of the answers; that it will be a modest contribution to the important task of passing on the beliefs we cherish and the tradition we guard to the generation which follows us. Perhaps it may also point the modern pilgrim towards the contemporary staging posts which will provoke us to ask deeper questions about ourselves, the lives we live and our relationship with God.

From the earliest times Christians have revered the memorials and sanctuaries of the martyrs and the hallowed ground of the faith. In the fourth century, the early Church Fathers – St Jerome, St Augustine, St John Chrysostom, St Ambrose – abound with examples of pilgrimage. St Jerome describes the zeal with which Christians gathered in Rome around the tombs of the martyrs. Britons travelled to Rome and they travelled to Jerusalem. In rediscovering the purpose of pilgrimage we might haltingly rediscover something of ourselves.

As they journey along their pilgrim way all pilgrims stumble, lose their bearings or reach some crucial crossroads. Rabbi Menahem Mendl of Kotsz pithily summed up the never-ending nature of the journey: "He who thinks he is finished *is* finished", he said.

At the heart-breaking times of our lives, we particularly need to encounter the sacred. When pilgrims quietly observe and then enter the pilgrim way, their lives are irrevocably changed. When we ask the simple question, what happened to the monks, or why did Christians make this site holy ground, we are striking out on the first tentative steps of our journey. St Catherine of Sienna said that "All the way to heaven is heaven itself, because Christ said, 'I am the Way.'" In treading the paths of the pilgrim way, we find the Way to God.

Let me end by recording my thanks to various people who have provided help or encouragement in bringing this text to a conclusion. Annabel Robson of St Pauls first discussed the project with me and then commissioned this book; Professor Jack Scarisbrick, Christopher Graffius, Derram Attfield, Jim Fagan-King, Ronan Mullin, Wilfrid Wong, Antony Tyler, Stephen Settle, Canon Frank Deeney, Fr Michael Seed, Simon Caldwell of the *Catholic Herald*, Tara Holmes and Kevin Flaherty of the *Catholic Times*, Nick Baty, Patricia Hardcastle of the Catholic Media Office, Professor Keith Hanley, Peter Garrett, Greg Grimer, Barbara Mace, the staff of the House of Lords Library, who are always so courteous and patient, and the indefatigable Joan Bond and her team at the Catholic Central Library. I am grateful, also, to my wife, Lizzie, for her encouragement throughout.

Although the book was written about Catholic pilgrim sites I hope that anyone who reads it will find something here for them. Perhaps it will also act as a spur to local parishes, deaneries and dioceses, to map out the shrines, religious sites and pilgrim ways in their own area and encourage lay people locally to make an act of pilgrimage.

In the appendix which appears at the conclusion of the book there are some practical notes on additional reading material and places to stay.

David Alton
Lancashire, Summer 2000

Glastonbury

1

Glastonbury

THE arrival of St Augustine at Ebbsfleet, in 597, is frequently seen as the landmark event which entrenched Christianity in Britain. Yet evidence exists of a much earlier Christian presence.

In Canterbury itself the Roman Church of St Martin dates from around AD 320 while the Celtic Church boasts settlements of even greater antiquity. Bangor-on-the-Dee, in Clwyd, has been dated at around AD 180, but it was during the fourth century that the Celtic monastic movement claimed Britain and its people for Christianity. St Ninian, a British Roman, established the first Christian community outside the boundaries of Rome's fast-fading empire. The impact of the Celtic missionaries was to be far-reaching, but as Rome's hegemony was eclipsed and England was colonised by successive waves of invaders their influence was pushed back to the inaccessible and remote places. Yet, even before this, legend has it that Christianity first entered these islands in the earliest days of the faith – and that it came to the Somerset settlement at Glastonbury.

There is an aura which pervades Glastonbury. Whether it is the stories of the Holy Grail, the court of King Arthur, the plunder of the monastery and the murder of its abbot, the history of the nearby Tor, or the legend of Joseph of Arimathea, there is no doubt that Glastonbury draws upon

11

some of the richest folk memories of our British traditions. Edmund Burke well understood the basic impulse of all people to know something of their roots and origins when he wrote: "People will not look forward to posterity who never look backward to their ancestors." You cannot travel far in Glastonbury without being reminded of our British ancestors.

When I last visited Glastonbury it was on the last day of the last year of the last millennium. Some of the children stayed with their grandparents in Wiltshire and a small group from our extended family decided that it was a good day to visit Wells Cathedral and Glastonbury.

Wells

Wells is less than eight miles from Glastonbury and boasts one of the finest of the mediæval cathedrals. Its name comes from the profusion of holy wells which poured forth around a Roman mausoleum. This was the place which King Ina of the West Saxons chose for a Christian church. In the Anglo-Saxon the minster was first known as Wiela.

Bishop Jocelin Troteman de Wells was responsible for the present cathedral church. He was bishop between 1206 and 1242. Around his church he created a network of schools – a grammar school and a choir school – almshouses, hospitals, hospices and workplaces. The church is a magnificent building, truly beautiful. My children particularly enjoyed the cathedral's clock, and the characters who appear to strike the hours. This astronomical clock dates from the fourteenth century and was probably made by Peter Lightfoot of Glastonbury. The clock not only gives the time of day but also the phase of the moon, and at every quarter of the hour a small tournament takes place as four clockwork knights charge one another. At the battle's end one is always left dead. A figure called Jack Blandifer is situated on the wall above and he kicks his heels against a bell while striking another with a hammer. His nodding head nods away the hours.

On entering the cathedral the pilgrim should look eastward, down the nave, to where an arch was erected in the fourteenth century to support the tottering tower. It forms the initial of the Greek word *Christos* and is the shape of the cross on which St Andrew was martyred. The cathedral is dedicated to St Andrew.

The diffusion of light into the quire floods in gloriously through the Jesse or Golden Window. This window dates from about 1339 and depicts the genealogy of Jesus, linked in a family tree to King David and his line.

The Tor

The grandness of Wells Cathedral is a good preparation for the ruins of Glastonbury, not least because it reminds you of the scale of mediæval ecclesiastical building. It is said that the mediæval pilgrims who came here were drawn from all over Britain but that those who travelled from Ireland and Wales came to Barnstaple, in North Devon, which until the 1700s was a major port. Researchers have suggested that a series of holy wells and standing crosses marked stopping places at twenty-mile intervals, at Braunton, at North Molton, Barlynch, Cothelstone, Wembdon, Chilton Polden and Shapwick. On arriving in sight of Glastonbury the first thing that they would have seen – as modern pilgrims do – is the towering conical hill called the Tor.

The Tor, which is situated behind the ruins of the abbey, bears traces of an ancient maze pathway and has many associations with the occult. As a centre of pagan ritual it would inevitably have drawn early Christians who saw their mission as bringing light into the places of darkness. To reach the summit of the Tor pilgrims need to brace themselves for a steep climb. Best reached along the

Pilgrim's Path, which runs along the Tor's spine, the summit affords wonderful views of the surrounding countryside. All that remains of the fourteenth-century church of the Archangel Michael is a small tower which stands at the top of the Tor. Nearby is evidence of the cells which were once occupied by Celtic hermits who lived on and around the summit of the Tor. It is sometimes possible, depending on the light, to make out the remains of prehistoric circles of terraces which covered the Tor and whose religious significance can only be guessed at.

In some ancient Welsh bardic verses, the Triads, Glastonbury is identified with Stonehenge and Llantwit Major as one of the three places where perpetual choirs chanted their way through the cycle of the seasons. There is also evidence of an ancient spirit path through which pagans believed that the souls of the dead passed from an ancient temple (possibly situated where the abbey was built) westward to Avalon and from there to the world beyond.

England's Jerusalem

Glastonbury, sometimes known as England's Jerusalem, was originally called Avalon. It came by this name because of the abundance of apples – still so much a part of the staple of Somerset's rich productive tradition.

In many of the ancient folk stories of Avalon, particularly those associated with Merlin and the Arthurian legends, the old British name of Ynis Witrin is the one which is used. It means grassy island (in the Saxon becoming Glastney). The whole of this lowland area was regularly awash with water and Glastonbury lay at the heart of a maze of waterways. Geological changes, thought to have occurred in the ninth century, raised the lie of the land and the monks of Glastonbury were responsible for huge land drainage projects which reclaimed large areas of the Somerset Levels.

There are two legends which associate Glastonbury with the earliest part of church history.

One of these, celebrated in the great hymn of William Blake (1757–1827), "Jerusalem", claims that in those ancient days the feet of the Christ Child walked on these verdant green hills. Blake had been born in London but was familiar with the stories associated with Glastonbury, which he described as "the holiest ground on earth".

The story which Blake was celebrating has it that the uncle of the young Jesus was a wealthy trader, Joseph of Arimathea. He came to the west of England, famous for its tin and minerals, and while he was busy bartering his merchandise the young Jesus built a small church from wattle and there he prayed.

Joseph of Arimathea and Weary All Hill

The more common tradition is that after the Resurrection, Joseph came to Glastonbury to bring the Gospel to the Britons. He is said to have arrived at Pilton with a small band of evacuees, fleeing for safety from the persecution of Christians which was underway throughout the Roman empire. Joseph knew of Briton from his earlier travels as a merchant and believed it to be a safe haven. When they arrived at Glastonbury the small exhausted band rested by a small hill just outside the town which, to this day, is still known as Weary All Hill. The local king, Aviragus, gave Joseph a grant of land and this is where the small missionary band settled. They dwelt in circular cells in a ring around the wattle church. The gift and hospitable welcome are certainly curious unless Joseph were already known to and respected by Aviragus.

If Joseph was indeed a magnate who controlled the tin and lead industries of his day then there is no doubt that he would have been familiar with Britain's West Country. Most of the known world's tin was mined in Cornwall, smelted into ingots, and Joseph is reputed to have owned the largest fleet of private merchant ships trading in tin.

Diodorus Siculus, Julius Caesar and other writers of the period refer to the existence of this trade. In the Latin Vulgate version of St Mark's and St Luke's Gospels, Joseph is referred to as *Decurio* – a word often used by the Romans to describe the official who oversaw the metal mines. St Jerome's translation of the Gospel describes Joseph as *Nobilis Decurio*. We also know that as well as holding high rank among the Romans, he was a member of the Jewish Sanhedrin and a legislative member of a provincial Roman senate. He had homes in Jerusalem and in Arimathea (today's Palestinian town of Ramalleh). According to the Talmud, Joseph was the younger brother of the Virgin Mary – an uncle of Jesus.

There is also the intriguing possibility that if Mary's husband, St Joseph, died while Jesus was young – and we certainly hear nothing more of him after Jesus' early childhood – then under Jewish law Joseph of Arimathea would have become the child's legal guardian.

Joseph of Arimathea was not among those disciples who, apart from John, fled from Jesus when the High Priests and Pilate closed in on Him. Joseph became a unique and bold defender of Jesus at His trial and then he defied the Sanhedrin by demanding Christ's crucified body from Pilate. His were the arms that cradled the broken body as it was taken from the cross and he placed the body in his own tomb. The evangelists describe him as "a good man", "an honourable man", "a just man" and as "a disciple of Jesus". Clearly this was no casual acquaintance, but a friendship which led Joseph to take greater risks than anyone else caught up in the events of the Passion, Crucifixion and Resurrection.

There has always been a tradition that the child and the merchant uncle had travelled together, and it is easy to see how the legend grew. Whether the boy came or not, the persistent story that Joseph knew these parts and regarded

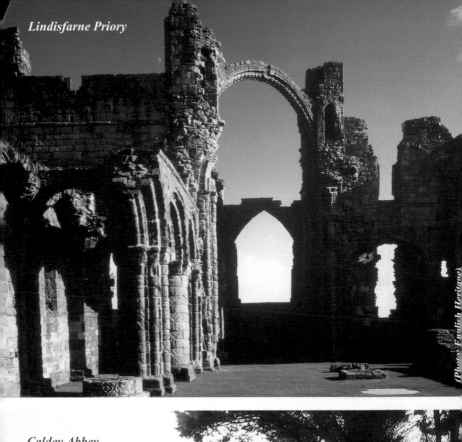

Lindisfarne Priory

(Photo: English Heritage)

Caldey Abbey

(Photo: Wales Tourist Board)

Durham Cathedral

(Photo: Durham County Council)

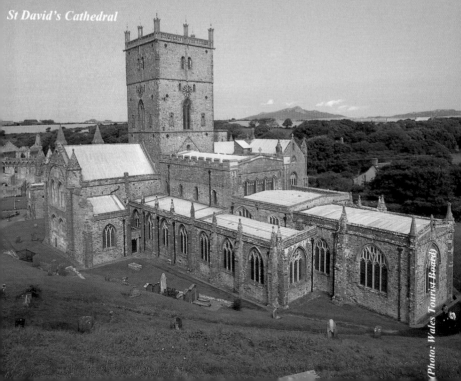

St David's Cathedral

(Photo: Wales Tourist Board)

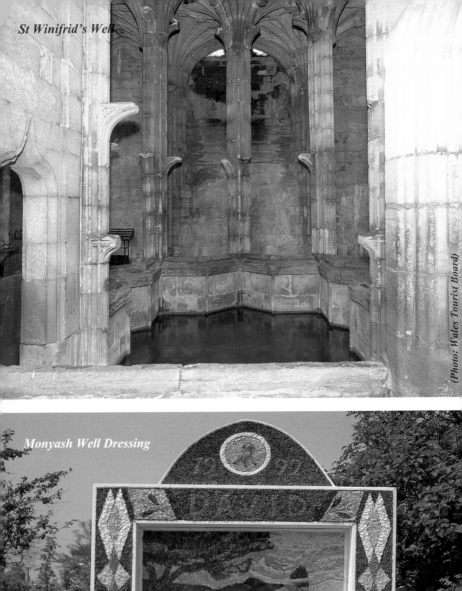

St Winifrid's Well

(Photo: Wales Tourist Board)

Monyash Well Dressing

(Photo: Derbyshire Dales District Council)

them as a quiet safe sanctuary in those dangerous times is a compelling one – though clearly neither provable nor essential to more fundamental questions of faith. For the pilgrim coming to Glastonbury, if it is a story which takes the heart and the soul back to the Cross and Resurrection then it more than serves its purpose.

In his book *The Drama of the Lost Disciples*, (Covenant,1961) (a second-hand copy of which I purchased in a Glastonbury bookshop, and which, at times, does tend towards flights of fancy), George F. Jowett quotes a former curator of the Vatican Library, Cardinal Baronius, writing in his Ecclesiastical Annals as saying: "In that year [AD 36] the party mentioned was exposed to the sea in a vessel without sails or oars. The vessel drifted finally to Marseilles and they were saved. From Marseilles Joseph and his company passed into Britain and after preaching the Gospel there, died."

Centuries later, St Augustine wrote to Pope Gregory (*Epistolas ad Gregorium Papam*) confirming the tradition of a wattle altar said to have been built by Jesus at Glastonbury and stating that the altar still existed. He continued:

> In the Western confines of Britain there is a certain royal island of large extent, surrounded by water, abounding in all the beauties of nature and necessaries of life. In it the first Neophytes of Catholic Law, God beforehand acquainting them, found a church constructed by no human art, but divinely constructed, or by the hands of Christ himself, for the salvation of his people. The Almighty has made it manifest by many miracles and mysterious visitations that he continues to watch over it as sacred to himself, and to Mary, the Mother of God.

It is from this association, and from an ancient inscription on a Glastonbury stone which simply refers to "Jesus – Mary", that England became known as Our Lady's Dowry.

The Glastonbury thorn

Another Glastonbury tradition holds that as this band of the earliest of all Christian pilgrims rested, Joseph struck his staff into the ground. It immediately took root and blossomed, and its descendants continue to bloom at Christmas time until this very day. A sprig of the Glastonbury thorn is cut and taken to the monarch to decorate the table on the feast of the Nativity.

During the regime of Oliver Cromwell (1649–60), the Puritans regarded the thorn tree as a part of Catholic superstition and they cut it down. However, local people took cuttings of the thorn and concealed them. It is from these cuttings that today's blooms are taken.

On arriving in Glastonbury, the pilgrim enters the ruins of the abbey church. This is where Joseph of Arimathea is reputed to have built his wattle church – the first church in Britain. The legend also has it that he brought with him the cup which Our Lord used at the Last Supper. In this cup Joseph is said to have caught some of the blood which Christ shed on Calvary. Again, what we know for certain is that Joseph was close to Jesus and his mother and that he was sufficiently wealthy to have his own sepulchre into which he arranged for the body of Christ to be laid after the body was take from Calvary.

Pilgrim in pursuit of the Holy Grail

The Holy Grail is reputed to have been buried with St Joseph on Chalice Hill, which is situated between the abbey and the Tor (close to Chalice Well; the Hill and the Well were so named nearly two thousand years ago, presumably for some good reason). The tradition holds that one day the Grail will be found and that this day will mark the beginning of a spiritual renaissance for our country.

The facts and the tradition always have to be

disentangled. Whether or not Joseph brought the communion cup with him to England, it is at least curious that the Holy Grail should become such a persistent and unique part of our history: synonymous with the quest of every pilgrim, striving for the apparently unobtainable, rich in symbolism and allegory, always associated with the pursuit of virtue. All the legends state that Joseph brought with him twelve travelling companions – and their spiritual descendants were to become the twelve knights of Arthur's Round Table who quest for the Holy Grail.

Alfred Lord Tennyson immortalised the tradition of the Chalice Cup in these verses:

> *The cup, the cup itself, from which our Lord*
> *Drank at the last sad supper with his own;*
> *This, from the blessed land of Aromat –*
> *After the day of darkness, when the dead*
> *Went wandering o'er Moriah – the good saint*
> *Arimathean Joseph, journeying brought*
> *To Glastonbury.*

William of Malmsbury and the ancient church

A fire destroyed the abbey in 1184, and with it perished the documents which referred to the abbey's foundation. However, William of Malmsbury, a scholarly monk, had seen the documents which referred to the ancient traditions and in 1130 he incorporated them in his *On the Antiquity of the Church at Glastonbury*. Quoting from the ancient texts, William states that "the church at Glastonbury did none other men's hands make, but actual disciples of Christ built it". He adds:

> It was the first formed of wattles, and from the beginning breathed and was redolent of a mysterious divine sanctity which spread throughout the country. The actual building was insignificant but was so holy. Waves of

common people thronging thither flooded every path; rich men laid aside their state to gather there, and men of learning and piety assembled there in great numbers.

The Abbot of Glastonbury was always given precedence over other ecclesiastical figures because the church in England accepted Glastonbury's claims to ancient foundation. It is also established that the Old Church of Glastonbury was rededicated by legates of Pope Eleutherius (175 to 189 AD), the thirteenth pope to follow St Peter.

Saints at rest

William of Malmsbury also describes Glastonbury as "the resting place of so many saints, deservedly called a heavenly sanctuary on earth". The most famous of the abbots of Glastonbury is St Dunstan. Canterbury's claim to his earthly remains is more convincing. Possession of bones and their subsequent allure in attracting pilgrims led to many false or unlikely claims.

Dunstan was born in or close to Glastonbury around the year 909, and after a career at court he became a monk. As abbot, in 943, he introduced strict reforms insisting on the practice of the Benedictine Rule, and with the active support of King Edmund I and King Edred he reformed monastic life throughout Britain. He was an educator, a liturgist, a lover of church music, an æsthete and a builder. He created new monasteries or re-founded old ones at Exeter, Peterborough, Ely, Bath, Malmesbury and Westminster.

Tradition has it that those who were buried here included St Patrick and St Bridget – although there are also more compelling claims made by other locations.

St David is said to have been at Glastonbury and to have arrived with a retinue of bishops intent on rededicating the church. In a vision it was revealed to him that the chapel had already been dedicated by Christ Himself to

Mary, His mother. David built an oratory, instead, at the east end of the Old Church.

King Aviragus had originally granted Joseph 1440 acres of land, and although by the time the Domesday Book was compiled the monastic lands had grown well beyond the area of the "twelve hides", within the perimeters of the original land the abbot enjoyed tax exemptions and sovereign powers.

Although the Vikings never desecrated Glastonbury, and the British, Saxon and Norman rulers respected its antiquity and sanctity, fire proved its most daunting enemy. On 25 May 1184, the wattle church, which had been enclosed by a wooded structure, caught light and a fire swept through the abbey. The abbey was rebuilt but its reputation as a centre of pilgrimage declined.

The Arthurian legend

The abbey saw its fortunes restored a few years later when two ancient oak coffins were discovered sixteen feet below the surface of the earth in the burial ground to the south of the abbey. Here, it was said, were the remains of Queen Guinevere and King Arthur. Their coffins were reburied at the heart of the abbey church and today's pilgrim can still see the location, which is marked with an inscription.

Of the mediæval buildings few now remain. The Abbot's Kitchen is a fourteenth-century octagonal building in which a few artifacts and photographs are exhibited. At the corner of Chilkwell Street and Bere Lane is the abbey's tithe barn – dating from around 1420. It is used as a museum of rural life.

The vast site and the scale of the buildings still stand testimony to the wealth and importance which monasteries such as Glastonbury came to symbolise. This was ultimately to be their undoing. The thousand-year tradition of annual pilgrimage to Glastonbury – during August to celebrate the feast of St Joseph – was about to come to an abrupt end.

Abbot Whiting: death and dissolution

Henry VIII, jealous of the wealth, independence and power of monastic foundations, and embittered by his acrimonious arguments with the Pope over his determination to divorce his wife, decided to destroy the monasteries. The last abbot of Glastonbury was Abbot Richard Whiting (see also chapter 3). Henry VIII's agents called on him in 1539 and began the confiscation of the abbey's possessions. Henry's agents accused Abbot Whiting of concealing abbey treasures. He was brought to trial on these trumped-up charges, and on 15 November he was taken with two of his monks to the summit of the Tor, where they were hanged, drawn and quartered. The bodies of the three monks were left suspended on the gallows as a warning to others, and then parts of the abbot's body were taken on a gruesome pilgrimage to the towns and cities and placed on exhibition. With his companions, Richard Whiting was beatified by Pope Leo XIII in 1888.

The foremost historian of the period, Professor Jack Scarisbrick, believes that Whiting had refused point-blank to surrender his house: "Grasp that," he says, "and the story falls into place. The usual tactics – forcible retirement, bribes, faction stirring inside the community – having failed, there was only one thing for it: a treason charge so that, like the abbots of Reading and Colchester, he could be declared forfeit of his house. This was still not water-tight, because he did not 'own' the house and its lands. God did. So it was crucial that Parliament should have passed an act in 1539 confirming the King's title to any religious houses which had 'happened' to come into his possesion or would do in the future. Whiting was a very brave man. He probably *had* been hiding the abbey's most precious treasure – rightly!"

The abbey was laid waste and the stones ripped out and used for new buildings. The holy objects disappeared – some doubtless concealed to this day in hiding places chosen to prevent their desecration by Henry's agents. Others passed into private hands. One, the Glastonbury Cross, which had marked the burial place of King Arthur, turned up at the British Museum in 1981, but once the owner had identified its provenance he concealed it and despite a brief spell in prison refused to give it up.

Perhaps that incident sums up the enigmatic past of Glastonbury.

New beginnings

There are occasional sightings or glimpses of reality which lie concealed beneath unexcavated legends and mythology. Like the quarry which tantalisingly appears out of the undergrowth only to quickly conceal itself again, it all adds to the appeal of the chase. For the modern pilgrim, Glastonbury continues to intrigue and to inspire. The practical details are all competently explored in the visitor centre, which was officially opened by Dr George Carey when he was Bishop of Bath and Wells.

For Catholics, there is also the story of return. In 1903 the exiled French Sisters of Charity founded an orphanage in Glastonbury, complete with chapel. In 1940 the foundation stone of the new church of St Mary was laid, on a site adjacent to the convent, close to the entrance to the abbey. The Bishop of Clifton consecrated the building one year later. This church is home to the restored shrine of Our Lady at Glastonbury. The statue was blessed by the Pope's representative in 1955 on the feast of the Visitation, and a gathering of pilgrims took place which was probably the greatest number assembled since the royal visit of Edward I. Here and in the quietness of the magnificent grounds, answers abound to most of the questions which haunt our lives.

The Ammerdown Study Centre is the ideal contemporary setting in which to ponder the continuing implications of Glastonbury. It was founded in 1967 by Lord Hylton, an independent Catholic crossbench peer, well known for his ecumenical work in Northern Ireland and for championing human rights, especially those of asylum seekers, domestic workers and exploited children.

Faced with a large mass of buildings, some very dilapidated, he consulted with Dom Aelred Watkin OSB, a former headmaster of the nearby Downside School, and with Dr John Coulsen, then lecturer in theology at Bristol University. In the climate of the post Second Vatican Council years, Raymond Hylton and a small steering group hit on the idea of a centre committed to the renewal of the Church and of society.

Bishop Butler, one of the major figures of the Council and former Abbot of Downside, gave considerable encouragement to go ahead. The Sisters of Our Lady of Sion provided the nucleus of a resident community at Ammerdown, and with the support of other denominations, the Centre was born.

Underlining its role in drawing together people of differing religious backgrounds, Rabbi Lionel Blue and, latterly, Rabbi Mark Solomon, have been involved as governors and lecturers at the Centre. The Ammerdown Centre follows papal teachings in working towards the goal of a kingdom of justice, mercy and peace.

Among the Catholic leaders and lecturers who participated in programmes at the Centre during 2000 were Fr Gerald O'Collins SJ, Sr Elizabeth Rees OCV, Fr Gordian Marshall OP, Fr John McCluskey MHM, Sr Teresa Ridge PBVM, Fr Tony Horan SJ, Bruce Kent, Fr Tony Ford, Sr Magdalen Lawler SND, Fr Richard Rohr OFM, Fr Michael Barnes SJ, Fr Robert Murray SJ, Dr Tina Beattie, Kathleen Hopkins and Dr Lawrence Freedman OSB.

Details of how to find Ammerdown and contact details appear in the Appendix.

A meditation

Jerusalem

And did those feet in ancient time
Walk upon England's mountains green?
And was the holy Lamb of God
On England's pleasant pastures seen?

And did the Countenance Divine
Shine forth upon our clouded hills?
And was Jerusalem builded here
Among these dark satanic mills?

Bring me my bow of burning gold!
Bring me my arrows of desire!
Bring me my spear! O clouds unfold!
Bring me my chariot of fire!

I will not cease from mental fight,
Nor shall my sword sleep in my hand,
Till we have built Jerusalem
In England's green and pleasant land.

(William Blake)

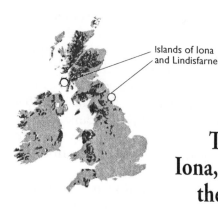

Islands of Iona and Lindisfarne

The Celtic Sites –
Iona, Lindisfarne and
the northern saints

IN May 2000 Newcastle City Council announced that it had chosen a design for a public memorial of the late Cardinal Basil Hume. Designed by the sculptor Nigel Boonham, it will stand prominently in the city centre.

The sculpture will be cast in bronze and depicts the Cardinal in his Benedictine habit with a cardinal's skull-cap on the back of his head. It will stand in a memorial garden outside the city's Catholic cathedral, opposite the central station.

The sculpture will stand on a plinth in the shape of Holy Island, Lindisfarne, recalling the Cardinal's great devotion to the hermit saints of the island, the monks Aidan and Cuthbert. This will be the ideal point to conclude a pilgrimage intent on discovering the Celtic sites and the northern saints. The best companion to take is the Cardinal's *Footprints of the Northern Saints* (Darton, Longman and Todd, 1996) and which is based upon the television programme *Return of the Saints* (available in video format from St Pauls Multi-Media).

This is a pilgrimage which winds from its point of disembarkation on the Scottish island of Iona, through the lowlands to Melrose, on to Lindisfarne and thence to Durham, Jarrow, Newcastle and possibly south to Ripon and the ruins of Whitby Abbey. What are the essentials in understanding this part of our rich Christian tradition?

Wherever the Romans extended their empire, Christianity was not far behind. Thus, Christianity took root in Britain and found a fertile soil and congenial climate in which to grow. It was to a largely Christian land that waves of Angles, Saxons, Jutes and Frisians came, and, as peoples never conquered by the Romans, they brought their pagan gods and kings who claimed descent from the god Woden.

It would be a second wave of Romans – notably St Augustine of Canterbury and his successor, Theodore of Tarsus, who established schools of Latin and Greek in Kent and began the evangelisation of the Anglo-Saxons.

Iona

But the ancient faith, having taken root among the British, had never died out and from the north, at the beginning of the seventh century, there came a deep spiritual renewal. British, mystic spirituality had been transplanted to Ireland by the Romano-Briton, St Patrick (see chapters 9 and 10). It returned to Britain with St Columba and his monks, who established a monastic foundation on the Hebridean island of Iona in 563. It was to Iona that Oswald, future king of Northumberland, fled during dynastic wars and where he fell under the influence of Celtic Christianity. When Dr Samuel Johnson visited Iona in the 1770s, he wrote: "That man is to be envied, whose patriotism would not gain force upon the plain of Marathon, or whose piety would not grow warmer among the ruins of Iona." What captivated Dr Johnson has captivated successive generations of pilgrims who have travelled to that remote and windswept place.

Columba was a descendant of the High Kings of Ireland. After precipitating a spate of blood-letting he was banished and came to Iona to begin a new life. He spread the Christian message of mercy and peace and had the great joy of seeing the message accepted by many of the Pictish and Celtic peoples of Strathclyde. This legacy is the one upon which St Ninian and St Mungo built. They spread the Gospel throughout Scotland, and Mungo (also known as Kentigern) travelled deep into Cumbria. Even the Vikings who came to Iona inter-married and accepted the faith. It was from Iona that the dynasty of Scottish kings emerged and many of these early sovereigns, and others from Ireland and Norway, were brought here for burial. Iona has a special place in the hearts of Scottish people; it was not surprising that even in our own times when John Smith, the Leader of the Opposition, died, his family asked that the Christian politician should be buried on Iona.

Iona's rocky promontories, its rugged hills and grassland, its beautiful beaches and wild coastland and the ancient stones all speak of God's presence and His abiding commitment to the human race. The only motor vehicles allowed on Iona are those of the residents; visitors must leave their cars at Mull. Each Wednesday a pilgrimage group trace the steps of the island saints. The pilgrim needs to travel lightly in a practical sense as well as spiritually.

Here, on the road to the abbey, lie the ruins of a nunnery founded as a Benedictine house in the twelfth century by St Margaret. The nearby Cathedral of the Isles was restored at the beginning of this century by the Duke of Argyll. The restoration of the abbey was the work of the Very Revd Lord MacLeod of Fuinary, who founded the ecumenical Iona Community in 1938. In both buildings there are quiet places for prayer and contemplation.

Lord MacLeod sought to fulfil the prophecy of St Columba – the mound of whose cell stands a little inland from the cathedral – that "where once there was the singing of monks there shall only be the lowing of cattle, but before the world comes to its end things shall be as they were".

On taking the ferry from Mull to Oban, the pilgrim will also pass the island of Lismore, where the earliest bishops of Argyll lived. It was called the Bishop's Isle because those offering themselves for priesthood needed to be ordained by a bishop. Columba was an abbot, and his friend Moluag the bishop ordained the candidates for the priesthood. A rough-cast church stands on the site of the early church which survived the Vikings.

When King Oswald – later canonised as Saint Oswald – assumed his Northumberland throne after the battle of Heavenfield, he asked Iona to send him a monk to come and teach his people about Christianity. An Irish monk, Aidan, accepted the challenge and ventured forth, establishing a monastery off the north-east coast of England at Lindisfarne, which was an island under the protection of Oswald's royal hall at Bamburgh. Lindisfarne would become known as Holy Island.

A Scottish peregrination

In striking out for Lindisfarne, following in St Aidan's footsteps, the modern pilgrim may wish to take a number of detours to take in important sites of Celtic Christianity.

At Hoddam, in Dumfries and Galloway, there are traces of St Mungo. Recent excavations unearthed an early baptistery with Roman-style plaster, brick and mosaic. At the rear of Hoddam Bridge is Repentance Hill – where King Roderick of Strathclyde and St Mungo are reputed to have addressed the crowds who had assembled to see their spiritual and temporal leaders.

In the same county lies Ruthwell – where the Ruthwell Cross was discovered. In the eighth century it watched over the Solway marshlands and may be found today in the parish Kirk. On it appear some words from *The Dream of the Cross*:

I was reared up a rood
I raised the great King,
liege-lord of the heavens...
They drove me through with dark nails;
on me the deep wounds manifest,
wide-mouthed hate-dents...
I was all moist with blood
sprung from the Man's side
after he sent forth his soul.

(quoted in *Sacred Britain* by
Nigel and Martin Palmer, Judy Piatkus, 1997)

Brow Well lies a mile to the east of Ruthwell and was visited by Robert Burns during the last month of his life.

On the coast, to the south and west of Dumfries at New Abbey, lie the ruins of Sweetheart Abbey, which takes its name from a thirteenth-century political marriage between Devorgilla, a Celtic princess, and John Balliol, a Norman Baron. Defying the predictions of the day, the nuptials led to true love. Beyond lies the Whithorn Pilgrim Way, opened in 1993. It is thirty-six miles from New Abbey to Kirkcudbright (meaning the church of Cuthbert). This takes the pilgrim to the ruined abbey of Glenluce and thence to Whithorn and St Ninian's Cave, just under four miles south of Whithorn. It was at Whithorn that Ninian established a community which cultivated the shared life of love, work and learning. It became known as the Shining Place.

In the city of Glasgow, St Mungo is celebrated in the city's thirteenth-century cathedral where his tomb lies. Next to the cathedral stands the St Mungo Museum of Religious Life and Art, which houses, most famously, Salvador Dali's painting *Christ of St John of the Cross*.

To the north-east of Iona lies Inverness, where the solitary pillar from the burying ground of the Dominican friars marks the site of their thirteenth-century priory. Further north still, the twelfth-century murder, on Easter Sunday 1116, of Magnus, Earl of Orkney, led to the celebration of this Christian leader as a local patron saint. At Dornoch, Fortrose, Tain and Portmanhomack there are ancient Pictish centres of Christianity. Local dedications to St Ninian show how far the influence of Iona and Whithorn had spread. Tain was the eleventh-century birthplace of Duthac, the Irish "Primus Anamchara" (first among soul friends), who died in Armagh. His birthplace became a centre of pilgrimage and the church at Tain was dedicated to his name.

At Brechin, in Angus, there is a tenth-century round tower, standing alongside the restored cathedral. These towers were places of refuge for the Celtic monks when the Vikings attacked and plundered their monasteries. Fifteen miles away, at Arbroath, are the wonderful ruins of Arbroath Abbey, while St Vigean's Museum (off the A92 to the north-west of Arbroath) rewards the pilgrim with artefacts from the Pictish and Celtic period.

In Perthshire, north of Loch Tay and west of Aberfeldy, lies Fortingall. Local legend has it that while a Roman embassy stopped off here, the ambassador took a Scots woman, a Menzies, as his wife. The legend claims that these were the parents of Pontius Pilate and that Pilate's famous question to Jesus, "What is truth?", is a central Druidical riddle. The Royal Scots add further intrigue by claiming descent from Pilate's bodyguard.

In Fife, the pilgrim will want to visit St Andrews (see chapter 8) and Dunfermline, which was home to St Margaret. Her greatest memorial, Dunfermline Abbey, was built in the eleventh century. A descendant of King Alfred the Great and brought up in Hungary, Margaret married Malcolm Canmore (who defeated Macbeth) and dedicated her life to drawing together the Celtic tradition of Scottish Christianity and Roman Catholicism. Queen Margaret and her children encouraged Benedictine and Cistercian foundations and granted them land on which to develop their monasteries. At Edinburgh Castle the chapel of St Margaret is eleventh-century and named after the Scottish queen.

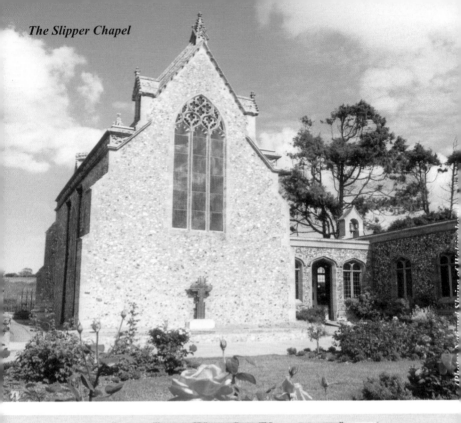

The Slipper Chapel

*Statue of Our Lady
of Walsingham*

Melrose Abbey

(Photo: Scottish Viewpoint)

St Andrews

(Photo: Scottish Viewpoint)

Croagh Patrick
The Author and his daughter,
Marianne, climbing Croagh
Patrick (known as 'The Reek')

Croagh Patrick

Twenty-one miles away, in Stirling, one-time capital of Scotland, lies a church established by St Ninian. The Monymusk Reliquary, which held the remains of St Columba, was kept here.

As the pilgrim travels on towards Lindisfarne, there are opportunities to travel to Haddington (see chapter 8), to see some of the Scottish holy wells (see chapter 5) and the remains of Melrose Abbey, where St Cuthbert was first a monk (see below). From Berwick-upon-Tweed it is ten miles to Holy Island and a beautiful walk for those who are so inclined.

Lindisfarne

Celtic Christianity was entirely monastic, and Iona and Lindisfarne both represent the Celtic love of seclusion and solitude.

Lindisfarne is a crescent-shaped spike of land whose sand dunes are linked to the mainland by a causeway twice a day at low tide. I first visited the island at the suggestion of the local Member of Parliament for Berwick-upon-Tweed, Alan Beith. Berwick lies about ten miles to the north and Bamburgh Castle is about the same distance to the south.

St Aidan organised his work around the ebb and flow of Lindisfarne's tides, going out to Oswald's people to evangelise and teach, and then returning to his fastness to pray. In his long narrative poem, *Marmion*, Sir Walter Scott creates the impression of an idyllic life. The rugged realities were very different:

> *For, with the flow and ebb its stile*
> *Varies from continent to isle;*
> *Dry-shod, o'er sands, twice every day,*
> *The pilgrims to the shrine find way:*
> *Twice every day, the waves efface*
> *Of staves and sandalled feet the trace.*

Aidan and his followers lived simply and placed poverty above worldly success. Their mission attracted such numbers of followers that St Aidan retreated to the nearby Farne Islands, where he could only be reached by boat. St Bede described Farne as "cut off from the landward side by very deep water and facing, on the other side, out towards the limitless ocean. The island was haunted by devils."

Cardinal Hume wrote that Aidan's spiritual energy was directed towards saving souls, towards helping people understand the great richness of life with God in their lives here on earth as well as in heaven.

Aidan began a school at Lindisfarne, where he educated twelve young Anglo-Saxon boys to train for the priesthood. Among them were the future St Eata, who would become fifth Bishop of Lindisfarne, St Cedd, who evangelised the East Saxons (and founded Lastingham Abbey, East Yorkshire), and St Chad, who became Bishop of Mercia (and consecrated the cathedral at Lichfield in 700).

In August 651 St Aidan died (just twelve days after the death of his beloved friend, Oswine, who had succeeded his brother Oswald). On the night of his death a young shepherd, Cuthbert, was tending his sheep on pastures in the Scottish Lowlands. He saw a streak of light breaking through the sky and he believed that he was being called to follow the departed Abbot of Lindisfarne. Setting out to become a monk, he joined the monastic community at Melrose. He became renowned for his visits to neighbouring hamlets and for dropping in at the cottages of the poor. He would gather the people around him, preaching, hearing confession and doing whatever he could to alleviate their suffering.

Farne

Ultimately, Cuthbert became Abbot of Lindisfarne, living on Inner Farne. St Bede the Venerable says:

Cuthbert was the first man brave enough to live there alone... Having routed the enemy, Cuthbert became monarch of the place, in token of which he built a city worthy of his power and put up houses to match. The structure was almost circular in plan, from four to five poles in diameter, and the walls on the outside were higher than a man... so that with only the sky to look at, eyes and thoughts might be kept from wandering and inspired to seek for higher things. This same wall he built not with cut stone or bricks and mortar but with rough stones and peat dug out of the enclosure itself.

The Farne Islands are extraordinarily bleak. They comprise about twenty-five pieces of rock protruding from the North Sea – and are about two miles off the Northumberland coast. At low tide Inner Farne is about sixteen acres with about five acres capable of bearing some vegetation. There are precipitous cliffs and a tiny patch of sandy beach, St Cuthbert's Cove, where small boats can make a landing. Thousands of birds, including terns, shags, cormorants, guillemots, razorbills, kittiwakes, fulmars and eider ducks, and puffins all call Farne their home.

A succession of hermits followed Cuthbert to live in these inhospitable conditions. In the thirteenth century Geoffrey of Coldingham wrote about the twelfth-century hermit, Bartholomew, and the spiritual foes he met on Farne: "their countenances most hideous, their heads long, the appearance of the whole troop horrible".

Nothing remains of Cuthbert's cell but it is thought to have stood on the site of the Tower, built in 1500 by Prior Thomas Castell of Durham. The seepage well is thought to have been Cuthbert's original well. The Tower was later used as a beacon lighthouse and now provides accommodation for the wardens of the National Trust.

In the nineteenth century the Chapel of St Cuthbert, which dated from the fourteenth century, was restored by Archdeacon Charles Thorp of Durham, and by the landing stage stands a small stone building, Fishe House, thought to be the remains of the Benedictine guest house.

Bede described Cuthbert as a man of great holiness:

> He was so full of penitence, so aflame with heavenly yearnings, that when celebrating Mass he could never finish the service without shedding tears. In his zeal for righteousness he was fervid to reprove sinners, yet he was kind hearted and forbearing in pardoning the penitent, so that sometimes when the wrong-doers were confessing their sins to him, in his pity for their weakness he would be the first to burst into tears and thus, though himself righteous, by his own example would show the sinner what he ought to do.

King Egfrid, accompanied by a large retinue, travelled to Inner Farne to persuade Cuthbert to become Bishop of Lindisfarne. Initially reluctant, he was persuaded, but although successful, two years later he relinquished office and returned to his cell on Inner Farne. After celebrating Christmas with the community at Lindisfarne he set off for Farne, and to a questioner who asked: "Tell us, Lord Bishop, when may we hope for your return?" Cuthbert replied: "When you bring my body back here."

As he had prophesied, after his death in 687, Cuthbert's remains were taken to Lindisfarne. When they were exhumed for their removal to a reliquary eleven years later, the body was found to be completely undecayed, and the joints and limbs still flexible. St Bede described him as more like a sleeping man than a dead man. His garments also seemed to be perfectly new and wondrously bright. Many miracles were recorded.

North Eastern Monasticism and Whitby

Aidan and Cuthbert had a magnetism which attracted the Anglo-Saxons, who came in significant numbers to these remote places to seek out the wise counsel of the saints. In turn this triggered an extraordinary renaissance of Christianity. At Jarrow, Wearmouth and Flixborough, monastic foundations would be created from which scribes crafted the wonderful Lindisfarne Gospels. The Celtic mission in the north and Augustine's Roman mission in the south were like a pincer movement which swept through England, although temperament and style, and differences in organisation and liturgical practice, inevitably led to the creation of tension between these two rich Christian traditions. This came to a head in 664 at the Synod of Whitby (see chapter 3).

On Lindisfarne, Aidan had been succeeded as abbot by Finan and he, in turn, by Colman. During his tenure the Whitby Synod was convened. Principal protagonist for the Celtic tradition, Colman's arguments were marshalled against those of Wilfrid, Abbot of Ripon.

This thirty-year-old monk, renowned for his erudition and learning, championed the Roman cause. A whole host of liturgical, theoretical and practical questions were ultimately singled down to a central question put by King Oswy to Colman and Wilfrid: "Is it true that special authority was given to St Peter?" Colman replied: "It's true, Your Majesty." Then the king continued: "Do you both agree that these words were indisputably addressed to Peter in the first place, and that our Lord gave him the keys of the kingdom of heaven?" Both answered that they did. At this the king concluded: "I tell you, Peter is guardian of the gates of heaven, and I shall not contradict him. I shall obey his commands and everything to the best of my knowledge and ability. Otherwise, when I come to the gates of heaven, there may be no one to open them because he who holds the key has turned away."

The controversy was thus settled; although argument about church authority and obedience to Christ's teaching continue to our own day and will doubtless persist until the Kingdom comes. Oswy perceived the issue very clearly.

Whatever the arguments about the date on which Easter was celebrated, or how monasteries and dioceses were organised, or, in our own context, questions of women's ordination or the re-marriage of divorced people in church buildings, was the Christian Church in this island going to be separate from the universal Church? Was it going to follow its own whims and fancies or was it prepared to break communion with the universal church in order to follow its own path?

As Cardinal Hume put it: "The Synod of Whitby and King Oswy's allegiance to the authority of St Peter united all of Christian England in one tradition and practice of the faith, and also united England with the greater universal tradition of the Roman Church."

Yet here, too, was the humility of acceptance. Although Colman left Whitby, returning to Iona to continue his disagreement, Cuthbert accepted the outcome and brought the brethren at Lindisfarne with him. Cuthbert became the focus for reconciliation, preferring to get on with living his life by the Gospel rather than worrying unduly about the shape of the tonsure or the date of Easter. As he lay dying in his cell on Farne, on 20 March 687, Cuthbert told his brethren to "have no communion with those who depart from the unity of the Catholic peace".

The Whitby decision was also accepted by the remarkable woman who presided over the Synod, Abbess Hilda of Whitby. A descendant of King Edwin of Northumberland, Hilda had been Abbess of Hartlepool but in 657 founded a double monastery (of men and women) at Streanaeshalch – later called Whitby by the Danes. The men and women lived separately but came together in the abbey church to pray. The monastery had its own school and established learning as an important part of its mission.

It was to Whitby that Hilda brought Caedmon, a poor, elderly, illiterate cowherd. One night he had a vision and was told to sing of the creation of the world. As Caedmon began to sing, the farmer who employed him took him to

Abbess Hilda. She commissioned Caedmon to set scriptures to music – which he did, to a superlative setting. Caedmon then entered the monastery and set the works of the monastic scribes to music and verse.

Hilda became renowned for drawing out hidden talent and for developing potential. Her advice was sought by pilgrims from all over the country. In our own context it is perhaps instructive that although she never sought to be a priest, her leadership and ministry were decisive.

Nine years after the Synod of Whitby the combination of faith and learning came to great fruition in the birth and subsequent development of "the father of English history", St Bede the Venerable (recognised as a doctor of the Church in 1899).

St Bede, Wearmouth and Jarrow

At the age of seven Bede was sent to the monastery at Wearmouth. From here he went to Jarrow where he remained for the rest of his life. Although he was firmly of the Roman, Latin tradition, he showed impeccable objectivity and integrity as he recorded the achievements of both the Celtic and Roman traditions, and to this day his *History of the English Church and People* remains the decisive account of these times.

Bede wrote:

> When we compare the present life of man on earth with that time of which we have no knowledge, it seems to be like the swift flight of a single sparrow through the banqueting hall where you are sitting at dinner on a winter's day with your thanes and counsellors. In the midst there is a comforting fire to warm the hall; outside, the storms of winter rain or snow are raging. The sparrow flies swiftly in through one door of the hall, and out through another. While he is inside, he is safe from the winter's storms; but

after a few moments of comfort, he vanishes from sight into the wintry world from which he came. Even so, man appears on earth a little while; but of what went before this life or of what follows, we know nothing. Therefore, if this new teaching has brought any more certain knowledge, it seems only right that we should follow it.

Bede died at Jarrow, seated on the floor of his cell, surrounded by the monastic community, having completed his translation of the Gospel of St John.

Lindisfarne had also blossomed into a centre of learning and study. In the little scriptorium master-scribes like Eadfrith – later Bishop of Lindisfarne – created Holy Island's most famous manuscript: the breathtaking Lindisfarne Gospels. He and the other scribes used vellum sheets of scraped and cured calfskin. Pens were cut from goose quills; ink was mixed from soot and the whites of birds' eggs; mineral pigments provided colouring; and a bronze or bone stylus would be used to sketch a design onto wax and to prick the design onto the vellum. The Lindisfarne Gospels are now on permanent display in an exhibition case at the British Library.

Viking vicissitudes

These beautiful manuscripts were very nearly lost when this golden age of learning came to a sudden and brutal end. The Vikings sacked Lindisfarne in 793 and again in 875. In 870 the community tried to flee to Ireland by boat, and the story is told that when the ship was overwhelmed by a storm a copy of the Gospels fell overboard and sank into the sea. It is said that the monks received a vision and were told where to search at low tide. The Gospels were duly found and appeared never to have been touched by water.

Although the manuscript survived to remind us of this

celebrated time, it was an era which was drawing to a tragic end. Some historians argue that the *Anglo-Saxon Chronicle* hyped the story of Norse/Viking barbarism, but even allowing for the distortions of propaganda, which doubtless occur in every generation, the writers describe the year 793 as a particularly harrowing time:

> In this year terrible portents appeared over Northumbria, which sorely affrighted the inhabitants: there were exceptional flashes of lightning, and fiery dragons were seen flying through the air. A great famine followed hard upon these signs; and a little later in the same year, on the 8th of June, the harrying of the heathen miserably destroyed God's church on Lindisfarne by rapine and slaughter.

Two hundred and fifty years after the onslaught of the Vikings a new monastic foundation was created on Lindisfarne. This survived until the dissolution of the monasteries in 1537.

Sir Walter Scott, in Canto II of his *Marmion* captures the totality of these devastating events:

> *In Saxon strength that abbey frown'd*
> *With massive arches broad and round*
> *That rose alternate, row and row,*
> *On ponderous columns, short and low,*
> *Built ere the art was known,*
> *By pointed aisle, and shafted stalk,*
> *The arcades of an alley'd walk*
> *To emulate in stone.*
> *On the deep walls, the heavy Dane*
> *Had poured his impious rage in vain;*
> *And needful was such strength to these,*
> *Exposed to the tempestuous seas*
> *Scourged by the wind's eternal sway,*
> *Open to rovers fierce as they,*
> *Which could twelve hundred years withstand*
> *Winds, waves, and northern pirates' hand.*

Not but that portions of the pile,
Rebuilded in a later style,
Shewed where the spoiler's hand had been;
Not but the wasting sea-breeze keen,
Had worn the pillar's carving quaint,
Had moulder'd in his niche the saint,
And rounded, with consuming power,
The pointed angles of each tower:
Yet still entire the Abbey stood,
Like veteran, worn, but unsubdued.

Where to find the northern saints: Lindisfarne, Durham and Ripon

In 1888 the owner of Lindisfarne, Major General Sir William Crossman, excavated the Priory, and after it was transferred to the Ministry of Works more excavation was undertaken in the 1920s. Substantial renovation of the mediæval parish church of St Mary the Virgin was completed in the nineteenth century and a small museum was created. In the churchyard, overlooking the ruins of the Norman Priory, is an eleven-foot-high statue of St Aidan, bearing aloft a torch which symbolises the light of the Gospel, and in his right hand is his bishop's crozier. His head is framed against a Celtic cross.

Apart from Fridays in winter, the museum is open all year round and attracts some 50,000 visitors a year.

Today's pilgrim will need to travel south should they wish to pray at Cuthbert's grave. The monks exhumed Cuthbert's body to prevent its desecration and in 995 brought it to Durham (see chapter 3). According to the twelfth-century chronicler, Simeon of Durham, St Aidan's relics were placed in the coffin-reliquary of St Cuthbert in Durham Cathedral. When the Normans opened Cuthbert's tomb they found his body uncorrupted, and when he was reburied the head of his friend the king, St Oswald, was placed beside him. To this day, St Cuthbert's body lies in the cathedral. St Bede was brought here in 1370 and buried in the Galilee Chapel.

Elsewhere in the north east, at Tynemouth, are the remains of a priory associated with St Oswald, a church which contains the sites of the shrines of St Oswyn and St Henry. St Wilfrid is to be found at Ripon Cathedral; his shrine is beneath the east window of the church. The crypt contains some of his belongings and continues to act as a focus of interest in Wilfrid. Each year there is a procession on the first Saturday in August led by a man dressed as St Wilfrid; portraying his purity, he rides astride a white horse. Close to Ripon lies Fountains Abbey and further to the east lies Whitby (see chapter 3).

A meditation

The Celtic Benediction

> *Deep peace of the running wave to you*
> *Deep peace of the flowing air to you*
> *Deep peace of the shining stars to you*
> *Deep peace of the quiet earth to you*
> *Deep peace of the Prince of Peace to you.*

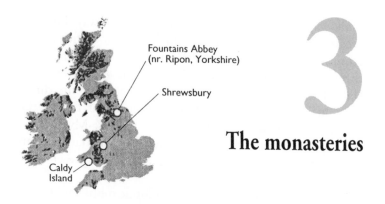

Fountains Abbey
(nr. Ripon, Yorkshire)

Shrewsbury

Caldy
Island

The monasteries

IN 1534 Henry VIII made himself head of the Church of England and severed the unity of the Church. Systematically he set about the destruction of the authority of the Pope and the elimination of those institutions and individuals who remained loyal to the Catholic Church. Elsewhere (see chapters 12 and 13) I have set out some of the consequences. Here I want to record the sites of some of the great monastic houses which for eight hundred years had done much to provide the people of Britain with employment, shelter for travellers, schools, hospitals and a whole host of social and religious services. The rich tapestry of abbeys, priories and friaries – occupied by a variety of monks: Benedictines, Cistercians, and Carthusians; and friars of various varieties and hues – black, white, brown and grey – Franciscan and Dominican – was simply ripped apart. Their colossal impact in developing local economies and fostering learning and education made them inevitable targets for a jealous king who coveted their wealth and their influence. If he was to destroy Catholicism he had to destroy the monastic communities.

Copts and Celts

These communities first sprang up in Britain when St Ninian, a Roman citizen, built Whithorn at Dumfries and

Galloway. Here, on the shores of the Solway Firth he created a remote community which was self-sufficient and committed to working the land and to reaching God through prayer (see chapter 2). In *Signs of Contradiction* (Hodder and Stoughton, 1996) I wrote about the direct links between the ancient Coptic Church of Egypt, the Desert Fathers, and the early Celtic monks. My interest was triggered after I wrote a report for the Christian Human rights Group, the Jubilee Campaign, about the present-day persecution of the Copts.

All the early writers describe the Coptic monks as "God's Athletes" seeking to be "alone with the Alone".

Coptic monasticism passed through three stages:

- The first was complete solitude. The person seeking a life of prayer, fasting and meditation, went alone into the desert, found some natural cave or dug one for his own purpose and lived there for the rest of his life.

- The second stage was the Antonian Rule. Antony is known as "the Father of Monks" because he gathered a group of disciples around him and they lived part of their time in solitude and part of their time in companionship.

- The third stage of Coptic monasticism was coenobitical or communal life, which was inaugurated by Abba Pakhom. The first monastery for men was built by him in Tabenissi in the upper reaches of the Nile. These ideas were transfused by the visits of Copts to Ireland and Wales and vice versa. Those early links are still celebrated in some of the ancient Catholic liturgies.

The Celtic forms of monasticism closely mirrored those of the Egyptian church. Men and women fortified themselves for the battles which lay ahead by seeking out remote places in which they might be alone with God. Thus strengthened, the missionaries ventured out into a hostile world and, as we have seen in chapter 2, the Celtic monks had a phenomenal impact on these islands – particularly through their belief that every person has a profound duty to respect creation which God has entrusted to our care; to be good stewards and custodians of the land; to be in harmony with all aspects of life; and to weigh the spiritual alongside the material.

The Benedictines: Crowland and Shrewsbury

This love of the land and its careful and sensitive cultivation blossomed in the monasticism which came to Britain with the Romans. The Benedictine Order and the Cistercians, and a whole host of smaller Orders, brought new agricultural methods which increased the fertility of the land. They encouraged greater diversity and cultivated the landscape as an expression of their love of God, believing that the land and the waters which had been entrusted to them were God's gift.

Benedictines live by the rule of St Benedict which he drew up at his Italian monastery of Monte Casino in about 540. As standards of discipline and devotion waned, reformers created new orders – the most successful of which were the Cistercians – who were particularly insistent on situating their abbeys in remote places.

The first Benedictine house in which I stayed was Prinknash Abbey in Gloucestershire. One of their most venerable monks, Dom Alban Leotaud, writing in *What Is a Monk?* (a pamphlet published by Prinknash Abbey) says that:

> The Benedictine monk should have three notable traits in his character. He should be genuine and authentic in his search for God. He should have a love of the Eucharist and the Liturgy and he should be obedient and able to fit into the daily round of community life. These would be signs of a Benedictine vocation and no novice would be acceptable without them.

Dom Alban goes on to write a succinct account of the Rule of St Benedict – which has produced five thousand saints in the course of its long history.

Crowland Abbey, Lincolnshire, was a typical Benedictine abbey. The foundation stone was laid by Aethelbald, King of Mercia, on 24 August 716. It was named for his friend, the "green" martyr, St Guthlac (who probably created the first religious community at Crowland).

The abbey was also dedicated to the Virgin and to St Bartholomew. Guthlac represented one of the three forms of martyrdom in the early Catholic Church. "Martyr" comes from the same root as the word "witness" and implied surrender of life – the dying of the old life, not necessarily violent death.

White martyrdom came by leaving your family and possessions and taking the Gospel to unevangelised places; red martyrdom represented the blood shed by those who were killed for their faith; and green martyrdom represented the fate of those who went into the "desert" – the wilderness or remote fastness – where, in their isolation, they prayed and worshipped God.

Closeness to creation inevitably led to the monks becoming celebrated bee keepers, herbalists, horticulturalists and farmers. They named many of the plants – which is why so many bear the name of the Virgin Mary or have Christian associations: white and yellow archangel, lady's fingers and lady's mantle, Jacob's ladder, Canterbury bells and rosemary are amongst the most obvious. Other plants which might be included in a contemporary sacred garden include Christ thorn, myrtle, cedar, myrrh, fig, turmeric and the saffron crocus (*Plants of the Bible* by Michael Zohary, Cambridge University Press, 1982).

The monastery garden was crucial for the kitchen but also for the cure of ailments. There were also areas given over for the cultivation of wild flowers for use during the celebration of Mass and other liturgies and religious festivals.

The Brother Cadfael Centre at Shrewsbury Abbey (where

Ellis Peters' fictional monastic sleuth cultivated the medieval monastic herb garden in between solving devilish mysteries) captures the essence of what went on in the Giardini Sacristi. Among the plants cultivated in the monastic sacred garden were lady's mantle, chives, garlic, dill, arnica, southernwood, chervil, borage, coriander, fennel, Christmas rose, hyssop, lavender, lovage, lemon balm, spearmint, apple mint, honeysuckle, catmint, peony, field poppy, parsley, primrose, rue, sage, houseleek, white rose of York, red rose of Lancaster, rosemary, sweet violet, onions, horehound, wormwood, white lilies, poppies, mandrake, lettuce, shallots, daffodils, beetroot, marigolds, celandine, acanthus, orache, smallage, clary and grape vine. Other old roses cultivated by the monks included maiden's blush, blush damask, the apothecary's rose (*rosa gallica officinalis*), *rosa mundi, rosa eglanteria*, and *rosa phoenicia*. Roses represented the blood shed by Jesus and the Virgin's purity was symbolised by the white lily.

The World Wide Fund for Nature (WWF UK) has initiated a Sacred Land Project which, as well as encouraging the rediscovery of ancient pilgrim routes, urges the recreation of monastic medicinal herbal gardens, using the traditional plants. Along with St Peter's Abbey at Shrewsbury, Gloucester and Peterborough Cathedrals have recreated their monastic herb gardens. Others have survived in parish churchyards.

Crowland and Shrewsbury were both Benedictine foundations. One of my favourite Cistercian monasteries is Valle Crucis Abbey in North Wales.

The Cistercians: Valle Crucis and the Welsh houses

For the pilgrim undertaking an expedition to St Winifrid's Well or St Beuno's (see chapter 5), or visiting the Marian shrines of mid and north Wales (see chapter 6), the additional journey to Llangollen to see Valle Crucis is well worth the trouble. The abbey lies about two miles north of Llangollen on the west bank of a stream which flows down to the River Dee. The Latin phrase *Valle Crucis* means quite literally the valley of the cross and took its name from the ninth-century Pillar of Eliseg, which stands a quarter of a mile to the north of the abbey. This cross was set up by Cyngen, last of the kings of Powys (who died on a pilgrimage to Rome in 854, when Powys passed to the kings of Gwynedd). The inscription on the historic cross records his descent from Brydw, the son of Gwrtheyrn (Vortigen) and grandson of the Roman emperor, Magnus Maximus, a Spanish-born general who seized power in Britain in 383.

Throughout the nearby hills there are stunning walks (particularly towards World's End) which I have enjoyed visiting since my student days. Above the abbey are old footpaths which were doubtless used by the monks who first came here in 1201 when it was established by Madog ap Gruffudd Maelor, the ruler of northern Powys.

A group of Cistercian monks came from Strata Marcella Abbey near Welshpool to create this daughter house. Their buildings and furnishings were to be plain and they eschewed elaborate decorations. Their clothes were woven with undyed wool (hence the epithet "white monks") and they observed strict rules of silence and diet. They established a series of outlying farms, or granges, which were close enough to the abbey for monks to get to them on a daily basis. The labourers at the granges were called *conversi* (lay brothers) and were not required to live such a strict rule as the professed monks.

Unlike the more autonomous Benedictines, the Cistercians held a General Chapter each year and formed a federated network of houses and daughter houses. This led to significant growth: more than 300 Cistercian monasteries created in Europe by 1155.

In Wales the Cistercians founded Tintern (1131), Whitland (1140), Margam (1147), Strata Florida (1164), Strata Marcella (1170) and Valle Crucis (1201). Whitland was the most important mother house. Other monasteries were later created in south Wales at Grace Dieu, Abbey Dore, Llantamam and Neath; in mid-Wales at Cwmhir; and in north Wales at Cymer, Aberconwy, and Basingwerk.

Valle Crucis was ravaged by fire in the thirteenth century and was made to suffer during the wars of Edward I because of the abbot's Welsh sympathies. In 1274 he was one of seven Welsh Cistercian abbots to write to the Pope defending the reputation of Prince Llywelyn ap Gruffudd. Part of their contribution to sustaining Welsh culture was the subsequent compilation by monks of the abbey, of *Brut y Tywysogion* (*The Chronicle of the Princes*) for the years 1282 to 1332.

Valle Crucis again suffered during the Welsh uprising under Owain Glyndwr but recovered during the fifteenth century.

This way of life, along with the gentle rhythms of feasts and fasting which regulated national life, would also soon disappear. Using the excuse of purging corruption, but entirely driven by his determination to seize their land and wealth, Henry VIII set about the ruthless extermination of the holy houses of England and Wales.

In the case of Valle Crucis, a visitation was made by the King's Commissioners in 1535 and within two years it had been closed. The abbey's communion plate was either sold for cash or sent to London to be melted down and sequestrated into Henry's coffers. Some of its bells found their way into the Shropshire churches of Baschurch and Ness. The estate was granted to Sir William Pickering, who stripped the lead and robbed the stones. After several changes of owner it eventually became part of the Coed Helen estate. Proving that nothing much changes, a report appeared in *The Times* in May 2000, reporting the theft of more of the abbey's historic stones, probably to be sold on at garden centres.

In 1872 the services of the great Victorian Catholic architect, Sir Gilbert Scott, were retained for the repair of the west front of the church. In 1950 the Ministry of Works bought the ruins and they passed on responsibility to Cadw, Welsh Historic Monuments, who make the site available for public access.

As well as attacking the monasteries, Henry also attacked the traditional patterns of religious observance. At one stroke, in 1536, the Crown wiped out a multitude of local festivals and celebrated feast days: St Winifred, St Edward the Confessor, St Augustine of Canterbury, the feasts of the Holy Cross and the Transfiguration and Holy Name of Jesus were among those abrogated or abolished. Henry's new Archbishop of Canterbury complained bitterly when he discovered that the king's own court had continued to celebrate St Laurence's Day in 1537 and wrote to Thomas Cromwell objecting to the example which was being set.

Henry's principal agent in decimating the old religion was his minister, Thomas Cromwell. The topographer and King's Antiquary, Thomas Leland, acted as chronicler of these tempestuous events. From 1534 until 1542 he traversed the length and breadth of England and Wales, detailing the final days of the Middle Ages as he made his "laborious journey". The modern pilgrim can take Leland's survey and follow in his footsteps, pondering the way of life which was eradicated. Even as he journeyed, events would overtake him.

Following in the footsteps of Thomas Leland

Leland began his first great journey in Cambridge, where he noted the magnificent Carmelite friary, the half-circle of monasteries on the far side of the town, and the new colleges which had taken over old monasteries. Crowland Abbey was the most northerly of the monasteries and was Benedictine. It had its own theological college (now Magdalene College). Jesus College had been the Benedictine Priory of St Ragmund until 1496, and south of it stood the

Franciscan priory. Blackfriars stood on the site of Emmanuel College (the Dominicans' theological college).

After completing his survey of monastic holdings in Cambridge, Leland rode on to the Benedictine priory of St Neots before crossing the River Ouse. His next objective was Northampton, where there was a circle of monasteries and friaries: Greyfriars, "the best built and largest house of all the friars, a little beyond the main market place"; Blackfriars, north-east of Northampton Castle; the Austin friars "hard against St John's Hospital"; and over the river was a Cluniac foundation, Delapre Abbey.

Next, at Leicester, he noted Greyfriars, within the town's walls, and outside them the Austin friars (Leicester Abbey) and the Dominicans. Today's pilgrim, following the meanderings of Thomas Leland, should pause at St Mary de Castro church – the jewel of Leicester's churches. It stands within the royal castle of Leicester and was founded in 1107. It had a dean and canons until the Reformation and survived because it had been adapted as a parish church. Prince Charles, the Prince of Wales, recently visited the church and described it as "a special place which is so clearly loved by those who worship in it. It deserves to be conserved and preserved for future generations to enjoy and treasure." Sadly, Henry VIII's survey undertaken by Thomas Leland had no such intentions of conservation in mind.

Leland left Leicester to ride east to Launde Priory, Leicester Abbey's daughter house, and from here to Stamford, where he found an abundance of religious houses: Browne's Hospital; the Carmelites at Whitefriars Priory on the Spalding Road, the Benedictines at St Leonard's Priory and several other foundations.

Yorkshire and its great monastic houses

Riding north to Grimsthorpe Castle, Leland recorded the dilapidated Vaudley Abbey before arriving at Lincoln. Here, he noted Whitefriars Priory on his left, and the Guild of St Mary on his right as he entered the city and stopped at the cathedral.

After riding on through the rain to Torskey Abbey, Leland forded the River Trent at Gainsborough and headed for Doncaster. He described the Whitefriars' priory as "a right goodly house" in the centre of the town, while the Greyfriars were to be found at the north end of the bridge.

Travelling west to Wakefield he noted St Oswald's Abbey before setting off in a northward direction for York. Fiercely Yorkist and Catholic, the city was not to the protestant Leland's tastes.

The largest of its religious houses was the Benedictine Abbey of St Mary's which William Rufus had founded. Nearby was St Leonard's Hospital; Austin friars were by the River Ouse; Whitefriars close to Layerthorpe Gate; Greyfriars close to the castle; Gilbertines at St Andrew's Priory, outside Fisher Gate; and the Priory of the Holy Trinity by Mickle Gate. Leland spent a month here, travelling out to monasteries and nunneries at Beverley, Kingston-upon-Hull, Scarborough, Whitby and Pickering.

Apart from visiting the magnificent York Minster, today's pilgrim will wish to spend some time at the Bar Convent where there is an exhibition of Catholic history. York is also home to a monastery of Poor Clares, women who spend their lives in poverty and prayer. The present foundation was enlarged four years ago when the Poor Clares closed their monastery in Liverpool and some of the nuns moved here. The community is made up of some remarkable women who are always extremely welcoming. To the north of York is Ampleforth Abbey, continuing the Benedictine tradition in these parts, especially through its provision of Catholic education. Its former abbot was Cardinal Basil Hume.

York Minster

The dominance of York as a regional centre originates in the third century when Constantine was proclaimed emperor at York. There was a Christian community in the city at that time, and when Paulinus baptised King Edwin in 627 it led to the construction of the first church in the city. Paulinus became the first bishop and was followed by Chad in 664 and Wilfrid in 669. It was York which subsequently produced Alcuin, commissioned by Charlemagne to organise education throughout his European empire.

In 1075, Archbishop Thomas began the building of a Romanesque church and it was given the name Minster, the Saxon word for monastery. However, it was always served by a secular clergy, many of whom were more than ready to stand up to temporal leaders. William Fitzherbert, bishop in the twelfth century was deposed by a hostile king but received his reward in heaven – being canonised by the Pope as St William of York. In the thirteenth century Archbishop Walter de Gray began the extensive rebuilding of the minster – a project which stretched over the next 250 years. His tomb lies in the south transept.

If, like Thomas Leland, modern travellers take York as a base, they can strike out to see some of the finest remains of Britain's monastic tradition.

Whitby, Rievaulx, Mount Grace and Fountains

Out to the east, at Whitby, the town's abbey stands as "the beacon on the hill". Standing on a cliff high above the town this is what remains of the double monastery for men and women created by St Hilda in 657. From Anglo-Saxon stock, Hilda was taught by Paulinus, In 664 Whitby was the dramatic setting for the Synod which settled the Celtic and Roman disputes, and Celtic and Roman traditions determined the future shape of Britain's ecclesiastical government. These themes are captured sensitively and accurately by Melvin Bragg in his historical novel, *Credo*.

In 867, Hilda's monastery was destroyed by Viking invaders, and it was not rebuilt until the eleventh century when Reinfrid, a monk from Evesham, refounded it as a Benedictine monastery.

Inland, in the Rye Valley, there are more monastic ruins. These are what remain of the magnificent Rievaulx Abbey, a Cistercian community which came here in 1132. It became one of their most important monasteries and a mission centre. One of its great abbots was Aelred, theologian and administrator. He carefully set out his vision of how the monastic life should be lived. The substantial ruins allow the modern pilgrim to grasp the scale and nature of monastic life, and to grasp the enormity of what was done.

In total contrast, the ruins of Mount Grace Priory, to the north west of Rievaulx, reveal an entirely different form of monastic life. Here, in this Carthusian house, monks lived as hermits, gathering together for some community worship. The priory was founded in 1398, when the first aisleless church was constructed. The tower, built as part of an expansion programme in the fifteenth century, still stands. It is also possible to see the clear outline of the buildings and the reconstruction of one of the monastic cells. These were placed around a great cloister.

Most famously of all, in 1132, in the valley of the Skell, Abbot Richard founded Fountains Abbey, the greatest of England's Cistercian houses. The ruined remains speak eloquently of the scale of the religious community, and the commitment of those who were a part of it.

The Cistercian rule was created by St Stephen Harding at Citeaux and developed by St Bernard of Clairvaux. It took the Benedictine community life and built onto it self-sufficiency, asceticism, poverty, simplicity and isolation. At Fountains, alongside 120 monks, about 600 lay brothers helped to run the farms and ensured the monastery's survival. Fountains was so successful that it became the mother house for eight new abbeys. Designated now as a World Heritage Site, Fountains Abbey is in the ownership of the National Trust. During a visit in May 2000 my children were enthralled by Super Sleuth and his hunt for Br Ambrose and his fellow monks, enlightened by the excellent video presentation available at the Visitor Centre, and entertained by the games at the educational centre. For at least two weeks after our visit my just-turned three-year-old son repeatedly asked the perceptive question "Why did the king kill the monks and break the house?"

Regular tours, recitals and children's trails are organised at the abbey (see appendix for details).

Bolton Abbey Priory

To the west of Fountains and York, en route for Skipton, is the beautiful Bolton Abbey Priory. As a pilgrimage in its own right, a day-long walk across the hills from Fountains to Bolton would temper most troubles of the spirit.

Set close to the River Wharfe, Bolton was an Augustinian priory created in 1155 by Alicia de Romilly of Skipton Castle. Three hundred years after the priory's dissolution in 1539, the great Victorian Catholic designer, Augustus W.N. Pugin, created the glass in the six windows on the south side of the priory. Of all the sites which I visited in connection with this book, the stunning location of Bolton Abbey affected me the most. The Anglican community who, since the destruction of the monasteries, have continued to use the nave of the priory as their parish church, deserve to be congratulated on the way in which the priory church of St Mary and St Cuthbert has been maintained and preserved. A sanctuary lamp burns above a stone altar which local people saved and cherished from destruction as altars were smashed and stripped all over

Britain. Five consecration crosses are engraved into its surface and hand-made mediaeval tiles from the now ruined choir surround it.

The last prior, Prior Moone, saved at least part of this great foundation by ensuring its transition to parochial use, and in the 1970s when the parish congregation was down to single figures Canon Maurice Slaughter performed a similar function. Prodigious effort and vision led to new restoration work and to spiritual renewal.

At Bolton Abbey, look for the east wall painting and for the five Madonna lilies, all slightly different, which refer to the priory's dedication to Our Lady. Alternating with the lilies are six symbolic plants. There is barley to represent Jesus as "the bread of life"; the olive to signify His suffering in the Garden of Olives, Gethsemane; the vine, recalling Our Lord's metaphor that He is "the vine and you are the branches"; the passion flower, which is a traditional folk symbol of Christ's suffering on the cross – the flower head has three nails and a crown of thorns; the rose, with its thorny branches and its red pigmentation signifying the crown of thorns and the precious blood; and the palm, recalling the short-lived triumph as Jesus rode into Jerusalem. Catholics burn the Palm Sunday palms, and the ashes are used during the liturgies at the next Ash Wednesday, as a reminder of how quickly in our fickle world triumph can turn to disaster.

The lily appears again between Mary and the Archangel Gabriel on the first panel of Pugin's stained glass window, looking from the right of the east wall.

On leaving the church look over the door of what is still Prior Moone's unfinished tower, at his engraved prayer asking for God's mercy on his soul. Look also to the south-west corner of the tower and see a small stone statue which somehow survived the ravages of those who destroyed so many of the representations which adorned these buildings. This small survivor is a pilgrim, complete with his staff and scrip, or purse, the emblems of the mediæval pilgrim.

Bolton Abbey Priory stages a series of public concerts throughout the summer months, including a musical extravaganza entitled "The Mystery Tour", telling the Bible stories.

The abbey is one of fourteen pre-Reformation churches listed in a pamphlet produced by the Anglican diocese of Bradford, entitled *Discover Churches in Wharfedale*. No holiday in this stunningly beautiful area – Bolton Abbey is at the gateway to the Yorkshire National Park – would be complete without a visit to some of these buildings (details in the appendix).

Beverley Minster and Selby Abbey

To the south east of York lies Beverley Minster, referred to by the Venerable Bede in his *Ecclesiastical History*. A monastery was formed by Bishop John of York and then, in the tenth century, it was refounded as a collegiate church of secular canons.

To the south of York stands Selby Abbey, the successor to a wooden building erected by Abbot Benedict in 1070. A Benedictine community flourished here until the Reformation.

The North East

Leland noted all of these religious houses for the reports which he was diligently preparing for his masters. After his four-week sojourn in York he went north to Bishop Auckland and then to Durham. Here he encountered the grandeur of the monastic cathedral with its great shrine to St Cuthbert, buried first on the Holy Island of Lindisfarne, when he died in 687. When it was feared that his remains would be desecrated by invading Danes, over the next 300 years his relics were moved to various locations before finally being interred in a shrine at Durham. A Benedictine monastery was established and served the cathedral, with the cloister adjoining the cathedral on the south side. Since the Reformation and the destruction of the shrine the monastic buildings have been used for various purposes – the refectory, for instance, is now the library, the undercroft is home to a restaurant and permanent exhibition ("The Treasures of St Cuthbert"). The dormitory houses the museum. This beautiful location was declared a World Heritage Site in 1987.

Leland spent most of his time in the library, which at the time contained over 500 printed books and 1,000 manuscripts.

From Durham via Chester-le-Street to Gateshead and Newcastle, he then retraced his steps travelling south to Teesdale and to Barnard Castle. The road through the Yorkshire Dales took him to Richmond, where he noted a Franciscan friary and a Premonstratensian abbey dedicated to St Agatha.

After a twenty-mile journey he arrived in Ripon. Here, in 672, the cathedral's tiny crypt had its origins as part of St Wilfrid's church. A Northumbrian, Wilfrid embraced the Roman pattern of monastic life and became one of the leading missionaries. The abbey could boast the Venerable Bede as part of its history, but during Leland's visit it had fallen on hard times. The Cistercians had taken many of its stones to build the tower at Fountains. In addition to its cathedral and abbey Ripon boasted three hospitals: St Anne's, St John's and St Mary Magdalene's hospital for lepers.

The home run

At Knaresborough Leland noted a Redemptionist priory, at Worksop an Augustinian priory, and at Welbeck – a Premonstratensian abbey. He then journeyed to Mansfield to Newstead Abbey – founded by Henry II, to Nottingham,

Belvoir Castle, Stamford and Bedford. Here he listed two Augustinian houses, Newnham Priory and Caldwell Priory, and a community of Greyfriars. His first journey almost over, Leland continued through Ampthill to Berkhamstead, Windsor, Datchet and to London's Hampton Court. He came armed with valuable information, which was set alongside the valuations made by the Lord Chancellor, Sir Thomas Audley. He had asked commissioners in every shire to make an inventory of each abbey, friary, nunnery, monastery or religious house in their area. Their six-volume *Valor Ecclesiasticus* would be the basis for the systematic eradication of Britain's religious communities.

Leland, meanwhile, did not tarry for long. By the summer of 1535 he was undertaking the same task of gathering information. This time he was in the West Midlands – in Oxford, Bicester, Banbury, Warwick, Stratford-upon-Avon, the Vale of Evesham, Tewkesbury, Cheltenham, Gloucester, Hereford, Leominster, Ludlum, Shrewsbury, Worcester, Birmingham and Lichfield. His last entry before returning to London was the Carmelite house in Coventry.

As 1535 passed into 1536 inventories were replaced by interrogators. On 11 March 1536 the House of Commons did the king's bidding and allowed the seizure of any religious house of fewer than twelve people. Most became manor houses for the rich. Knowing that time was running out, Leland accelerated his work.

Going west: London to Scilly

Going west this time, Leland visited the friars at Hounslow, who cared for the sick and poor; he went to Maidenhead, to Reading Abbey, to Oxford, Faringdon, through the Cotswolds to Cirencester's Augustinian abbey, to the famous Benedictine abbey of William of Malmesbury, to Chippenham, Corsham, and Bath, with its enormous abbey of Saxon foundation. Next he set off for Wells and Glastonbury, where he met the new abbot, Richard Whiting, whom he described as "a most candid and friendly man". That would not save the good abbot from execution in due course (see chapter 1).

At Sherborne he saw another abbey of Saxon origin. Today's pilgrim will be captivated by John Hayward's west window, which has the Madonna as the central focus. On to Ilchester, Bridgwater, Dunster, Minehead, Exmoor, Barnstaple, Torrington, Launceston and Catholic Cornwall, where in 1537 Cromwell expressed alarm at the degree of unrest. The parish of St Keverne had, for instance, commissioned a banner of the Five Wounds – like those carried in the Pilgrimage of Grace – to illustrate their unhappiness at the revolution which was underway. The new Bishop of Exeter, Bishop Veysey, issued an angry circular in 1539 admonishing the clergy because people such as blacksmiths and fishermen continued to observe their occupational feast days.

Like William of Worcester, who left an earlier account of his journeying in the West Country, Leland stayed at Bodmin, but already its religious houses had been suppressed. At St Michael's Mount, the Brigettine nuns had been evicted. Perhaps to ensure that no corner should be left unobserved, Leland then sailed for the Isles of Scilly, from where the Benedictine monks of Tresco had already disappeared. He passed back to Penzance, Penryn, Falmouth, Truro, Fowey and Plymouth, noting all the time any holdings owned by monks such as those at the abbey of Plympton and Torre Abbey. By the time he reached Exeter he recorded the empty Benedictine priory, the abandoned hospital of St John, the evicted Franciscans and Blackfriars and the last remaining foundation of six men caring for the sick on the Honiton Road.

Before completing this journey of 1,000 miles he took in the towns of Salisbury, Winchester, Southampton and Portsmouth. Leland's work was fast being overtaken by the juggernaut of destruction which the state had propelled into motion. His role as King's Antiquary was superfluous as the bigger religious houses followed the smaller ones. In a frenzy of activity Leland continued his great survey, undeterred that the buildings were now broken and the communities fractured. His subsequent travels took him into Wales, Cheshire, Lancashire and Cumbria.

Cumbria: Cartmel Priory

Typical of the religious houses he noted was Cartmel Priory, in the Furness Peninsular, now in Cumbria, once in Lancashire. Founded in about 1188 by William Marshall, who later became Earl of Pembroke, this was a priory of Black Canons of St Augustine. Although at the time of the dissolution the lead was stripped from the roof of the cloister and other buildings, the town choir was allowed to be retained as a parish church.

Leland would have recorded the presence of ten brethren – although there are twenty-six carved seats for the community in the choir. The Commissioners hanged four of the canons and ten laymen.

This was not the end of the priory's sufferings. Although a little of the east window still remains, most of the mediæval stained glass was destroyed by Oliver Cromwell's Puritans. The "Cromwell Door" to the church is pitted with holes said to have been made when local people shot at Roundhead soldiers who had decided to stable their horses in the nave.

Cartmel's choir stalls date from about 1450 and with the aid of Eric Rothwell's pamphlet, *The Misericords and Screen in Cartmel Priory*, my children were easily able to identify the symbolism and provenance of the unusual carvings. Throughout the summer months the priory stages public concerts and stages a festival weekend in September.

Perhaps it was as Leland grasped the enormity of the events which he had helped set in motion that his mind began to go. He fell into a terrible depression, and this precipitated his death in 1552. In any event, by then a whole way of life had been destroyed, and Britain would have to wait another three hundred years before new monastic houses and religious communities could be openly founded. What Leland's pilgrimage illustrates is the vast scale of the network of religious communities which existed in Britain and which would be ruthlessly crushed.

Monks today

If Leland were starting out today on a survey of Britain and Ireland's monastic foundations his task would be made considerably easier by two books in particular. Fr Gordon Beattie OSB, a monk of Ampleforth, travelled over 50,000 miles to visit the abbeys, priories, parishes and schools of monks and nuns following the Rule of St Benedict in Great Britain, Ireland and their overseas foundations. He subsequently published Gregory's Angels (Gracewing, 1997). Another useful publication is the *Directory of Monastic Hospitality* (The Economic Commission, 1991) which contains all the contact details of the contemporary convents and monasteries.

The English Benedictine Congregation opened a common novitiate at Belmont in 1859, and in 1899 Downside, Ampleforth and Douai (then still in France) were raised to the status of abbeys. Other houses include Fort Augustus, Ealing, Buckfast and Worth. Their nuns have houses at Stanbrook, Curzon Park and Colwich. The Solesmes Congregation have houses at Quarr and Ryde; the Subiaco Congregation have houses at Ramsgate, Prinknash, Pluscarden, Farnborough, Fernham, Minster, Jamberoo and Lammermoor. The Congregation of the Annunciation has a house at Glenstal; the Olivetan Congregation have houses at Cockfosters, Turvey and Turvey Priory; the Congregation of the Adorers of the Sacred Heart of Montmartre are at Tyburn (see chapter

14), London, and Cobh, Ireland; the Benedictine Sisters of Grace and Compassion have priories at Brighton and Heathfield. Houses of nuns who come under no congregation exist at Oulton, Kylemore, Buckfast and Andover. There are Jericho Benedictines at Harelaw, Dundee, Girvan, Edinburgh and Derby. There are also twelve houses of Cistercians in Great Britain and Ireland, including Mount Melleray, Mount St Bernard, Roscrea, Caldey, Mellifont, Nunraw, Portglenone and Bolton, and nuns at Whitland and Glencairn.

There is also a Bridgettine house recently established at Maryvale, in Birmingham. Drawn from all over the world, including India, Italy and Mexico, this community of eight has an average age of about thirty-three. Only one house of this "double" Order (i.e. male and female on the same campus) existed in pre-Reformation England, at Syon, in Middlesex. They had a more or less continuous history thereafter, surviving for a long time in England and then on the Continent, eventually returning to England.

For the modern pilgrim, perhaps bewildered by the variety and diversity of the modern monastic communities, the following suggestions may provide a useful blend of disciplines as well as locations which might facilitate modern pilgrimages to places of Catholic interest. Buckfast Abbey and Convent is situated in the West Country at Buckfastleigh, Devon. Caldey Abbey is on Caldey Island, close to Tenby on the coast of South Wales, Pembrokeshire. I had not been to Caldey until I came to write this book and I combined a visit with a detour along the wild and beautiful Pembrokeshire coast to St David's Cathedral (see chapter 4).

Caldey Island

The monastery is situated three miles across the calm waters of the Caldey sound and sits alongside its little sister island, St Margaret's, sanctuary of birds and seals.

There have been monks of some sort on this island for 1,500 years. Its twenty-first-century owners are the Reformed Cistercian Order, who devote their lives to the worship and service of God. At a small visitor centre close to the walls of their Italianate monastery a video is repeated every twenty minutes or so. It is a wonderful introduction to the community, who live behind the whitewashed walls beyond the small village green.

The little boat which took me over to Caldey (and during the season they ply backward and forwards every few minutes) was called *Nemesis*. Quite why a boat named for the Greek goddess of vengeance should be carrying pilgrims to an oasis of Christian tranquillity and peace entirely escaped me. The island is a paradise of natural beauty, clothed in the peace which really does pass understanding.

On disembarking the pilgrim should avoid taking a trip in the trailer pulled by a tractor and instead take the short walk to the abbey. One path, which I followed, is marked "Calvary", and there is a tiny chapel nearby dedicated to Our Lady of Peace. Here, in this little turret, were the hand-written prayers and petitions of pilgrims who had passed this way before, testimonies of a deeper faith which sceptics would probably be surprised to find alive and well in a country which too often thinks it can dispense with God.

About twenty monks follow the Rule of St Benedict and attend seven services each day, the first at 3.15 am. In addition the monks maintain a prime beef herd, bake shortbread in the monastery ovens and produce hand-made chocolate from the abbot's kitchen. They also manufacture the famous range of Caldey perfumes, made from the island's abundant flora, everything from gorse to lavender.

Signposts allow for easy walks to the parish church of St David; dry stone walls and fuschia hedges, reminiscent of the west of Ireland, line the paths to St Illtud's Church and the old priory; and on to the lighthouse which perches above Chapel Point. Beaches in Britain don't come much better than the one at Priory Bay, and if you are as fortunate as I was on my one day excursion you may even imagine for a moment that you have arrived in a Mediterranean Eden.

Prinknash Abbey and other houses

At the turn of the twentieth century Caldey was home to the monks of what is now Prinknash Abbey. Their journey from the island and from their Anglican roots is another fascinating story, well recorded in the monastery's records housed in their library. Among their community in the 1930s was Dom Bede Griffiths (for a time Prior) who, as Richard Griffiths, was the undergraduate who challenged C.S. Lewis, his atheistic English tutor at Oxford, about his unbelief. Lewis was present at Fr Bede's ordination and dedicates his book, *A Pilgrim's Regress*, to his former pupil. Prinknash Abbey is in Cranham, near Gloucester, and is set in stunning countryside.

Other abbeys to visit include Quarr Abbey, on the Isle of Wight. Stanbrook Abbey is at Callow End, near Worcester; Mount Saint Bernard is at Coalville, Leicester; Belmont Abbey is in Hereford; Ampleforth Abbey is close to York; Colwich Abbey is near Stafford.

In Scotland, Nunraw Abbey is situated in East Lothian, near Haddington; and Pluscarden Abbey is at Elgin, in Moray.

In Ireland, Bolton Abbey is at Athy, County Kildare; Mellifint Abbey is at Collon, County Louth; Kylemore Abbey is in Connemara, County Galway; Glenstal Abbey is at Murroe, County Limerick; and Glencairn Abbey is at Glencairn, County Waterford.

Details of some other religious houses also appear in the appendix.

Meditation

Zones of silence

In a civilisation which is more and more mobile, noisy and talkative, zones of silence and of rest become vitally necessary. Monasteries – in their original format – have more than ever, therefore, a vocation to remain places of peace and inwardness. Don't let pressures, either internal or external, affect your traditions and your means of recuperation. Rather make yourself educate your guests and retreatants to the virtue of silence. You will know that I had occasion to remind the participants in the plenary session of the congregation of Religious, on 7th March last, of the rigorous observance of monastic enclosure. I remembered the very strong words on this subject by my predecessor, Paul VI: "Enclosure does not isolate contemplative souls from communion of that mystical Body. More than that, it puts them at the very heart of the church."

Love your separation from the world, which is totally comparable to the biblical desert. Paradoxically, this longing is not for emptiness. It is there that the Lord speaks to your heart and associates himself closely with his work of salvation.

(John Paul II, 1980)

York

Canterbury

St Davids,
Wales

4

The Cathedrals
of England and Wales

SEMINAL in the development of European civilisation
were the great monastic houses and their cultivation of
learning and culture. They were providers of work,
guardians of literacy and custodians of creation. The sheer
number of religious houses which covered these islands
still confounds the non-believer anxious to dismiss the
centrality of Catholicism to the historic development of
our nation.

Alongside the monastic orders and the charterhouses of
the Carthusians and priories of the Augustinian canons,
there were mendicant Orders – such as the Franciscans
and Dominicans, founded in the thirteenth century – who
owned no property. Their special charism was urban
evangelisation and missionary work.

Yet the bulk of the Church's work was undertaken – as
it is today – by the secular diocesan priests living in their
parishes, ministering to the daily needs of the faithful,
administering the sacraments, and celebrating the holy
Mass. These priests looked towards their bishop who
exercised authority over them. The seat of his authority
became his cathedral church, *cathedra*, meaning the bishop's
throne.

The early cathedrals

The earliest cathedrals were basilicas, oblong buildings culminating in a semi-circle where the bishop would sit, surrounded by his advisers. These were later superseded by the cruciform shape, representing the Cross.

Almost uniquely, many English cathedrals – such as Ely, Canterbury and Durham – were administered by Benedictine monks, who provided the liturgy, especially the beautiful Gregorian chants. While the prior exercised authority over the monks, the bishop had ultimate jurisdiction and lived separately from the monastic community.

In other cathedrals – such as St Pauls, Lincoln and York – the clergy have always been secular, with a group of canons presided over by a dean.

For the modern pilgrim seeking pre-Reformation Catholic cathedrals, or some of those built since the Victorian emancipation of Catholics, I have geographically grouped together some of the key buildings.

The South East

I have written separately about Westminster Cathedral and Westminster Abbey (chapter 16).

Today's Catholic pilgrim will inevitably want to follow Chaucer's Canterbury pilgrims and visit the cathedral of Augustine and Becket. In the bibliography I list two ideal literary companions, Hilaire Belloc's *The Old Road*, and Shirley Du Boulay's *The Road to Canterbury: A Modern Pilgrimage*. These can hardly be bettered. In travelling the northern route to Canterbury from London the pilgrim might make a stop at Rochester Cathedral.

First, though, as they pass through Southwark, there lies the cathedral church of St George.

Southwark's Catholic cathedral had its origins in St George's Chapel in London Road, which, by the mid-nineteenth century was serving a congregation of 15,000 people. A collection for a new church was organised by the chaplain, Fr Thomas Doyle. By 1839 this enabled the church to acquire a site in St George's Fields and to commission the celebrated architect of Gothic revival, Augustus Welby Pugin.

In 1840 the foundation stone was laid and in 1848 St George's Church was ready to be opened by the Vicar Apostolic for the London District, Nicholas Wiseman.

In 1850, when the Catholic Hierarchy was restored, St George's became the cathedral of the new diocese of Southwark. It was here that Cardinal Wiseman was enthroned as first Archbishop of Westminster and Administrator of Southwark on 6 December of that year. It was here, and also at Westminster on 4 May 2000, that the Sesquicentennial Anniversary of the Restoration of the Hierarchy was celebrated, along with events at Westminster. During the celebration of Vespers for the Feast of St George, the congregation sang a hymn written by Marty Haugen, "Let Us Build a House Where Love Can Dwell":

Let us build a house where prophets speak,
And words are strong and true...
Here the cross shall stand as witness
And as symbol of God's grace;
Here as one we claim the faith of Jesus.

Let us build a house where love is found
in water, wine and wheat...

Let us build a house where hands will reach
beyond the wood and stone
to heal and strengthen, serve and teach
and live the Word they've known.

Let us build a house where all are named,
their songs and visions heard...
Built of tears and cries and laughter,
prayers of faith and songs of grace.

In 1941 St George's was severely damaged by German firebombs. In 1953, rebuilding began and the cathedral was ready to be re-opened in 1958.

From Southwark's Gothic revival the pilgrim's next cathedral offers glimpses of Norman Gothic architecture.

Rochester makes claim to be the oldest diocese in England, only after Canterbury. In 604, Augustine sent the first bishop. The remains of the northern missionary, St Paulinus, are buried here.

In 1077, the Saxon church was built by Gandulf, the first Norman bishop, and some of his Romanesque building is still visible, as are parts of the twelfth-century monastic cloister and chapter house.

Throughout the twelfth and thirteenth centuries the building continued in the Gothic style. In the fourteenth century, Bishop Hamo de Hythe constructed the central tower and spire, although these were remodelled by the Victorians. The cathedral produced two martyrs, Bishop John Fisher (see chapter 12), executed by Henry VIII and, during the reign of Mary Tudor, the Protestant martyr, Nicholas Ridley (who was Bishop of London by then). The latter is commemorated in the quire screen.

Elsewhere in the South East, pilgrims following the southern route to Canterbury will commence their journey at Winchester, which had its origins in the seventh century when Catholic missionaries, led by St Birinus, baptised King Cynegils of the West Saxons. In 643, Cenwalh built a minster and thirty years later Bishop Haeddi made Winchester the seat of his diocese.

As a religious, political and royal centre of power, Winchester became incredibly important – and the royal remains of Alfred the Great, King of Wessex, who was buried here along with many other great Saxon leaders, bear testimony to its political centrality.

In 1079, the first Norman bishop, Walkelin, began the replacement of the Saxon church, and in 1093 the dedication took place. Building and re-ordering continued over the centuries, with the re-vaulting of the Lady Chapel taking place in 1500. The chantry chapels of Cardinal Henry Beaufort and Bishops William Waynflete, Richard Fox and Stephen Gardiner (the last Catholic bishop), where daily Mass would have been celebrated by the monks, are particularly beautiful. Sadly, the famous shrine of St Swithun was desecrated at the Reformation.

Like Winchester, Chichester Cathedral has its origins with the early missionaries to the Anglo-Saxons. Following his disputes in Northumbria (see chapter 2) St Wilfred came to minister to the southern Saxons. In 681 he established a cathedral in Selsey. Four hundred years later the Normans moved the cathedral to the old Roman town of Chichester and the principal builder was Bishop Luffa. The most well known of his successors was Bishop Richard of Wych (1245–53), later canonised by the Pope as St Richard of Chichester. His shrine was destroyed in the Reformation but pilgrims continue to come here, not least to see the two Romanesque stone carved panels dating from the twelfth century.

In 1244 Richard of Wych was elected bishop, but Henry III and part of the cathedral chapter refused to accept him. After an appeal to the authority of Rome, Pope Innocent IV consecrated Richard bishop at Lyons. He is often depicted with a chalice at his feet, in memory of the time he dropped the chalice at Mass, when the wine remained miraculously unspilt.

The prayer of St Richard of Chichester is still widely used:

Thanks be to Thee my Lord Jesus Christ,
for all the benefits which
Thou hast given me;
For all the pains and insults
which Thou hast borne for me.
O most merciful Redeemer,
friend and Brother,
May I know Thee more clearly,

Love Thee more dearly,
And follow Thee more nearly.

Three post-Reformation Catholic cathedrals in the South East are worth visiting: Portsmouth, Arundel and Brentwood Cathedrals.

Arundel is close to Arundel Castle, the family home of the Howards (see chapter 12) whose patriarch, the Duke of Norfolk, is England's leading Catholic layman. The Cathedral was built through the generosity of the fifteenth Duke and is a magnificent example of nineteenth-century Gothic revival, although its architect, Joseph Hansom, is perhaps better known as designer of the hansom cab. In the north transept are the remains of St Philip Howard, Earl of Arundel, martyred in 1595 (see chapter 12). The cathedral is seen at its best on the feast of Corpus Christi (22 June) when the nave is decked with flowers sent from Covent Garden and a wonderful procession takes place through the grounds, in which the duke and many of the knights of the Catholic Orders walk behind the Blessed Sacrament. It is a truly memorable occasion.

Brentwood Cathedral has special associations for me, as my parents were married and buried from here. I made my First Communion and was Confirmed at Brentwood, served as an altar boy and went to primary school in the parish school, administered by the Sisters of Mercy, and my sister, Deirdre, was baptised here. The earliest part of the cathedral dates from 1861 and is mock-Gothic in style. Insufficient space led to an undistinguished extension being erected in the 1970s and this was happily removed when work began, in 1989, on its replacement. Quinlan Terry came up with a superb classical building, a blend of early Italian Renaissance and Wren. The new structures sensitively take the eye into the earlier church, where the Blessed Sacrament is housed in the traditional sanctuary area. The building is surmounted by a dome lantern and cross and entirely achieves its purpose.

Bishop Thomas MacMahon, who oversaw the construction of the work, will bequeath to his successors and the laity a building which truly seeks to praise God in the best traditions of church architecture.

The South West

Bath Abbey was built in a well-known Roman town, and we know that from 757 the monastic community of St Peter was established here. The Benedictines would come here in due course. In 973 Edgar was crowned at Bath as first king of all England. The abbey's most famous abbot was St Alphege, consecrated Archbishop of Canterbury and martyred in the eleventh century.

The cathedral was commenced in the eleventh century but in 1244 its influence waned when the seat of the diocese was transferred back to Wells (see chapter 1).

Elsewhere in the South West, the pilgrim should visit Salisbury Cathedral, Exeter Cathedral, Wimborne Minster and Clifton Cathedral. In addition, Malmesbury Abbey and Sherborne Abbey are in delightful settings and might be reached during the same expedition.

Exeter has always been one of my favourite cathedrals. The young Saint Boniface, missionary to the Germans, was educated at a monastery on this site. Pope Leo IX allowed Bishop Leofric to transfer the See from Crediton to Exeter, and when the Normans arrived they created the Romanesque cathedral, including its distinctive twin towers. The thirteenth century saw the construction of the Lady chapel and the neighbouring chapels dedicated to St Gabriel and St John the Evangelist. To the south of the cathedral some of the old monastic cloister remains, although the cathedral's life was ordered by a dean and canons rather than by a monastic community.

Clifton Cathedral, in Bristol, is dedicated to St Peter and St Paul. Its altar stands at the centre of a quadrant and is surrounded by some beautiful internal fittings. William

Mitchell designed the stations of the cross and the font, made out of Portland stone, is the work of Simon Verity.

East Anglia

In 633 the Roman mission to Canterbury sent St Felix to establish the Church in East Anglia. The diocesan seat was founded at Dunwich and then moved to North Elmham, Thetford and, in 1096, to Norwich.

In the seventh century, Celtic missionaries came from Ireland and established a monastery in Great Yarmouth at Burgh Castle, in the ruins of the ancient Roman fort. St Cedd built the stone church at Bradwell, in Essex.

Benedictines had an abbey church at Bury St Edmunds, whose ruins may be seen near the present cathedral, and monasteries at Peterborough, Binham and Ely. There was a Cluniac priory at Castle Acre.

In 1096 the cathedral was begun in Norwich and boasts the largest monastic cloister in England. The ambulatory, the bishop's throne and the almost circular St Luke and Jesus chapels are all unique to Norwich in their design.

Nearby is the post-Reformation Catholic cathedral of Norwich. Built by the fifteenth Duke of Norfolk, it was begun in 1882, designed by George Gilbert Scott and his brother John Oldrid Scott. The north aisle of the sanctuary contains a chapel dedicated to the Precious Blood while the south aisle houses the chapel of the Blessed Sacrament.

At Ely stands the cathedral which crowns what was once an island. First settled by Etheldreda, here she built her double monastery for men and women. When this was destroyed by the Danes, Benedictine monks re-established the monastery and, in 1093, Abbot Simeon began the construction of the Romanesque church.

The fourteenth-century Lady chapel is the largest chapel of its kind in any of our cathedrals. Although the cloister was destroyed at the dissolution, the twelfth-century Prior's Door remains. The board ceiling was constructed in the nineteenth century to a design of Sir Giles Gilbert Scott.

Peterborough Cathedral can trace its origins to the seventh-century monastery founded by Peda, the King of Mercia. After its destruction by the Danes, the Benedictines founded a community and, in 972, the abbey church was consecrated in the presence of King Edgar. The present building, with its unique Gothic triple portico dominating the west front, was begun in the thirteenth century.

The Midlands

St Chad brought Christianity to Lichfield (see chapter 2), which, in the eighth century, briefly achieved metropolitan status having its own archbishop. Elsewhere in the East Midlands there was a minster at Southwell, an abbey at Newstead and a cathedral at Lincoln. In Coventry Earl Leofric of Mercia, and his countess, Lady Godiva, founded the Benedictine monastery of St Mary, which became the cathedral of the diocese of Coventry and Lichfield.

In the West Midlands stand the great cathedrals of Hereford, Worcester, Gloucester and Christ Church, Oxford. There were abbeys at Tewkesbury, Hailes and Dorchester-on-Thames.

Lichfield has its origins in a church built in 700 as a shrine for St Chad. This Saxon church was replaced in the twelfth century and the present building was erected in the fourteenth century. The fourteenth-century Lady chapel originally housed the shrine of St Chad. Some of his bones were rescued from the mediæval shrine before its destruction at the Reformation and hidden, and they are now above the High Altar at St Chad's Cathedral, Birmingham. This was the first post-Reformation Catholic cathedral by A.W. Pugin.

Lincoln Cathedral stands high on a limestone cliff and dominates the skyline. In 1072, Bishop Remigius moved his see here from Dorchester-on-Thames. In 1185, after an earth tremor damaged the Romanesque cathedral, St Hugh of Avalon, a Carthusian monk, rebuilt the cathedral – and in due course his shrine would become a place of pilgrimage (which was housed in the Angel Choir).

Hereford Cathedral dates from the seventh century when a Saxon Church replaced the wooden church of St Mary the Virgin. The construction of today's cathedral began in the thirteenth century. Pilgrims came here to honour St Thomas Cantilupe, canonised by the Pope in 1320.

Born in Hambleden, near Great Marlow, St Thomas was the son of the Norman baron, William Cantilupe. In 1261 he became Chancellor of Oxford University, and, in 1265, he rose to be Chancellor of England. In 1275 he was appointed Bishop of Hereford and became locked in a struggle over the rights of his diocese with the Archbishop of Canterbury, John Peckham. He died at Montefiascome, in Italy, where he had gone to plead his case before the Pope and to have his excommunication overturned. Some parts of his remains were returned to Hereford and the memory of his personal holiness and pastoral zeal led to his canonisation. His feast is celebrated on 2 October.

Hereford's refurbished cloister and library house some magnificent treasures, including the thirteenth-century Mappa Mundi, the Limoges reliquary, and the Anglo-Saxon Hereford Gospels.

Worcester Cathedral's first bishop was the seventh-century Bishop Bosel. The cathedral was rebuilt by the Normans and the crypt is the largest remaining Norman crypt in England. Among the surviving monastic buildings are the chapter house and the cloister.

Gloucester Cathedral owes its origins to King Osric of Mercia, who established a monastery in the seventh century. The Benedictines came during the reign of Cnut. In 1089, the foundation stone of what became the abbey church, and, in the sixteenth-century, a cathedral, was laid. The Romanesque nave, the Perpendicular choir and great cloister (probably the finest in England) and the fifteenth-century Lady Chapel are breath-taking. The great east window depicts the mediæval hierarchy with Christ and the angels, Mary and the saints, and the knights and the bishops in their descending order. The magnificent tomb of the murdered Edward II lies in the north ambulatory of the east end.

Christ Church Cathedral, Oxford – a college chapel – was raised to cathedral status by Henry VIII, enabling him to suppress the abbey which had been raised to the status of cathedral church in c.1542. Approached through the Tom Quad, commenced by Cardinal Wolsey, and by the Tom Tower, added by Sir Christopher Wren, Christ Church was the priory church. Legend holds that St Frideswide founded the monastery which preceded the later Augustinian foundation.

St Frideswide was the daughter of Didan, the prince (*subregulus*) of a district bordering the Upper Thames. She was the abbess–foundress of the nunnery of St Mary's under the Rule of St Benedict. She is said to have had as her maxim "Whatever is not God is nothing." She is patroness of the city and university of Oxford. Her relics are extant, although disturbed at the Reformation. In art she is depicted as a nun with a crown, crozier and sceptre, and with an ox beside her. She died in 735 and her feast is celebrated on 19 October.

In 1004 her church was rebuilt by King Aethelred, who had a manor in nearby Headington. Then, in the twelfth century, Augustinian canons refounded the priory, and a church, chapter house and cloister were built. The cathedral spire is thirteenth-century, and in 1338 the Latin Chapel was built (where there is some later stained glass by Sir Edward Burne-Jones).

The North

Chester Cathedral can trace its origins to around AD 79 when the Romans built their fortress on the River Dee. Later, it would become associated with St Werburgh and become a place of pilgrimage.

St Werburgh was a devout and holy woman, a nun, who lived in the seventh century. She was the daughter of St Ermenilda and King Wulfhere of Mercia. She became a nun of Ely under St Etheldreda and later founded the nunneries of Hanbury, near Tutbury, Trentham, near Staffordshire, and Weedon, in Northamptonshire. She died at Trentham but the remains of this Mercian saint were brought to Chester to protect the citizens from the marauding Danes. Her remains were placed in the Saxon minster – and this was enlarged to become her shrine. Her feast day is celebrated on 3 February.

The Normans refounded the church as a Benedictine abbey under St Anselm, Abbot of Bec and later Archbishop of Canterbury. Henry VIII destroyed the monastic community although much of the monastic complex, including the cloisters, survives. He then created the new diocese of Chester, and the monastic church became the diocesan cathedral.

Elsewhere in the region, Manchester Cathedral has its origins in the collegiate church of Henry V (1421) and probably in a Saxon church of St Mary. The discovery of the "Angel Stone", with its carving of the Annunciation, appears to authenticate this claim. For the Catholic visitor, time is well spent at the diocesan Salford Cathedral, at the city-centre "Hidden Gem" church (with special attention to the modern Stations of the Cross), and with a visit to Manchester Cathedral's Lady chapel (rebuilt after World War II bombing) to see there the stone carving of the Christ Child by the Catholic sculptor, Eric Gill.

Liverpool, of course, boasts two cathedrals, linked by the famous Hope Street, along which Pope John Paul II made his own pilgrimage. The Catholic architect, Giles Gilbert Scott, who died in 1960, was twenty-two when he was chosen to design Liverpool Cathedral (a project which was completed amidst great celebrations and royal visits the year after I entered the House of Commons, in 1980). Scott came from a dynasty of religious architects. His father was George Gilbert Scott (see Norwich Catholic Cathedral) and his grandfather was the redoubtable Sir Gilbert Scott, the great Victorian exponent of the Gothic style. His uncle, John Oldrid Scott, also worked on many ecclesiastical projects including St Mary's Cathedral, Edinburgh, and restoration at St David's.

An Anglican, Frederick Gibberd, was the architect commissioned to complete Liverpool's Catholic cathedral of Christ the King. The original design had been executed by Sir Edwin Lutyens, and his crypt was completed just before the Second World War (see chapter 15). It houses the tombs of the archbishops of Liverpool (apart from Archbishop Derek Worlock, whose tomb is in the chapel of St Joseph) and some of the memorabilia and artifacts of the cathedral's early days.

Shortage of money led to the abandonment of the Lutyens design and in 1959 work began on the familiar circular edifice, crowned by the lantern of glass by John Piper and Patrick Reyntiens. For many visitors, uncertain about the exterior appearance of the cathedral, the interior is a wonderful surprise. Over the years during which I represented Liverpool in Parliament this was the setting of great civic services and memorable events – from the service to commemorate those who died at the tragic Hillsborough football match to the papal Mass (celebrated by a magnificent wall hanging). A close friend was a priest of the cathedral, and having presided at our wedding he baptised our two eldest children in the cathedral's baptistery. The work of the late Fr Paul Thompson has been recognised through the double eagle lectern by Sean Rice. The statue of Abraham and Isaac, also by Rice, and the stations of the cross, along with the tapestries, and side altars, are themselves a wonderful spiritual pageant. The presence of the Blessed Sacrament, and the comings and goings of the faithful, calling in to offer a prayer, remind today's pilgrim of the real point of these great buildings.

In the far north west lies Carlisle Cathedral. It is the

only mediæval cathedral to have its origins in an Augustinian rather than a Benedictine community and was founded in 1122 by Henry I, ten years before the diocese of Carlisle was created. Cruciform in plan, the remains of the nave are part of the earliest Romanesque building, which was constructed by the first bishop, Bishop Adelulf. The north transept is St Wilfrid's Chapel and includes the Brougham Triptych, which is early sixteenth century and carved in Antwerp. The fine stalls in the quire are fifteenth century. On the rear of the stalls in the south aisle is the story of St Augustine, and those in the north aisle tell the stories of St Cuthbert and St Antony of the Desert.

Elsewhere (see chapters 2 and 3) I have told the story of Durham Cathedral, Ripon Cathedral, York Minster and Beverley Minster. York Minster has the greatest wealth of mediæval glass in England. The Five Sisters window, with its grisaille colouring, has been described as one of the wonders of the world. Taken together, and with the monastic foundations of the region, this wonderful collection of buildings could form the basis for a stunning walking holiday or a pilgrimage commencing at Lindisfarne and culminating at York and Beverley.

Wales

On a beautiful day in the early summer of 2000 I made my first visit to the stunning cathedral of St David's, on the west coast of Wales. Of all the ancient Catholic sites this is perhaps the most arresting. It stands in a remote and beautiful setting and recalls a time when faith was an integral part in the daily lives of all people.

For more than a thousand years this spot has been associated with the patron saint of Wales. David died in about the year 589 after founding a monastery on this site. The tradition holds that his mother, St Non, gave birth to him on the nearby cliffs to the south of the cathedral and that he was baptised at Porth Clais, where the River Alun enters the Irish Sea. A holy well bubbled up and the waters gave sight to the Irish bishop who had christened him. After being educated by St Paulinus, David returned to Vetus Rubus where his uncle had a monastery. He then founded another monastery at Vallis Rosina (the valley of the little marsh) and became renowned for his asceticism. The monastic community became a centre of learning and sanctity.

In the tenth and eleventh centuries Viking raiders frequently attacked the monks and their cathedral. In 999 Bishop Morgenau was slain and in 1080 Bishop Abraham suffered a similar fate. By the eleventh century even St David's shrine was covered in undergrowth.

In 1081 William the Conqueror came here and prayed, and a combination of ecclesiastical and military interests led to the Normans appointing Norman bishops in place of the indigenous Welsh. In 1115 Henry I appointed Bishop Bernard as the first Norman bishop of St David's and created a chapter of canons. In 1123 Pope Calixtus II agreed to canonise David and this led to St David's becoming a centre of pilgrimage (*Roma semel quantum: bis dat Menevia tantum*: once to Rome is equal to twice to St David's).

Bernard's cathedral was rebuilt by Bishop Peter de Leia and Giraldus de Barri in the twelfth century. Giraldus was scheduled to succeed Bishop Peter but his independent spirit and insistence on an independent Welsh church led to a stand-off with Canterbury. His failure to be elected bishop is reflected in the Holy Trinity Chapel statue which shows him with the bishop's mitre at his feet, rather than on his head.

During the thirteenth century the Chapel of St Thomas Becket and a Lady chapel were constructed along with a new shrine on the north side of the presbytery.

In the middle of the fourteenth century Bishop Henry Gower carried out a further transformation, including the construction of the Bishop's Palace. The last significant addition was the College of the Blessed Virgin Mary, built in 1365 by Bishop Adam Houghton. During the centuries which followed, frequent re-ordering and renewal occurred, especially the provision of flying buttresses and props to prevent the collapse of walls affected by poor foundations and subsidence.

The Reformation brought Bishop William Barlow to St David's (bishop, 1536–48). A lackey of Thomas Cromwell, he sought to remove the episcopal centre from St David's to Carmarthen and stripped the shrines of St David and St Justinian. Justinian was a sixth-century martyr who went to the Isle of Ramsey, off the coast of South Wales, where he became a recluse and was later murdered. His feast is celebrated on 5 December.

In 1538 Barlow wrote to Cromwell confirming that he had been to St David's and removed two skulls, two arm bones and a "worm eaten book". This may have been a copy of the Gospel of St John written in St David's own hand.

The cathedral's Catholic canons are thought to have hidden many other relics. In 1866, when Sir Giles Gilbert Scott (and, later, Oldrid Scott) came to restore the cathedral, a recess containing a collection of bones was found in the Holy Trinity Chapel, directly behind the High Altar. Mortar had been poured over them. Early in the twentieth century Dean Williams had the bones, which he believed to be those of St David and St Justinian, placed in a reliquary.

St David's is also home to the shrine of St Caradog. Details of his life are found in *Journey Through Wales* (1188) by Gerald of Wales (Giraldus Cambrensis). Gerald was born in Manorbier in 1146, educated in part in the cathedral school, and knew the stories of St Caradog. In 1077 Caradog was sent from Breconshire to the court of the king of South Wales.

Valued as a harpist, Caradog fell foul of the king and departed to Llandaff to become a monk. After a time in

Gower he was ordained priest at St David's. After living for a time on Ynys Ary, possibly Barry Island near Llanrahian in Pembrokeshire, he suffered at the hands of Norse raiders. He went to take charge of a cell founded by St Ismael, now St Issells, near Haroldston, where he finished his life. In accordance with his wishes he was taken for burial at St David's, and Gerald of Wales records that his body was "the cause of many miracles". Gerald investigated these miracles for Pope Innocent III and recorded that Caradog's body was incorrupt. His feast day is celebrated on 13 April.

During the Civil War the Parliamentary soldiers stripped the lead off the roof, wrecked what remained of the mediæval library, destroyed the organ and bells, smashed the stained glass and tore up the brasses on the cathedral's tombs. For two centuries the east end of the cathedral was without a roof.

It would not be until the end of the eighteenth century that restoration would commence. William Butterfield, John Nash and Sir Giles Gilbert Scott gradually accomplished the extraordinary feat of restoration. Remarkably, Scott managed to lay new foundations for the tower and to rebuild it without having to demolish the existing structure. Scott's son, Oldrid, oversaw the restoration of the Lady chapel.

In commencing a pilgrimage to the cathedral of St David's, the visitor may care to start at the font, which stands close to the entrance, and which denotes the beginning of every Christian pilgrimage.

A renewal of the baptismal vow may be said:

I believe and trust in God the Father
who created all that is.
I believe and trust in His Son, Jesus Christ,
who redeemed mankind.
I believe and trust in His Holy Spirit
who gives life to the people of God.
I believe and trust in one God:
Father, Son and Holy Spirit. Amen.

At the Chapel of the Most Holy Trinity the pilgrim may wish to reflect upon the life of St David and on the Latin text on the reredos:

Ecce Qui Tollit Peccata Mundi...
Behold the Lamb of God,
who takes away the sins of the world.

In the Lady chapel there are several decorated bosses placed where the ribs of the vaulted roof meet. One has three hares sharing three ears – a symbol of the Trinity – and another depicts a pelican feeding her young. When food is short a pelican will peck her breast and give her own blood as nourishment for her children. The pelican has been used as a representation of Christ, shedding his blood that we might live. Here we might remember the prayer of St Benedict:

Hail O Queen of heaven enthroned,
Hail by angels mistress owned.
Root of Jesse, gate of morn,
Whence the world's true light was born.
Glorious Virgin, joy to thee.
Loveliest whom in heaven they see.
Fairest thou, where all are fair,
Plead with Christ our sins to spare.

Pray for us, O holy Mother of God.
That we may be made worthy
of the promise of Christ.

O gracious and holy Father, give us wisdom to
*   perceive thee,*
intelligence to understand thee,
eyes to behold thee,
and a life to proclaim thee,
a heart to meditate upon thee,
through the power of the Spirit of Jesus Christ
*   our Lord.*

Meditation

St David's Cathedral

Eight hundred years the stones
have borne attendance on Majesty
Here in this echoing House:
Stones from the cliff foot,
Wrought and hammered by a million years
Of sea and hurricane,
Cut and tooled in skilful pride
For vault and moulding.

Hallowed, time moved in them
As prayers ascended, and the rain
Beat its patterns
on the cloud-cold roof and aisles
Stripped of their covering
through the wanton years.

Eyes that measured time, and hands
honed by toil
Are irrecoverable dust;
And yet,
while this House stands
Not wholly can they die
who built it:
Within the stillness of a summer day
A shaft of sunlight will with gold
Burnish afresh each shadowed arch,
tracing its curve
as once
Some mason traced it with his
dreaming eye.
And it will stand afresh against the dark.
his living testament.

(Mary Denyer; from *An Alternative Order for Morning and
Evening Prayer*, Church in Wales Publications, 1992)

St Winifrid's Well,
Holywell, Flintshire,
North Wales

5

The holy wells

SINCE Celtic times, British Christians have attached symbolic importance to holy wells. Through immersion in the waters of baptism comes admission into the Christian Church. Water is the very source of life, and without it we perish. Tradition also has it that this life-giver could be endowed by God with special curative and restorative powers. Christ sought baptism at the hands of his cousin, John the Baptist, in the waters of the River Jordan. Jesus asks the Samaritan woman at the well for water and then sits by the well to talk to her about her past life. He promises that whoever drinks of his water will never thirst again.

Our ancestors regularly called wells by the names of the saints, and this practice was especially common in Ireland, Wales, Cornwall and the north of Scotland. Many of the wells which were colonised by the early Christians had been sacred to pre-Christian religions. The hot springs at Bath and Buxton were thought to have curative powers as well as religious significance. The running waters were seen as sacred messengers. Up until the nineteenth century many villages enjoyed the custom of well-dressing, which led to magnificent displays of flowers being used to dress the well.

Well-dressing In Derbyshire

Well-dressing usually took place on the day which commemorated the saint to whom the well was dedicated, and there would be a procession and festivities. The tradition was revived in Derbyshire, and one of my more pleasant recollections from a parliamentary by-election in West Derbyshire was stealing away to see some well-dressing in local Peak District villages. Some of the finest displays are said to be at Tideswell, Youlgreave and Tissington.

Stunning floral arrangements depict scenes from Bible stories; a favourite inevitably is the Samaritan woman at the well encountering Jesus. The High Peak Tourist Authority encourage interest in well-dressing and can provide details of when the ceremonies take place.

St David's, East Dereham and St Withburga

In early Christian times wells are often associated with the stories of individual saints, with wells such as those at Pistyll Dewi, Gweslan and Eliud, close to St David's Cathedral, in Pembrokeshire, said to have had their origins from the prayers of holy men and women. In the case of St Withburga's Well, East Dereham, in Norfolk, and St Winifrid's Well, in Flintshire, wells appeared as part of a miracle story.

East Dereham, which was also the birthplace of the great English poet and composer William Cowper who wrote hymns such as "God Moves in a Mysterious Way", was where St Withburga founded a nunnery in the eight century. She was the youngest daughter of King Anna and sister of the forceful St Etheldreda of Ely and St Sexburga. In 473 she died and was buried in the abbey grounds, and for two hundred years her remains were honoured and venerated by many pilgrims. In 974, Brithnorth, the Abbot of Ely, decided to have her remains uprooted and taken to

Ely, where he wanted her to lie with her sisters. Her forced removal led to a spring of water appearing in the churchyard, which was said to have flowed from her grave. The healing power of the waters became immensely valued, and they are still sought by the sick.

St Winifrid's Well

Best known of all the holy wells is St Winifrid's Well at Holywell in North Wales. This is one of the few shrines which remained a place of secret pilgrimage throughout the Reformation and penal times and has always been sacred in the Catholic tradition. The site remains tranquil and holy, still frequented by many people, especially women seeking the intercession of St Winifrid in support of their own prayers to God.

The best account I have seen of the story of the Well was published by Rev Christopher David in 1971. He was a curate at Holywell between 1955 and 1964 and his updated illustrated history and guide is available at the Catholic bookshop at St Winifrid's Well.

The first printed text, setting down the details of Winifrid's life appeared in 1485, printed by William Caxton, but the story was one which had been handed down by word of mouth from generation to generation. In Caxton's text appear the memorable words:

> ...and after the hede of the Vyrgyn was cut off and touchyd the ground, as we afore have said, sprang up a welle of spryngyng water largely enduring unto this day, which heleth al langours and sekenesses as well in men as in bestes, which welle is named after the name of the Vergyne and is called St Wenefrede's Welle.

Caxton's account was probably instigated by Lady Margaret, Countess of Richmond, wife of Thomas Stanley, Earl of Derby, and mother of Henry VII, whose generosity was probably also responsible for the construction of the fifteenth-century Well Chapel which stands to this day.

The first chapel was constructed here in wood and erected by her uncle, St Beuno, in the seventh century. His memory is captured in the dedication of the nearby Jesuit retreat house, from where the great Jesuit poet, Gerard Manley Hopkins, came to bathe in St Winifrid's Well on Boxing Day 1879, before beginning an unhappy ministry at Liverpool's St Francis Xavier's parish.

In honour of the saint he penned his poem: "St Winefride's Well" (*Poems*, Oxford University Press, fourth edition, 1967):

Oh now while skies are blue, now while seas are salt,
While rushy rains shall fall or brooks shall fleet from
*   fountains,*
While sick men shall cast sighs, or sweet health all
*   despairing,*
While blind men's eyes shall thirst after daylight,
*   draughts of daylight*
Or deaf ears shall desire that lipmusic that's lost upon
*   them,*
While cripples are, while lepers, dancers in dismal
*   limb dance,*
Fallers in dreadful frothpits, waterfearers wild,
Stone, palsy, cancer, cough, lung-wasting, womb not
*   bearing*
Rupture, running sores, what more? In brief, in burden,
As long as men are mortal and God merciful,
So long to this sweet spot, this leafy lean-over,
This dry dene, now no longer dry nor dumb, but moist
*   and musical*
With the uproll and the downcarol of day and night
*   delivering*
Water, which keeps thy name, (for not in rock written
But in pale water, frail water, wild rash and reeling
*   water,*
That will not wear a print, that will not stain a pen,

Thy venerable record, virgin, is recorded)
Here to this holy well shall pilgrimages be,
And not from purple Wales only nor from elmy
   England,
But from beyond seas, Erin, France, and Flanders
   everywhere,
Pilgrims, still pilgrims, more pilgrims, still more
   pilgrims
What sights shall be seen when some that swung,
   wretches, on crutches
Their crutches shall cast from them, on heels of air
   departing,
Or they go rich as roseleaves hence that loathsome
   came hither!
Not now to name even
Those dearer, more divine boons whose haven the
   heart is.
As sure as what is most sure, sure as that spring
primroses shall new-dapple next year, sure as tomorrow
morning, amongst come-back-again things,
things with a revival, things with a recovery.
Thy name Winefride will live.

So, who was Winifrid and what was her story?

She was the daughter of a local Welsh prince, Tewyth; her mother was known as Gwenlo. Caradoc, a chieftain from Hawarden, attempted to seduce the beautiful Winifrid, and she sought sanctuary in her uncle Beuno's church. Before she could reach the church, Caradoc attacked her and severed her head from her body. At that spot a spring of water erupted. Beuno then emerged from the church. Picking up the head of his niece, he placed it by her body and through earnest prayer he raised her back to life. Throughout her life a white scar encircled her neck. Caradoc sank into the ground and was never seen again.

Subsequently Winifrid took the veil, and having joined the community at Gwytherin she later became the abbess. It was here that she remained for the rest of her life. She was buried in the churchyard, but in 1138 her remains were removed to Shrewsbury Abbey. In her entertaining accounts of that abbey's Benedictine sleuth-monk, Brother Cadfael, published by Futura Publications, the late Ellis Peters has reminded a new generation of readers of the devotion which the Welsh virgin generated among people of all walks of life.

Initially, the well was in the care of the monks of Basingwerk, who had come from Savigny in 1131 and adopted the Cistercian rule in 1147. Evidence at Basingwerk suggests an earlier monastic presence during Saxon times. Disputes over guardianship erupted from time to time, with the abbey at Chester staking its right to maintain and possess the well.

The fame of the shrine spread. Many pilgrims followed the lead of kings, such as Henry V, who placed himself under Winifrid's care at the battle of Agincourt and subsequently made the pilgrimage to her shrine, walking from Shrewsbury Abbey. Tudur Aled recorded the pilgrimage of Edward IV who, after making his devotions, placed some of the soil on his crown. Tudur Aled, who died in 1526, wrote his poem "The Story of St Winefride and Her Well", (*Stori Gwenfrewy A'I Frynnon*) to commemorate the life of the saint but also to celebrate his own faith:

> *While the Son was offering his sacrifice,*
> *And his prayer in God for her was strength,*
> *He led a river from heaven,*
> *And a channel of grace – it was a holy place.*
> *How fit it was, when Gwen was raised,*
> *That Jordan's bath sprang up.*
> *There is less of a surge in Aeron's current,*
> *Or in the Eurphrates than in this stream.*

Aled's enthusiasm for this holy well was shared by the poor and powerful alike. Lady Margaret's son, Henry VII, had a statue of Winifrid placed in his chapel at Westminster.

With Glastonbury and Walsingham, St Winifrid's Well was the third point on the triangle of popular pilgrimage in Britain.

Pilgrims using the well follow the custom of passing through the water three times. In the twelfth century, Robert, the Prior of Shrewsbury, recorded the prayer of St Winifrid and the hope that the pilgrim will be heard "at least at the third time". In fact, the custom goes back to Celtic times when a candidate for baptism was immersed three times. Pilgrims saw this as a penitential way of renewing their baptismal vows.

With the onset of the Reformation the shrine's days were numbered. Nicholas Pennant was the last Abbot of Basingwerk at the time of the abbey's dissolution in 1537. Control of the site passed to Henry VIII who appointed William Holcroft to oversee it. During Queen Mary's reign the shrine was briefly placed under the care of the restored Catholic bishop of St Asaph, Thomas Goldwell.

Then, remarkably, during the reign of Elizabeth I a series of Catholic priests were based at Holywell. In 1574 John Bennet arrived from Douai, where he trained. In 1582 he was caught and condemned to death. Imprisoned for three years, he was ultimately banished and escaped execution. His trial is believed to have taken place in a room over the Well Chapel.

Fr John Gerard SJ made the pilgrimage in order to be there on St Winifrid's feast day, on 3 November 1593. He wrote that "for a quarter of an hour I lay down in the water and prayed. When I came out my shirt was dripping, but I kept it on and pulled all my clothes over it and was none the worse for my battle." Fr Gerard was subsequently arrested and was one of the few to successfully escape from the Tower of London. A gripping account of his life appears in *The Autobiography of John Gerard: the hunted priest* (Fount Books, 1959).

Many other Catholics who visited the well during those years were tortured and killed, among them Edward

Oldcorne, executed in 1601. Henry Garnet, the Jesuit Superior, and St Nicholas Owen, (the "Little John"), who made many of the hiding holes which saved the lives of fugitive priests, came in 1605. One year later both were dead.

Elizabeth gave instructions for special measures to be taken to suppress Catholicism in the Welsh Marches and "to pay particular attention to the pilgrimages to St Winifrid's Well". The ineffectiveness of their persecution is exposed by judicial complaints that a resident of Chirk was known to have been secretly attending Mass at Holywell and that several priests were known to operate in the vicinity. A letter sent in 1590 complains that pilgrims "still goe in heapes to the wonted welles".

The Lord President of Wales sought further reports of Catholic activity and learned in 1624 that "every year about midsummer many superstitious Papists of Lancashire and other more remote places go on pilgrimage". The informer complained that such was the confidence of the pilgrims that they openly heard Mass in the chapel "without contradiction". Some of the names which emerged in 1629 as present on St Winifrid's Day included some of the leading recusant families. Among them were Lord William Howard of Shrewsbury, Sir Thomas Gerard, Mr Scarisbrick of Scarisbrick, Mr Blundell of Crosby, Lady Falkland and an estimated gathering of 1,500 people. Lancashire Catholics would come in pilgrimage across the Mersey, walk over the Wirral, cross the sands of the Dee at low tide and make their way up the narrow valley. Beacons would be lit on the Wirral to signal for a boat to be waiting to take the pilgrims home (see chapter 15, "Lancashire and Liverpool").

Inscriptions and dates carved into the pillars around the well bear witness to these post-Reformation pilgrimages. One shows the Greek *Khi Ro* inscription – Christ's name – alongside the date 1627. Another shows the Jesuit monogram, IHS, and the date 1687.

In 1636 further attempts were made to suppress the use of St Winifrid's Well and Sir John Bridgeman, Chief Justice of Chester, gave orders for the statue of St Winifrid to be disfigured, and for the names of all pilgrims to be reported to the Assize.

This did not prevent George Petre, the youngest son of Lord Petre, who died as a prisoner in the Tower, from buying the Star Inn. It was to be used for pilgrims but in reality it became a Jesuit house.

During the Civil War the statue of the saint is thought to have been finally destroyed. The niche remained empty for 250 years until 1888 when St Winifrid was restored to her place. Her Victorian effigy depicts her with the crook of an abbess in one hand and the palm of martyrdom in the other. She has a double crown symbolising her lineage as the daughter of a prince and as a saint of the Church.

Desecrated statues can be replaced but, tragically, real life cannot be. In the upheavals which followed the Civil War there was another wave of persecution, costing one Holywell priest, Fr John Plessington, his life. He was executed on the gallows at Chester.

In 1686 James II and Queen Mary of Modena came to pray at the chapel in the hope of a son. Although their prayer was answered – and the queen clarified the ownership of the chapel by formally giving it to the Jesuit priest Fr Thomas Roberts – the birth of a son triggered the landing at Torbay, on 5 November 1688, of William of Orange. In Holywell it led to a crowd breaking into the Star Inn and evicting Fr Roberts, and to the public burning of books and a cross in the market place.

Still pilgrims came, provoking Bishop Fleetwood of St Asaph to complain that pilgrims were arriving from all parts of Britain and Ireland: "the enemy we have to deal with grows more numerous, is active, vigilant and daring, daily pushes on its conquests, is in good heart and under no discouragement but that of laws...". Even those laws, which barred Catholics from the professions, from the right to vote, and from inheriting or purchasing land, could not destroy the old faith. Nor did the public humiliations. The Jesuit superior at Holywell, Fr Thorold, and a lay brother, William Christopher, were stripped in mid-winter and thrown into prison for the better part of a year.

After a protracted and painful battle for possession, Catholics were prohibited from using the chapel and in 1723 it was converted into use as a school room. This simply led to pilgrims hearing Mass privately in the town's inns: records show that there was always a priest at Holywell throughout the sixteenth, seventeenth and eighteenth centuries, and there were always more and more pilgrims.

In 1808 the long night finally ended when Flintshire's Clerk of the Peace agreed that Mass could be said publicly at the Star Inn. The inn remained in use until part of the present church was built in 1832. It is now part of St Winifrid's Presbytery.

In 1859 the Sisters of Charity created a convent in Loyola Cottages and St Winifrid's Convent was built on the site of the Cross Keys. In place of Basingwerk, friars and nuns had moved into Pantasaph around the same time, and the Jesuits to St Beuno's.

In 1870 a new hospice for pilgrims was opened and in 1873 the Jesuits obtained a lease on the well from the Town Council. In the 1890s an 11.30 am daily service was initiated at the well, beginning when the pilgrimage season begins, at Pentecost, and ending on the last day of September. It has continued ever since.

Other Welsh wells

Elsewhere in Wales there are many other examples of holy wells. One, used for baptism, is the well of Llanfyllin in Powys: St Myllin's Well is set on a hillside overlooking the town. St Myllin was said to have carried out baptisms here in the sixth century. Francis Jones' *The Holy Wells of Wales* (University of Wales Press, 1992) is the ideal hand-book for anyone wishing to discover the holy wells of the principality. It includes a full list of the Welsh wells and where to find them. Among those listed is St Seriol's Well, at Penmon on Ynis Mon, the island of Anglesey. Close by are a monastic cell and a hermit's cave. From the well the pilgrim can see Puffin Island ,which is where St Seriol, a local holy man and preacher, is buried.

At Colwyn Bay, in Conwy, a beautiful chapel, probably of twelfth-century origin, is constructed over the well of St Trillo, a well which rises below the altar. St Trillo is a sixth-century saint whose feast day is celebrated on 15 June. In Gwynedd a famous healing well is located at Llanberis and is dedicated to St Beri; and in Pembrokeshire, at Llandyfan, close to Llandeilo, the Baptists have adopted an ancient holy well as their baptismal pool, for use in baptisms of adults by total immersion. Elsewhere in the county, at Nevern, there is a holy stream set alongside the church, and the famous wells of St David's.

St David's

Twyddewi, or St David's, is the smallest of our cathedral cities (see chapter 4). David's mother, St Non, was an exemplary woman who prayed for her young son's priestly vocation and ministry. When Dewi, or David, set off on his missionary travels, the young monk founded twelve new monasteries, including Leominster, Crowland and Mynyw (later known as St David's). Tracing his footsteps would make a wonderful summer pilgrimage.

He built a church at Glastonbury and many churches, especially in the west of Britain and in Brittany, are dedicated to him. The cathedral of St David's ultimately became the seat of Welsh ecclesiastical authority and many of the places nearby were made sacred by the saint's presence. To the south of the city lies a holy well dedicated to his mother. From St Non's Well, the pilgrim can make their way to the chapel of St Justinian – St David's confessor – who is buried here. St Non was probably born into a ruling family in Dyfed. A chapel was dedicated to her at Altarnun, in Cornwall, and after her death in Brittany her relics were preserved at Altarnum until the Reformation. Her feast day is celebrated two days after that of her son, on 3 March.

St David chose this site for his ministry because he wanted a place where he could perform baptisms and healing, and so he chose a place with a river close by and a place where there were many wells.

English sources

As in Wales, many of the early English churches and monastic foundations were built alongside wells which either had an existing sacred provenance or became known as holy sites because of their use in baptisms or for more miraculous reasons. Local guide books often detail their whereabouts. R.W. Morrell's *St Ann's Well and Other Medieval and Holy Wells in Nottingham* and J. Taylor Page's *Cumbrian Holy Wells*, which could lead the pilgrim to the Anchorites' Well at Kendal, are examples of the sort of local publications which can give clues to the whereabouts of holy wells; but within local place names and the oral tradition there are also usually plenty of clues. In his book, *The Ancient Crosses and Holy Wells of Lancashire* (1906), Henry Taylor lists many Lancashire wells, including St Helen's Well at Tarlton, St Helen's Well at Brindle, St Thomas's Well at Windleshaw, St Anne's Well at Inglewhite, and Ladyewell at Fernyhalgh (see chapters 6 and 15).

Give-away names include places such as Holywell-cum-Needingworth, in Cambridgeshire. The name of the village celebrates a well which was used for baptism. So, too, does Holywell in Oxford.

London

In London, the well at Willesden – meaning the spring or well at the foot of the hill – was a busy centre of Marian pilgrimage. A Saxon church pre-dated the foundation of St Mary's Church in Willesden and the shrine of the Black Virgin, along with the well, was a source of healing for the eyes and a popular place of pilgrimage during the horrors of the Black Death. The shrine was destroyed by Henry VIII but devotions were continued within the church, leading to the imposition of an annual fine on the church of £1.6s.0d. The fine continued to be levied until 1902. More recently still, in 1972, a new shrine was dedicated by the Anglican Bishop of Willesden and the ancient font is filled with water drawn from the holy well.

Elsewhere, the well at Muswell (meaning mossy well) was famous for the cure of a Scottish king.

Some other English wells

Some other well-known English holy wells are at St Anne's Well in Brislington, once a major centre for pilgrimage, and Whitchurch Canonicorum, near Bridport in Dorset; Chardown Hill and Morcombelake also have wells dedicated to St Wite. At Cerne Abbey, Dorset, there is a well dedicated to St Augustine. In Cornwall, near Penzance, there are the remains of an ancient chapel at St Madron and a well alongside it. In Devon, the well in the Cathedral Close at Exeter Cathedral is Roman in origin but subsequently given a Christian dedication to St Martin. In Worcestershire, St Richard's Well at Droitwich still feeds the spa.

In Oxford, St Bartholomew's Well may be found at

Cowley. This well, situated in the graveyard of the church, was a place of purification, shortening the time which the penitent pilgrim might spend in preparation for entry to heaven. In Staffordshire, St Chad's well at Stowe is associated with the seventh-century missionary saint. After the Council of Whitby in 664, St Chad was appointed as Archbishop of York but accepted a lesser role when conflict erupted between him and St Wilfrid. After becoming Bishop of Mercia Chad founded Lichfield Cathedral and undertook much missionary work. He was ultimately buried in his cathedral.

A nineteenth-century Anglican priest, the Reverend R.S. Hawker, captured the spirit of this devotion well in his poem "The Lady's Well". His child asks him a question about the well's origin and provenance:

Look at that spring, my father dear,
Where the white blossoms fell;
Why is it always bright and clear?
And why the Lady's well?

The remainder of the text appears at the end of this chapter but the answer to the question – what's in a name? – why "Ladywell" or "Holywell"? – reveals a great deal about our Catholic past.

The wells of Walsingham were as famous as the waters of Lourdes are today (see chapter 7).

Irish wells

In Ireland there are diverse numbers of wells and holy places connected with the saving and healing powers of water. Croagh Patrick and Lough Derg have been written about separately in other chapters (see chapters 9 and 11) but the pilgrim in Ireland will also want to visit St Bridget's Well at Clondalkin and many of the local wells which exist in every diocese.

The Dublin Diocesan Jubilee Committee, in their *Pilgrim's Handbook*, have this to say about the provenance of the holy wells: "As the water is the most important gift the earth provides and comes from deep within the earth it reminds us of God's presence within us. To visit a well can be a healing and calming experience and can help us to get in touch with deep resources within ourselves."

Many important stories in the Bible are centred around wells which were places where God was revealed and relationships were formed: for example, Moses to Zipporah (Ex 2:15-22), the Samaritan woman (Jn 4:6-30). Local areas have their own traditions and customs around holy wells. They are usually called after a saint, though there are some wells dedicated to Jesus.

In the Dublin diocese one of the finest pilgrimage sites is to be found at Glendalough, the Valley of the Two Lakes. Its founder was Saint Kevin (Coemgen/Caoimhin) who is thought to have died between 618 and 622. It is also associated with St Laurence O'Toole, who was Abbot of Glendalough in 1153 and Archbishop of Dublin in 1162.

The traditional pilgrim route begins where St Kevin began his search for God, near Wicklow's Hollywood. Cross-slabs and other markers still signpost St Kevin's Way to Glendalough. On arrival, St Kevin settled by the beautiful south shore of the upper lake and became totally absorbed in the spiritual life.

The Irish poet Seamus Heaney, in his poem "St Kevin and the Blackbird" (*The Spirit Level*, Faber and Faber, 1984), captures the spirit of the place:

> *Alone and mirrored clear in love's deep river,*
> *"To labour and not to seek reward," he prays,*
> *A prayer his body makes entirely*
> *For he has forgotten self, forgotten bird*
> *And on the river bank forgotten the river's name.*

Along the pilgrim way are the Healing Pool at Glendassan River and St Kevin's Well. The Poulanass Waterfall is a good place to stop and reflect on the hectic rush of our lives and to contrast the speed and force with the tranquillity of the deep pools and the wells.

Elsewhere in the Dublin Diocese there are other celebrated wells: St Bridget's Well, Castleknock; St Patrick's Well, Finglas; St Margaret's Well (St Canice's parish), Finglas; Lady's Well at Mulhuddart; St Donagh's Well at Kilbarrack; St Moling's Well, Tobar ba gCluas; and St Colmcille's Well, Ceile De; St Maelruin's Graveyard and Tree, Tallaght; St Kevin's Well, Kilnamanagh; St Begnet's Well, Dalkey; St MacCullin's Well, St Catherine's Well, and St Fintan's Well at Sutton; St Colmcille's Well, Swords; St Patrick's Well, Moone; and Holy Wells, Maynooth.

The diocese suggests a liturgy which may be used by pilgrims. It includes the prayer:

> *Bless again this water, source of life and nourishment,*
> *It gives fullness to all living things and*
> *Refreshes and cleanses us.*
> *Protect us from all danger, ill health and broken*
> *   dreams.*
> *May we always thirst for you, knowing that you*
> *Alone can satisfy our quest for freedom and wholeness.*
> *Give us living water,*
> *Today and always and bring us to*
> *Salvation and new life.*

The prayer is followed by a Scripture reading from St John's Gospel (4:11-14):

> The woman said to him, "Sir, you have no bucket, and the well is deep. Where do you get that living water? Are you greater than our ancestor Jacob, who gave us the well, and with his sons and his flocks drank from it?" Jesus said to her, "Everyone who drinks of this water will be thirsty again, but those who drink of the water that I will give them will never be thirsty. The

water that I will give will become in them a spring of
water gushing up to eternal life."

On drinking from the well the pilgrim is invited to say:

*May God give me to drink from the well that never
    runs dry.*
*May God who made wine of the water at the wedding
    of Cana,*
Fill this water with strength and vigour.

Go dtuga Dia deoch duit as an tobar nach dtrann.
An te a rinne fion den uisce ar bhainis Chana,
Go gcuire se bri agus spreacadh san uisce seo.

And to sing:

We shall draw water joyfully, singing joyfully,
We shall draw water joyfully,
From the well springs of salvation.

Scottish wells

In Scotland, one of the major centres for post-Reformation
pilgrimage was the Chapel of Grace, situated near Fochabers,
on the western bank of the River Spey. What remained of
the chapel was completely destroyed in 1638, but in 1775
one writer disapprovingly records that multitudes from the
Western Isles still made pilgrimage to the chapel and its
holy well, and "nothing short of violence" could stop
them. In the nineteenth century the observance continued,
and throughout the north of Scotland there are few ruins
of old churches or religious foundations without a holy
well in close proximity. Some of the finest examples include
St Finian's Well, Chapel Finian, located by the seashore;
St Drostan's Well at Aberdour Bay, near New Aberdour;
St Fillian's Pool, situated by the ruins of Strathfillan Priory
near Crianlarich, in Perth and Kinross, and famous for its

healing powers; and the wells at Lismore and Iona in Argyll and Bute. Lismore was one of the islands at the heart of Celtic Christianity and became known as the Bishop's Isle, for it was here that the first bishops of Argyll lived.

In 1608 the General Assembly, which was held in Linlithgow, wanted action taken against pilgrims frequenting the Chapel and Well of Grace and mentioned further miraculous wells of Our Lady at Ordiquhill in Banffshire. In 1630 Margaret Davidson was fined £5 by the justices in Aberdeen for permitting her sick child to be taken by her nurse to the Well of St Fiache. The Provincial Assembly meeting in Aberdeen in 1652 was equally perturbed by the continued use of the well at Seggett and called for punitive measures to be taken against those who used it. The Assembly ordered that any future pilgrim to a well "shall be answered in penalty and repentance in such degree as fornicators are" (Ecclesiastical Records of Aberdeen, Spalding Club).

The desecration of the wells

A nineteenth-century pilgrim, Mrs Hemans, penned these lines explaining her emotions and feeling about the desecration of holy wells. Her verse was inspired by the well at St Asaph – named after the sixth-century saint who succeeded St Kentigern as abbot and bishop. These lines were published by Rev T.E. Bridgett in his 1875 work *Our Lady's Dowry*:

> *Fount of the vale! thou art sought no more*
> *By the pilgrim's foot, as in time of yore,*
> *When he came from afar his beads to tell*
> *And to chant his hymn at Our Lady's Well.*
> *There is heard no Ave through thy bowers,*
> *Thou art gleaming lone midst the water-flowers;*
> *But the herd may drink from thy gushing wave,*
> *And there may the reaper his forehead lave,*

And the woodman seeks thee not in vain;
Bright fount! thou art nature's own again!

Fount of the chapel, with ages gray.
Thou art springing freshly amidst decay!
Thy rites are closed, and thy crosses lie low,
And the changeful hours breathe o'er thee now.
Yet if at thine altar one holy thought
In man's deep spirit of old hath wrought;
If peace to the mourner hath here been given,
Or prayer from a chastened heart to heaven,
Be the spot still hallow'd while Time shall reign,
Who hath made thee nature's own again!

A meditation

It flow'd like light from the voice of God,
Silent and calm and fair;
It shone where the child and the parent trod
In the soft and evening air.

"Look at that spring, my father dear,
Where the white blossoms fell;
Why is it always bright and clear?
And why the Lady's well?"

"Once on a time, my own sweet child,
There dwelt across the sea
A lovely Mother, meek and mild,
from blame and blemish free.
And Mary was her blessed name,
In every land adored:
Its very sound deep love should claim
From all who love their Lord.
A Child was hers – a heavenly birth,
As pure as pure can be:
He had no father of the earth
The Son of God was He.

He came down to her from above,
Who died upon the Cross;
We never can do for Him my love,
What He hath done for us.

And so to make His praise endure,
Because of Jesu's fame,
Our fathers call'd things bright and pure
By His fair Mother's name.

She is the Lady of the well –
Her memory was meant
With lily and with rose to dwell
By waters innocent."

(Rev R.S. Hawker)

Our Lady of Fernyhough,
Ladywell, nr. Preston

Our Lady of Evesham

The Marian Shrines

FOR reasons which have become clear in the earlier chapter on Glastonbury, England in the Middle Ages became known as Mary's Dowry, and all over the country there were many pilgrimages undertaken in honour of the mother of Christ.

In 1875 Rev T.E. Bridgett compiled his classic book on the subject, *Our Lady's Dowry; or how England gained and lost that title* (Burns and Oates), and in 1957 H.M. Gillett published *Shrines of Our Lady in England and Wales* (Samuel Walker). Both drew down on a tradition which is woven through centuries of Christian devotion in these islands. Using these same sources we can construct some of the paths which pilgrims took. In compiling this chapter I was struck by the sheer volume of places which were held sacred. In the space available I have chosen to list as many as possible but clearly can say very little about most.

Why Christians honour Mary

In 1399 Thomas Arundel, Archbishop of Canterbury, wrote that "the contemplation of the great mystery of the Incarnation has drawn all Christian nations to venerate her from whom came the first beginnings of our redemption. But we English being the servants of her special inheritance and her own dowry, as we are commonly called, ought to surpass others in the fervour of our praises and devotions."

Chaucer's prioress, one of the pilgrims on her way to Arundel's Canterbury Cathedral, had these words to say about the Virgin:

> *O Mother Maid! O Maid and Mother fresh!*
> *O bush unburnt, burning in Moses' sight!*
> *That down didst ravish from the Deity,*
> *Through humbleness, the spirit that did alight*
> *Upon thy heart, whence, through that glory's might,*
> *Conceived was the Father's sapience,*
> *Help me to tell it in thy reverence!*
>
> *Lady, thy goodness, thy magnificence,*
> *Thy virtue, and thy great humility,*
> *Surpass all science and all utterance;*
> *For sometimes, Lady, ere men pray to thee,*
> *Thou go'st before in thy benignity,*
> *The light to us vouchsafing of thy prayer,*
> *To be our guide unto thy Son so dear.*

Throughout Britain there were Guilds and Fraternities dedicated to Mary. These institutions reached back to the earliest Saxon times, and were organised for the performance of works of charity and piety. They would be used to gather people together for social and religious purposes and placed under the patronage of one of the saints. In Norfolk alone it was estimated that of 909 Guilds, 155 were dedicated to Our Lady. Each would usually have a priest assigned to them as a chaplain. On the great Marian feast days they would gather, walk in procession, hear Mass and lay flowers. In Yorkshire, the statutes of the Guild of Our Lady of Beverley (founded 1355) provided that "every year, on the feast of the Purification of the blessed Mary, all the brethren and sisters shall meet together in a fit and appointed place… and there one of the guilds shall be clad in a comely fashion as a queen, like to the glorious Virgin Mary, having what may seem a son in her arms." The statutes then describe how the players will continue their pageant, with the Virgin offering her Son to

Simeon at the High Altar. Perhaps the most famous of the confraternities was the Confraternity of the Scapular at Mount Carmel. The illustrious Order of the Garter has a similar origin, having for its patrons St George and the Virgin Mary. Clues to the enduring role of the Virgin in the nation's life may be uncovered at every level of British society.

Anglo-Saxon devotion

The earliest Christian writers all venerate and draw us closer to Mary.

The Anglo-Saxon church received and published the decrees of the Lateran Council (649) at its own Council of Hatfield (680) and stated that

> If any one shall not confess, in accordance with the teachings of the Holy Fathers, that the holy and ever-Virgin and immaculate Mary is properly and truly the Mother of God, since at the end of ages, without union with man, but of the Holy Ghost, she conceived God Himself the Word, especially and truly, who before all ages was born of God the Father, and brought Him forth without corruption, retaining indissolubly her virginity even after birth; let him be condemned.

In the eighth century the Venerable Bede quoted Sedulius, the Irish poet: "To her we sing, Who bore in time the world's eternal King, And peerless in the human race has found a mother's joys by virgin honours crown'd." St Bede describes her as the Mother undefiled, the Virgin blessed beyond compare. St Anselm calls her "the garden enclosed"; Alcuin names her "his sweet love, his honour, the great hope of his salvation, the Queen of Heaven, the flower of the field, the lily of the world, the fountain of life."

The Book of Cerne, which belonged to Ethelwald, the Bishop of Sherbourne in 760, contains a prayer to the Virgin, and names her as "the advocate for the sins of the whole world." Many of the other Anglo-Saxon Christian writers speak in a similar vein.

Leofric, Saxon Bishop of Exeter, in 1046, held a collection of Anglo-Saxon poetry in his cathedral library which reveres Mary's purity and urges her to intercede with God and to make known her Son to a needy world.

In the tenth century Aelfric wrote movingly about the anguish which Mary would face recalling the prophecy of Simeon to her that "His sword shall pierce through thy soul." Aelfric said that "Though Mary believed that Christ would arise from death, her child's suffering went, nevertheless, very deeply into her heart."

The Normans

In the twelfth century, Peter of Blois, Archdeacon of Bath, gave an eloquent sermon on Mary's Assumption into heaven and the joy with which she would be greeted. He reminds his congregation that John leapt with joy "while still in his mother's womb... at the coming of Mary. The infant's soul was melted when Mary spoke. Let them, the angels, also melt with joy, now that they will both hear the voice and possess the presence of Mary."

During the same century, St Aelred says that Mary is the Eastern Gate, "for a gate which looks towards the East is the first to receive the rays of the sun". His contemporary, Archbishop Baldwin, wrote a meditation on the prayer, the Hail Mary. He says that the salutation – *Ave Maria* – "was spoken by the angel, to be repeated by ourselves, as a jubilation to the heart that conceives it and a sweetness to the mouth that speaks it". He continues that "the more she was magnified by God, the more she did magnify God. The more she was magnified, the more did she dwell on her own lowliness." All generations would call her blessed; the Lord would be seen to be with her; and she would be blessed amongst all women.

The most common devotion to Our Lady in Old England was to Mary's joys but pilgrims would also meditate on her words, on her sadness and on her glory. Here are the origins of the "mysteries" on which Catholics set their hearts as they say the rosary.

In the thirteenth century, St Edmund said that she might apply to herself the words of the prophet: "Call me not beautiful, but rather call me bitter; for the Lord Almighty has filled me with bitterness and with great grief" (Ruth 1:20).

The Tudors

By the fifteenth century, hymns and carols were regularly dedicated to Mary: "Mother and maiden was never none but she; Well might such a lady God's mother be". Another, the *Alma Redemptoris Mater*, draws on St Luke's Gospel narrative of the angel Gabriel's dramatic intervention in Mary's life.

In the sixteenth century, sacred drama, intended to be represented on the afternoons of Good Friday and Holy Saturday, again recalled Simeon's prophecy and places Mary standing at the foot of her Son's cross. Typical of these are the Chester Plays, which include "The Lamentation of Mary": "I pick out thorns by one and one, for now lieth dead my dear Son dear".

While Bishop of Rochester, St John Fisher (see chapters 4 and 12), gave the funeral address following the death of Lady Margaret, Countess of Richmond (mother of Henry VII). In it he describes how this devout woman began her devotions at five in the morning, starting with the Matins of Our Lady, and continued throughout the day to use the Office of Our Lady. Fisher says, "The Lady Margaret in these devotions followed in the footsteps of her patroness, St Margaret, Queen of Scotland who, during Advent and Lent, after a short sleep she would rise at midnight, and going to the church, she would say alone Matins of the Most Holy Trinity, Matins of the Holy Cross, and lastly Matins of Our Lady."

After Fisher's execution and the Reformation, secret devotion to Our Lady continued. In the register of criminal proceedings in 1569, Thomas Wright, vicar of Seaham, admitted that he said daily in his house, with certain others, the Office of the Blessed Virgin Mary.

The breaking of the chain

Before these devotions were forced underground England had openly and enthusiastically celebrated the feasts and the fasts of Our Lady. In Anglo-Saxon times, four feasts were celebrated: the Purification (2 February); the Annunciation (25 March); the Assumption (15 August), and Our Lady's Nativity (8 September). These were gradually added to: St Anselm instituted the celebration of Mary's conception while Pope Urban VI, in the fourteenth century, instituted the feast of the Visitation. The office of this festival was drawn up by Cardinal Adam Eston, born at Hereford and later Bishop of London.

By the laws of King Alfred all freemen were exempt from servile work for twelve days before Christmas, seven days before and seven days after Easter, and for the whole week before St Marymass (the Assumption). King Ethelred reiterated these laws.

During the great holidays, pageants and processions would take place. In the sixteenth century the Council Register of the Borough of Aberdeen lists the roles of the town's craftsmen in preparing for the colourful pageant, and especially in the preparation of the costumes for the plays and procession through the town. Along with the pageant and the festivities there would be fasting and almsgiving to the poor.

This love of Mary extended to the naming of parish

churches in honour of the Virgin. During the Reformation some were renamed. St Saviour's, near London Bridge, for instance, was formerly St Mary's Ovaries. Many others were simply pulled down; and yet there is hardly a town in Britain or Ireland which does not have a St Mary's Church or a church dedicated to Our Lady. The many instances of Lady chapels within our churches is further evidence of the depth of the traditional devotion.

Dedication and the shrines

Apart from the dedication of the ancient church of Glastonbury to the Virgin, the custom of dedication began in England in the twelfth century and was widespread amongst Saxons and Normans alike. Previously, we know that St Augustine built a church to the ever-virgin Mary at Ely in the seventh century. It was destroyed by Penda and rebuilt and rededicated to Our Lady by St Etheldreda fifty years later. It was famous for miracles.

St Augustine's companion, St Lawrence, also Archbishop of Canterbury, built a church of the Holy Mother of God in the monastery of St Peter's at Canterbury. It was consecrated by St Mellitus. St Bede records that St Cedd, Bishop of London (died 664), was buried in the stone church of the monastery at Lestringham, dedicated to the Blessed Virgin. By 1500, Arnold's *Chronicles* record that of London's 118 parish churches and thirty-six non-parochial churches, eighteen were dedicated to the Virgin, including Mary Woolchurch, Mary-at-the-Bowe and Mary-at-the-Hill.

The reformers branded this traditional devotion to the Virgin as "superstition" and Henry VIII and Edward VI used the opportunity to grow rich from the plunder of the shrines dedicated to Mary.

The most famous of these shrines were the sanctuary of Our Lady at Walsingham (see chapter 7), and, in Scotland, the shrine of Our Lady of Haddington (see chapter 8).

London

In London, the church of All Hallows is situated at the east end of Thames Street, adjoining the Tower. It was called "of Barking" because it was dependent on the Benedictine monastery of St Ethelburga, at Barking, in Essex. Richard the Lion Heart had built a chapel dedicated to Our Lady in 1190 adjoining this church.

There was another shrine close to the Tower, Our Lady of Graces, at Eastminster (or New Abbey), founded by Edward III in 1349 as the completion of a vow which he had made during a tempestuous storm at sea.

At Muswell Hill within the parish of Hornsey there was an ancient chapel bearing the name of Our Lady of Muswell. It was a place of pilgrimage and healing.

A sanctuary was built to Our Lady of Willesden. The parish of St Mary of Willesden was well established in Saxon days. Norman sources show that the new church which they built was also dedicated to the Virgin. There is an ancient tradition that there was an apparition of Our Lady and that a well sprang up at which miracles occurred.

Islington also had a sanctuary; and at Westminster there was much devotion to Our Lady at the Abbey Church and the nearby chapel of Our Lady of the Pew. The crypt chapel within the Palace of Westminster is dedicated to Our Lady Undercroft (situated beneath the former St Stephen's Church – now the entrance to the Central Lobby).

In a narrow street running parallel to Regent Street, close to Piccadilly Circus, is the shrine of Our Lady of Warwick Street. To be found in the church of Our Lady of the Assumption and St Gregory, this is one of the oldest functioning Catholic churches in the London area. Mass was said in several secret centres, including a number of embassies. The chapel of the Portuguese Ambassador became the Royal Bavarian Chapel in Warwick Street and records show its regular usage from 1735. Burnt down in

1780 after the Gordon Riots (when Lord George Gordon protested against the repeal of the harshest anti-Catholic laws), it was rebuilt eight years later. In the nineteenth century the shrine to the Virgin was re-established and in 1908 Pope St Pius X gave the church an apostolic blessing.

Aylesford and some other shrines

Outside of London many towns chose Mary as their patroness. The seal of Stamford depicts Our Lady with the Divine Child; Lincoln was dedicated to her; Kent was famous for the sanctuaries of Our Lady of the Crypt at Canterbury, Our Lady of Chatham, of Broadstairs, Our Lady of Gillingham, and Our Lady of Aylesford. In 1246, the church at Aylesford was dedicated by its Carmelite builders to the Assumption of the Glorious Virgin Mary. St Simon Stock lived here as a hermit, perhaps for a time in the hollow of a great oak tree. At a General Chapter of the Carmelite Order held at Aylesford in 1247 St Simon was elected as Prior General, and he led the transformation of this Order from that of contemplative hermetical life to one of no less contemplative active mendicancy. On 16 July 1251, St Simon had a vision of Mary seeing her with the Holy Child on her knee, and holding out towards him the Scapular, which would thereafter be a mark of Mary's esteem and the symbol used to mark out the Carmelite Order.

In 1538 the Bishop of Dover, acting in Henry VIII's name, suppressed the Carmelite Order, and Thomas Cromwell wrote to Sir Thomas Wyatt – one of the king's favourites – that "I have reserved for you the house of the Friars of Aylesford." Suppression had been crowned by theft.

In 1926 a new chapter opened in the history of Aylesford when the Carmelites returned to Kent and established houses in Sittingbourne and Faversham. Then, in 1949, they quietly managed to purchase "The Friars" and on the Vigil of All Saints they returned in the company of thousands of pilgrims from all over the world. It was the first time since the Reformation that an English monastery had been restored to the Order which had built it.

In 1951, on the eve of the seven-hundredth anniversary of the Scapular Apparition, the Archbishop of Bordeaux returned the relics of St Simon Stock. As a place of prayer and pilgrimage, Aylesford has continued to draw many pilgrims right up to our present times.

East Anglia

Norfolk had many other Marian sanctuaries as well as Walsingham. There were shrines at Thetford, Reepham, Horstad and Our Lady of the Mount at Lynn. At Norwich there were sanctuaries in St Martin's Church, the church of the Austin Friars, and the statue of Our Lady of Pirt in the Franciscan convent.

Suffolk boasted a famous sanctuary at Ipswich and Our Lady of Stoke by Clare and Our Lady of Wulpit and of Woodbridge. The statue of Our Lady of Ipswich was carved in wood and during the Reformation it was sent to London to be burnt. Some people believe that the statue escaped this fate and was mysteriously smuggled out of the country, and taken to Nettino, near Anzio (in the same church as the body of St Maria Goretti). At least one modern copy of this Madonna and Child is now on display, in the new shrine in Ipswich town centre.

Bucks and Berks: Our Lady of Caversham

Berkshire boasted shrines to Our Lady of Windsor and Our Lady of Eton; Berkshire had Our Lady of Caversham, near Reading, a centre of great pilgrimage. This shrine developed in the thirteenth century after the Benedictines of Reading Abbey built a bridge across the Thames. The construction was made easier by a small island which linked the spans of the bridge. A Holy Well dedicated to the Virgin existed on the Caversham side and it was decided to erect a small church on the island dedicated to St Anne, Mary's mother.

Records reveal that a chapel of Our Lady had existed in Caversham a century earlier and probably stood close to the Church of St Peter. As to its fate we have to rely on the report of the notorious Dr London, reporting to his master Thomas Cromwell in 1538: "I have pulled down the image of Our Lady at Caversham, whereunto was great pilgrimage... I have also pulled down the places she stood in, with all other ceremonies, as lights, shrouds, crutches and images of wax hanging about the chapel, and have defaced the same thoroughly." Notwithstanding this violent suppression, Catholicism survived in these parts through the recusant strongholds at Stonor (see chapter 14), associated with St Edmund Campion and Blessed Adrian Fortescue, and at Mapledurham. As early as 1780 the district saw the restoration of a Catholic parish at Reading, that of St James.

By 1896 Mass was being said once again at Caversham, and by 1899 a school and chapel were ready to be blessed. In 1904 a church tower was built, and the Angelus rung from its bells (one of which is pre-Reformation and comes from Canterbury), and in 1933 a new church, dedicated to Our Lady and St Anne, was finally consecrated. Expansion of the congregation led to the erection of a new church, under the dedication of Our Lady of Caversham, being opened in the Marian Year, 1954.

Work on the bridge at Caversham led to the uncovering of the foundation of the ancient chapel. Some of the stones were subsequently incorporated in the construction of an altar on Caversham Heights and, in 1955, some were incorporated into the altar of a new Lady chapel, which, in accordance with the old traditions, was built on the "gospel side" of the church. This is to commemorate Mary's place at the right hand of Our Lord when she stood at the foot of the cross. A mediæval statue carved in oak, depicting the Virgin and Child, was obtained and incorporated into what has become once again a centre of pilgrimage and devotion.

Mary's rich legacy

The whole of England was peppered with sanctuaries where Christ's mother was honoured. Salisbury, in Wiltshire, had a shrine to Our Lady; Shropshire had Our Lady of Ludlow; Warwickshire, Our Lady of Warwick; Oxfordshire, Our Lady of Binsey and a statue in Oxford known through the devotions made there by St Edmund. While still a youth he made a vow of perpetual chastity and commended himself to the Virgin's protection.

Cambridge had an image of Our Lady which was a centre of pilgrimage. It was in the church of the black friars (where Emmanuel College now stands).

Since 1915 Staffordshire has held an annual devotion to the Virgin at Hednesford, near Cannock. The annual diocesan pilgrimage takes place on the first Sunday in July, with Mass at 4.00 pm followed by the Blessed Sacrament Procession and the Blessing of the Sick.

More ancient centres of devotion existed at Doncaster, Belcrosse, Himminburgh, Durham, Northampton, Sudbury, Cockthorpe, Hillbury, Truro, Marychurch and Deepdale.

Our Lady of Evesham

Worcestershire and Gloucestershire had ancient sanctuaries at Worcester, Tewkesbury and Evesham, celebrated for the apparition of Our Lady to Eoves, the swine-herd, and Egwin, the Bishop of Worcester, at the end of the seventh century.

Little remains of Evesham's monastic or pilgrim past. Vestiges include the bell tower, converted in 1745 into a campanile, and two churches sited in the same churchyard which the monks had built. All Saints was built to serve the local people and St Lawrence was erected for the use of the pilgrims.

Pilgrimage began after St Egwin established a church in honour of the Virgin on the spot where he and Eoves had seen the apparition. King Ethelred was one of the principal benefactors. His nephew, King Kenred, together with King Offa of Essex and St Egwin, went to Rome to ask Pope Constantine to grant important privileges to the new foundation, which he gladly agreed to do. On his return, St Egwin, with St Wilfrid, consecrated the new church and placed it under the care of the Benedictine monks. Although plundered and desecrated by the Danes, the foundation was rebuilt and maintained by Saxon Christians. The Normans subsequently rebuilt it on a massive scale.

After the destruction of the abbey small clusters of Catholics tried to hold on to the faith, but when the Passionists arrived at nearby Broadway in the late nineteenth century virtually none were left. Under the influence of men like Fr Dominic Barberi, a small chapel was opened at Evesham in 1889, and in 1913 a new church was opened, dedicated to the Immaculate Conception and St Egwin. In recognition of the renewed interest of pilgrims in Evesham a beautiful coloured glass window was incorporated into one of the two pre-Reformation churches which guard the approach to the former abbey and site of Our Lady's apparition.

Each year, on the second Sunday in June, Mass is celebrated on the site of the High Altar of the abbey in the presence of pilgrims from all over the Birmingham archdiocese and beyond. The procession starts from St

Mary's church at 2.30 pm and Mass is said at 3.00 pm, followed by the Blessing of the Sick.

Some historians have suggested that Evesham was a staging-post en route to the Cistercian abbey of Hailes, whose "glorious ruins" have been described by Professor Scarisbrick as "a haunting miniature version of Tintern or Fountains." It boasted the shrine of the Precious Blood and was undoubtedly an important centre for pilgrims. Perhaps because it is not such a famous tourist centre as Fountains, Hailes has a very special serenity and sense of the numinous about it.

Our Lady of Fernyhalgh: Lancashire

In Lancashire, the county which clung most tenaciously to the Catholic faith, a reminder of the past is to be found at Fernyhalgh Chapel, about four miles from Preston (see also chapter 15).

Fr Christopher Tuttell was a missionary priest at Fernyhalgh – pronounced "Ferny-huff" – between 1699 and 1727. He wrote a personal account of the origins of Fernyhalgh. The name comes from the Anglo-Saxon for "ancient shrine" and the site has been in use as a baptismal well since at least the seventh century.

Fr Tuttell wrote that in 1471 a wealthy merchant found himself in great distress during a passage on the Irish Sea:

> He made a vow, in case he escaped the danger, to acknowledge the favour of his preservation by some remarkable work of piety. After this the storm began to cease and a favourable gale wafted the ship into the coast of Lancashire… a voice somewhat miraculous, yet providential, admonished him to seek a spot called Fernyhalgh and there to erect a chapel, where he should find a crab-tree bearing fruit without cores, and under it a spring of clear water…

Having found the spot he discovered a statue of the Virgin and erected a chapel. The spring became known as Lady Well, usually written Ladyewell. There is a record of an earlier chapel having existed on this spot and the merchant may have discovered some of its remains. The chapel was pulled down during the suppression but Lancashire Catholics continued to throng there, shrine or no shrine. By 1685 a house of prayer was constructed next to the holy well, and made to look as much like an ordinary house as possible. Cuthbert Hesketh of the Whitehill in Goosnargh was responsible for procuring the house at Fernyhalgh and paid the rent on the property for the following sixteen years. The records reveal that a Madam Westy was another benefactor, as was Bishop James Smith, first Vicar Apostolic of the Northern District, who died in 1711.

In 1687 Bishop Leyburn confirmed more than a thousand people at Fernyhalgh, but the authorities did not always turn a blind eye. As late as the eighteenth century soldiers were sent to plunder the chapel, although they stopped short of destroying it. On one occasion, in 1718, a renegade priest, a Mr Hitchmough, led twenty soldiers to Fernyhalgh to plunder and strip it. By 1723, private and then public prayers began to be offered at the shrine.

Fr Tuttell records a "sweet melody they sung" at Fernyhalgh:

Of one that is so fair and bright,
Velut Maris stella,
Brighter than the day is bright,
Parens et puella;
I cry to thee, thou see to me,
I am pia,
That I may come to thee,
Maria.
All this world was forlorn,
Eva peccatrice,
Till Our Lord was of ye born,

De te Genetrice,
with ave it went away,
thus went night and cometh day
Salutis;
The well springeth out of thee
Virtutis.

Lady, flower of all things,
Rosa sine spina.
Thou bore Jesus, Heavenly King,
Gratia Divina,
Of all thou bearest as the prize,
Lady, Queen of Paradise,
Electa;
Maid mild, Mother sweet,
Effecta!

Fernyhalgh's sufferings were still not over. In 1745, as Prince Charles and his Highlanders pushed south to Manchester during the second Jacobite Rising, a hostile mob attacked the Lady Well chapel, sacked and burned it. Another priest, also by the name of Tuttell, rebuilt the chapel, and as numbers increased they began work on a new church, which was opened in 1794. Built to escape notice from the outside, the cruciform shape and interior design leave today's pilgrim in no doubt that this church, built thirty-five years before Emancipation and fourteen years after the Gordon Riots, represented a statement of enduring faith. It has continued since then to draw pilgrims who continue to give thanks from being spared the shipwrecks which threaten every life.

Even in our own times, on 8 September 2000, the feast of the birthday of the Virgin Mary, the shrine was desecrated. An effigy of Blessed Padre Pio, which had been brought from Rome by a Liverpool family, was ripped from its base and a chapel was daubed with blue paint. A priest at the shrine, Fr Benedict Rucsilo, described the attack as "sickening". The attack came after five churches in the same part of Lancashire had been torched by an arsonist.

Endurance is summed up by one other aspect of Fernyhalgh. Here, too, is the tombstone of the last of the English Carthusians of the old traditions: "Sacred to the memory of the Reverend James Finch, the last of the English Carthusian Monks. He died March 3rd, 1621, aged 72. Good Christian, on this Stone, shed not a tear for virtue lies entombed, enshrouded here. Religion, resignation both combine over these remains to raise a heavenly Shrine. R.I.P."

Mary is venerated at Fernyhalgh as Our Lady Queen of Martyrs. The statue depicting the Virgin holding her Son was brought to Fernyhalgh from Bolzano by the Sisters of the Holy Child of Jesus after the restoration of the English and Welsh Hierarchy. Beside the shrine is a prayer room called *Stella Maris*, built in 1996 in the shape of a ship. Nearby is the Martyrs Chapel, a modern building, beautifully simple, housing statues of Saints Thomas More and John Fisher. Around the walls are the names of more than three hundred Catholics from these islands who gave their lives for their faith.

Some of those martyrs lived very near to Fernyhalgh (see chapter 15). George Haydock came from Cottam, near Preston (martyred 1584, Tyburn); William Marsden came from nearby Goosnargh (martyred 1586, Isle of Wight); George Beesly was also from Goosnargh (martyred 1591, Fleet Street). Richard Herst was from Broughton (martyred 1628, Lancaster); John Southworth was from Salmesbury, a couple of miles to the south of Fernyhalgh (martyred 1654, Tyburn); John Wall was from Preston (martyred 1679, Worcester); and Germanus Helmes, the last priest to die for the faith, was martyred at Lancaster Castle in 1746.

Approaching Fernyhalgh, along Fernyhalgh Lane, today's pilgrim passes St Mary's Church and School, which was where Adam Butler, who wrote the famous *Lives of the*

Saints, was educated. It is possible to leave a car here or further along the lane at a small car park. Next to the shrine is Ladyewell House. Upstairs there is a reliquary which is home to the Burgess Altar, and which folds away as a sideboard. It was the secret altar on which many of the martyrs, including St Edmund Campion, St Edmund Arrowsmith and Blessed John Woodcock, celebrated Mass. There is also a display of the vestments which were used by many of the priests before their arrest and execution.

Three years ago another relic was brought to Fernyhalgh. This is part of the skull of St Thomas à Becket, murdered in 1170 in Canterbury Cathedral, and secretly taken to Castelfiorentino in Tuscany during the desecration of the shrines by Henry VIII.

During the last few days of May 2000 I visited Fernyhalgh with three of my children. I was enormously impressed by the quiet atmosphere of peace, characteristic of Our Lady's shrines. There is no doubting that this is hallowed ground.

I strongly agree with the journalist Simon Caldwell, himself a Lancastrian, writing in the *Catholic Herald* about Fernyhalgh. He said that travelling to Fernyhalgh proved for him to be an unexpected delight: "a walk up a timeless Arcadian path flanked by steep wooded embankments, in May cloaked with bluebells. This is England at its best. It puts the pilgrim in an ideal frame of mind for arrival at the shrine and without doubt as to why so many spiritual sons of the holy queen died *pro Petro et Patria*."

To get to Fernyhalgh (which is not marked on maps) , the pilgrim should leave the M6 at Junction 31A (accessible from the south only) and head east to Grimsargh (signposted Longridge) on the B6243. Here, take Whittingham Lane (signposted Haighton and Goosnargh) and then follow signs for Ladyewell. Other Lancashire pilgrim sites are nearby (see chapter 14). When travelling from the north go to Junction 31 and drive back the short distance to 31A to access the B6243.

Wales: Our Lady of the Taper

In Wales, Our Lady of Pen-Rhys, near Swansea, in Glamorganshire, was one of the most famous of the shrines. In Merioneth, a new shrine, intended to commemorate events at Fatima, was created at Bala. One of the first great pilgrimages was undertaken in 1949 by a small group who walked the sixty miles from Liverpool, following the route taken by the car cavalcade which had brought the statue of Mary to Bala (via the Mersey Tunnel and stops at the pro-cathedral of Our Lady of Dolours at Wrexham and the Catholic church in Llangollen).

At Cardigan, there is a shrine of ancient foundation. An early dedication, probably to the Holy Trinity, was confirmed in the twelfth century by Pope Alexander III, and Rhys ap Gruffydd encouraged a Benedictine foundation. It is likely that the new church of St Mary the Virgin had its foundation at this time. The shrine of Our Lady of the Taper became a place of pilgrimage. After William Barlow, acting on behalf of Henry VIII, had destroyed the shrine at Haverfordwest and desecrated St David's (see chapter Four) he set about the destruction of the Cardigan shrine, which depicted the Virgin holding a taper in her right hand.

In 1889 the Passionist Fathers came to Carmarthen and were given responsibility for Cardigan. By 1926 Carmelite nuns had opened a house nearby and in 1930 Bishop Vaughan blessed a new church and dedicated it to Our Lady of Sorrows. During the Marian Year, 1953-4, it was decided to restore the historic Cardigan shrine. In 1956 a new statue, carved at Farnborough Abbey, was blessed by Cardinal Griffin. It was taken first to Wrexham and then conducted solemnly through Wales and installed on 27 May at Cardigan.

Scotland and Ireland

Centuries-old devotion to Mary throughout Ireland is continued today at Knock (see chapter 10) and the restoration of the pilgrimage to Our Lady of Haddington (see chapter 8) revives equally venerable Scottish traditions of devotion to the Virgin.

In Scotland there were other shrines at Aberdeen, Scone, Dundee, Paisley, Melrose, and Jedburgh.

Mary and God

In the nineteenth century, in his classic work on Marian devotion, Rev T.E. Bridgett roundly refutes the idea that pre-Reformation Catholics had replaced God with Mary and that devotion to the Mother of God had become a superstitious cult. Listing what he calls its "beneficent influence" he describes how the devotion sprang from a lively faith in the Incarnation and in its turn acted as a safeguard of that faith:

> How the devotion was an exercise and a stimulant of Christian hope, whether in the sinner or the saint, looking as they did on Our Lady as the great channel of the mercies of God, purchased for us by Jesus Christ; how the devotion is one of the noblest acts of that charity which makes us love what God loves; how it led to innumerable works of love and mercy to men; and how it gave a charm and attraction to the Christian heart, without in any way substituting mere poetry and sentimentalisation for solid virtue.

Nor does Fr Bridgett, or other writers, hesitate to point to the effect which devotion to Our Lady had on developing a respect for women. In Mary a woman was elevated to her rightful position of respect; recognition, too, was given to the sanctity of weakness and of sorrow. Antiquity and modernity have no similar concept or subject of reverential devotion. The beauty and the charm of female excellence was given great expression through the Marian pilgrimage and devotion to Mary. In an often ignorant and dark world the ideals of gentleness, tenderness and purity, which she personifies, radiated a penetrating light. The old English poem recorded in the *Reliquiae Antiquae* captures this thought:

> *To unpraise women it were a shame,*
> *For a woman was thy dame;*
> *Our Blessed Lady beareth the name*
> *Of all women where that they go.*

A meditation

The Old English Version of the *Magnificat*
(published about 1400)

> *Mi soule magnifieth the lorde: and my spirit fulout*
>   *ioiede in god myn heethe.*
> *For he bihelde the mekenesse of his handmaide:*
>   *lo forsothe of this alle kynredis shulen seie me blessid.*
> *For he that is migti hath don to me grete thing is:*
>   *to men with the thougt of his herte.*
> *And his merci is fro kynrede in to kynredis:*
>   *to men that dreden him.*
> *He made mygt in his arm: he scatride proude men with*
>   *the thougt of his herte.*
> *He sette doun mygti men fro ceete: and enhauncide meke*
>   *men.*
>
> *He hath fulfillid hungri men with goodis: and he hath*
>   *lefte riche men voide.*
> *He havynge mynde of his merci: took up Israel*
>   *his child.*
> *As he hath spokun to oure fadris:*
> *to Abraham and to his seed in to worldis.*

(Taken from William Maskell's *Monumenta Ritualia*, 1846)

And here is a prayer of the great Archbishop of Canterbury of the eleventh century, St Anselm:

Of a certainty, O Jesus, Son of God, and thou, O Mother Mary, you desire that whatever you love should be loved by us. Therefore, O good Son, I beg Thee, by the love Thou bearest Thy Mother, and as Thou wishest her to be loved, to grant to me that I may truly love her. And thou O good Mother, I beg thee by the love thou bearest thy Son, as Thou wishest Him to be loved, to pray for me that I may truly love Him. Behold I ask nothing that is not in accordance with your will. Since then, this is in your power, shall my sins prevent its being done? O Jesus, lover of men, Thou wert able to love criminals even as to die for them; canst Thou, then, refuse me, who ask only the love of Thee and Thy Mother? And Thou, too, Mary, Mother of Him who loved us, who didst bear Him in thy womb, and feed Him at thy breast, art thou not able, or not willing, to obtain for one who asks it the love of thy Son and of thyself?

O then, may my mind venerate you both as you deserve! may my heart venerate you, as it ought! in your service may my life be spent! and may my whole substance praise you in eternity! Blessed be God for ever.

Amen, amen.

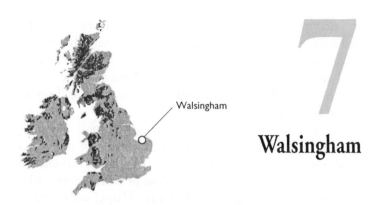

7

Walsingham

IN England the pre-eminent shrine to Our Lady was undoubtedly at Walsingham, in Norfolk. As a child I was brought here by my parents during one of our annual Norfolk holidays; but it was in 1989, when my friend, Ken Hargreaves, former Member of Parliament for Hyndburn, in Lancashire, and a close ally in the fight to protect unborn life, invited me to join him on a pilgrimage, that I really began to appreciate the treasure of Walsingham. When our little girl was diagnosed as having a congenital hip displacement, and, not long after, our oldest son's twin miscarried, Lizzie and I gained some comfort from a visit to Walsingham.

My first thoughts about Walsingham coincided with those of John Wesley, who during a preaching visit some two hundred years ago said: "I walked over what is left of the famous Abbey... had there been a grain of virtue or public spirit in Henry VIII, these noble buildings need not have run to ruin." Walsingham's story, however, is not about the study of archaeological remains. Its resurrection as a centre of pilgrimage is an apt metaphor for the endurance of faith.

Origins

The earliest evidence of Walsingham as a shrine is contained in a deed which declares that Geoffrey of Faveraches made it known that he had "given and granted to God and St Mary, and to Edwin his priest for the establishing of an Order which said Edwin was to find, for the health of his soul and the good of his parents and friends, the chapel which his mother had founded in Walsingham in honour of the Ever Virgin Mary."

Geoffrey's mother was the Lady Richeldis, who is thought to have lived in the twelfth century, or possibly a little earlier. One account places her at the tail-end of Saxon England. She was the widow of a landowner who held lands at Walsingham. She built a chapel dedicated to the Virgin on the estate, and Geoffrey, before heading off on pilgrimage to Jerusalem, attached a religious house to serve the chapel. The Bishop of Norwich subsequently established the Augustinian Canons at Walsingham and they became guardians of the chapel. This chapel was not rebuilt or enlarged but carefully retained in its original condition.

A ballad published in 1461, and published by Richard Pynson, gives the clue to the chapel's careful preservation and the importance of its original construction by Richeldis. The ballad describes how this saintly widow had received three repeated visions of Our Lady. Richeldis petitioned that she might be permitted to carry out some special work in honour of the Virgin. The widow was transported in spirit to Nazareth, was shown Mary's home and was greeted by Gabriel. Richeldis was invited to build another home like the house of the Annunciation and to set it at Walsingham. The ballad put it thus:

> O England great cause thou hast glad for to be
> Compared to the Land of Promise, Sion,
> Thou attainest my grace to stand in that degree
> Through the gracious Lady's supportacion,
> To be called in every realm and region
> The Holy land, our Lady's Dowry:
> Thus art thou named of old antiquity
> And this is the case, as it appeareth by likeliness,

In thee is builded New Nazareth, a mansion
To the honour of the Heavenly Empress
And of her most glorious Salutation,
When Gabriel said at Old Nazareth, "Ave",
This joy here daily remembered for to be.

No doubt the romantic spirit of the age and poetic license added embellishment to the Walsingham story. Yet at its heart is a simple story of personal piety and obedience. Richeldis did as she was bid and built a Holy House like the one which had been revealed to her. The story has it that the workmen could not complete the structure in its original site close to a well which was already regarded as holy, and after a vigil of prayer by the Lady Richeldis the structure was supernaturally removed to a different site alongside another well some two hundred feet away. The first site was used to build a chapel dedicated to St Lawrence while, in time, the Holy House became enshrined in an outer chapel adjacent to the north aisle of the Priory Church of the Canons.

Walsingham's miracles

Over the centuries which followed there were many benefactors who gave land and material support to Walsingham. Many also attributed miracles. One of the earliest is connected to Edward I, who believed that divine intervention had protected him as a young man from being crushed, when a large stone had fallen on the spot from which he had felt compelled to move moments before. His subsequent devotion accounts for twelve personal visits to the shrine at Walsingham. Over the centuries there is a long record of miraculous cures and remarkable answers to prayer – the lame healed, the blind restored to sight, lepers cleansed, and the ancient ballad even asserts that the "dede agayne reyved of this no doubt".

By 1291, the Taxatio of Pope Nicholas IV lists eighty-six parishes in Norfolk alone held by the Walsingham Priory. Other records reveal that monarchs from Henry III to Henry VIII came on pilgrimage to Walsingham and that the poor and wealthy alike saw the shrine as their refuge in time of trouble. Edward III, for instance, gave protection to Robert Bruce of Scotland, who travelled to Walsingham when taken by leprosy.

We cannot apply rigorous scrutiny to the claims made about eleventh-century healings but we can at least observe the same phenomenon in Lourdes and allow that miracles can and do happen. Just as miracles are not the final purpose at Lourdes, they were not the final purpose at Walsingham. Just as faith is not dependent on belief or scepticism about such occurrences, we can also allow that, for many, the miraculous can point the way to God.

When Erasmus came to Walsingham in the sixteenth century he described it as "graceful and elegant". He said that the Blessed Sacrament was housed in the main church and that the famous statue of Our Lady of Walsingham was housed in the Holy House. "The Virgin dwells", he wrote, "within a small chapel, made of wainscot, admitting devotees on each side by a narrow door. There is little light, indeed scarcely any but from the candles. A delicious fragrance greets the nostrils."

The Pilgrim Way

Erasmus described the statue as "a small image, neither excelling in material or workmanship, but in virtue most efficacious". He added "at the feet of the Virgin is a jewel" which he said symbolised "all filthiness, malice, pride, avarice, and whatever belongs to human passions." These excesses were subdued under the Virgin's foot.

In the time of Erasmus many pilgrims followed a "Pilgrims' Way", comparable to the pilgrimage route which led across the hills of Surrey and Kent to the shrine of St Thomas of Canterbury. Pilgrims travelling from Scotland and the north came through Lincolnshire and crossed the Wash at Long Sutton. They assembled at Bishop's Lynn (now King's Lynn) and travelled via the priories at Flitcham, Rudham and Cokesford.

Norwich to East Dereham

Pilgrims from the east travelled through Norwich and Attlebridge; some stayed at the Hospital of Bec, where free accommodation was provided each night for thirteen pilgrims. By taking this route, starting at Ely, the modern pilgrim can encounter some of the great women of the Church, St Etheldreda of Ely, one of the most single-minded of the Anglo-Saxon saints, and Mother Julian of Norwich, the great English mystic.

At Bury St Edmunds not only was there another of the great English shrines, to the Saxon king, St Edmund, but here, too, the English barons drew up Magna Carta in 1215. At East Dereham is the site of a nunnery founded by St Withburga, whose remains were stolen and removed to Ely in 974. A holy well sprang up at the site of her grave and still flows in the churchyard. From East Dereham the pilgrims may make their way to North Elmham, where the ruins of the vast Saxon cathedral may still be seen. From here it is fourteen miles to Walsingham.

The Walsingham Way

From London, pilgrims travelled through Newmarket, Brandon and Fakenham to East Barsham and Houghton. This route was called the Walsingham Way or the Walsingham Green Way.

Along the pilgrim routes chapels and shrines were

erected. Two survive: one at King's Lynn (the chapel of Our Lady of the Red Mount) and one at Houghton-in-the-Dale, dedicated to St Catherine of Alexandria, and also known as the Slipper Chapel.

Turbulent times

The huge numbers of people who followed the road to Walsingham contributed to its undoing. Undoubtedly by the fifteenth century there were plenty who were prepared to profiteer at the expense of the pilgrims. The picture has been coloured by retrospective attempts to justify what then followed. The Church has often been caricatured as wholly corrupt and capable only of reform by destruction. The subsequent ability of the Council of Trent to deal with reform and to tackle decay, and the launch of the counter Reformation movement, illustrates how excesses could successfully be dealt with. The real cause of Walsingham's undoing was the greed and pride of Henry VIII, who had found no fault with the practice of pilgrimage or devotion at Walsingham until months before the Pope, Clement VII, refused to sanction his divorce. Indeed, he had himself been there on pilgrimage.

His decision to defy the authority of the Church led him to establish himself as supreme head of the Church in England and through the appointment of Thomas Cromwell as his Vicar General, he then set about the sequestration of church lands and the destruction of religious communities that might defy his power. In 1538 Walsingham became the target for Cromwell's visitors. The armed gangs who carried out his orders were not interested in religious reform, only in destruction.

The Walsingham Rebellion

When one local man, George Gisborough, said he thought "it very evil done, the suppressing of so many religious houses where God was well served" it led to a protest which was dubbed the "Walsingham Rebellion." Free speech led to the execution of eleven Norfolk men who were hanged, drawn, beheaded and quartered, at various towns in Norfolk. For his "high treason" the sub-prior was burnt alive on Walsingham's Martyr's Hill.

The prior, along with fifteen other canons, capitulated on 4 August 1538 and signed deeds of surrender. The image of the Virgin had already been taken to London and publicly burnt at Chelsea. Henry VIII gave the priory to Thomas and Agnes Sydney, and as the building fell into ruins the stones were taken for new buildings.

Long Catholic memories

This might have been the end of the Walsingham story. However, Catholics never forgot Walsingham, and Walsingham never forgot its place in Catholic hearts. There was an old saying that "When England returns to Walsingham, Our Lady will come back to England."

The next three hundred years would be a time of waiting, or, in words familiar to Mary herself, for the storing of memories in the heart and for living through trials and suffering in the expectation of the life to come, when all things will be made new.

The gentle beginnings of revival occurred in the early nineteenth century. This followed a period of religious decline and abstention. Then, in the late eighteenth century, the Wesleys and other evangelicals experienced a dramatic renewal of interest. They by-passed the officially Established Church, which too often was regarded as a department of state. Not long after, in 1833, a Catholic revival began and this, too, found itself in conflict with the establishment. The Oxford Movement began as a protest within the Church of England against the decision of Parliament to suppress certain dioceses in Ireland.

This raised the more fundamental problem of authority: by what mandate and by what right does the state determine such matters?

At Oxford, Edward Pusey, John Keble and John Henry Newman would endlessly debate these issues and agonised over the implications.

At one level it resulted in controversial tracts expounding Catholic doctrine and engaging in polemical debate about the direction of the Anglican Church. At another level it expressed itself in formularies, rituals and pietistic religious practice. It led to deep study of the early Fathers of the Church – Clement, Origen, Augustine and Gregory of Nyssa. At another level it led to reconciliation with Rome.

Keble and Newman made the Catholic religion attractive and accessible to their generation and undergraduates in the 1830s were as likely to have been swept up by it as the generation, of the 1930s were swept along by pacifism and a dalliance with communism. They were also likely to be captivated by the Romantic movement – personified by Sir Walter Scott – or by artists like Burne-Jones and by the renaissance of arts and crafts.

At a theological level, Newman came to believe that the Holy Spirit is at work revealing God in every generation, and that while being open to the movement of the Spirit, there needed to be some arbiter capable of upholding orthodoxy. It became self-evident to Newman where that authority rested.

Scripture teaches that such authority was given by Christ to His apostles. For Newman the test was whether that authority had been handed on in apostolic succession or whether it rested in the monarch and on the bishops' benches of the House of Lords. On 9 October 1845, the conflict resolved itself when Newman became a Roman Catholic.

For those who remained Anglican the Oxford Movement led to the restoration of Catholic practice within the Church of England. In 1841 the Society of the Holy and

Undivided Trinity was founded, thus restoring the practice of communal religious life, suppressed three hundred years earlier. The Community of St Mary the Virgin was established at Wantage in 1848; at Clewer the Community of St John the Baptist emerged in 1852; the Community of St Margaret was born at East Grinstead, in 1854; the Community of All Saints followed in 1856; and the Society of St John the Evangelist was formed at Cowley in 1856. Anglican Orders of Benedictines and Franciscans were also created.

Notwithstanding all this, both Keble and Pusey were hesitant about dealing with the position of Mary in the Church.

It would be another thirty years before the emergence of groups such as the Confraternity of Our Lady Help of Christians(1880) and the later League of Our Lady (1904).

New Dawn at Walsingham

All these trends and movements would ultimately have huge implications for Walsingham.

In 1852 the ownership of the estate passed to Rev D.H. Lee-Warner, whose nephew, Rev James Lee-Warner, began the excavation of the site. It revealed the foundations of the priory church, the cloisters and the chapter house. Above ground all that remained of the church of the Augustinian canons were the great east window and the staircase turrets, rising to about seventy feet. There were also some arches of the refectory and the principal western gateway.

Subsequently, they found the two wells and what they believed to be the Lady chapel, which had enclosed the Holy House. Doubts have arisen about the authenticity of this identification.

Mr Lee-Warner also reproduced the seal of the Walsingham Priory which is illustrated with a Norman church of cruciform character, with a central tower, and two small towers both at the east and west ends. A supplicant is shown in prayer and at the side is the Virgin, seated on a high-backed chair, holding the infant Jesus on her knee, a low crown on her head and a foliated sceptre in her right hand. Around the margin appear the words: *Ave: Maria: Gratia: Plena: Dominus: Tecum.*

Fr Hope-Patten

During this period a succession of Lee-Warners were incumbents of the nearby Parish Church of St Mary. Their active interest in the bare archaeological history of Walsingham paved the way for renewed theological and spiritual interest. This had to wait until the arrival of Rev A. Hope-Patten, who was appointed vicar in 1921.

He placed an image of the Virgin, copied from that on the priory seal, in the Guilds Chapel of the church. He saw this as an act of reparation. Within six years it had become necessary to make available accommodation for the regular flow of pilgrims who had begun to return to Walsingham. The hospice of Our Lady Star of the Sea was opened and an old pilgrim inn put into use.

Concern was expressed that if the incumbency passed into less amenable hands the devotions and pilgrimages might again be terminated. This led to the construction of a purpose-built chapel enclosing a facsimile of the Holy House which the Lady Richeldis had built nine hundred years earlier.

During the building work an ancient well was uncovered, and evidence was unearthed that the site which had been chosen had been in regular use by earlier pilgrims. Preaching at the consecration of the new building in 1931, Rev Ernest Underhill, the vicar of St Thomas, Toxteth in Liverpool, said that this was a logical conclusion of the Oxford Movement when "God brought forth the old treasures of the Catholic faith, and was presenting them to the generations in which they lived". Such was the renewed interest that by 1938 an extension had been constructed, and more evidence uncovered of the early associations of this site with the Holy House.

Fr Hope-Patten, who died in 1958, ensured that the autonomy of the shrine was preserved by creating a Chapter of Guardians. It has been their responsibility to maintain and uphold the work of the shrine. Among their number in recent years has been the former Cabinet Minister, John Gummer MP. Vexed, like Newman a century earlier, over the question of the exercise of authority, he made his way to the Roman Catholic church in the 1990s, along with five hundred Anglican clergymen. As with Newman and Manning before them, their ministry has greatly enriched the Catholic Church in England.

Renewal

However, in a paradoxical way, Walsingham has helped to heal some of these decisions rather than exacerbate them. Frequently, the different traditions come together and share in devotion and the sense of being pilgrims on the same road.

That this should have happened may be traced back to Newman and Manning and those other Anglicans who brought their strong faith into the Catholic Church. Their leadership gave confidence to the Church in England and helped to create a deep renewal. This expressed itself in diverse ways. The creation of the Birmingham Oratory and the Catholic University in Dublin were Newman's inspiration, so were the ideas he expressed about Catholic schools and education. Manning took his ministry to the poor, to the working classes and into a whole variety of causes. Church building was undertaken on a scale without precedent since the Middle Ages. Catholics were also rediscovering their roots.

In 1879 Edmund Waterton published his *Pietas Mariana Britannica* and stimulated the desire for Catholics to return to their sources. A copy of this rare text is held at London's Catholic Central Library (see Appendix for contact details).

A Catholic shrine again

At Walsingham, meanwhile, there was a new development. Miss Charlotte Boyd, an Anglican, was trying to purchase the dilapidated but still intact Slipper Chapel, the ancient Chapel of St Catherine. Miss Boyd's story is well told by Kate Moore in her pamphlet *Walsingham: Charlotte Boyd, 1837-1906.*

She had become fascinated by the Slipper Chapel where pilgrims had stopped before entering Walsingham's Holy Ground. They removed their boots and shoes and were shriven. From Houghton St Giles to the Holy House is just one mile. Penitents and pilgrims often walked this holy mile barefoot.

Miss Boyd was born in Macao, China, in 1837. She founded an orphanage in Kensington (at 3 Lansdowne Place) in 1866 which was later moved to Kilburn. She combined her love of helping the homeless with a desire to see ancient ruins restored. This had been sparked by her visit to Glastonbury as a girl of thirteen. When she later consulted Dr John Mason Neale, an Anglican clergyman who wanted to restore religious life in the Church of England, his advice was to make such restoration her life work. Faithfulness to this call ultimately led her to buy the Slipper Chapel.

Miss Boyd had originally intended that the Slipper Chapel might be the focus for a community of Anglican Benedictine nuns. In 1894, however, before the negotiations for the purchase of the land were completed, Miss Boyd became a Catholic. With the support of the Bishop of Northampton, Bishop Riddell, restoration was placed into the hands of Thomas Garner who had built the choir of Downside Abbey. He, too, had recently been received into the Catholic Church.

In 1897, Fr H.E Ford OSB, Prior of Downside, Fr Fletcher, Master of the Guild of Ransom, and Fr Wrigglesworth, parish priest of King's Lynn, led the first official Catholic pilgrimage since the Reformation. Miss Boyd placed the chapel into the care of the Downside community. This was partly because, since her youth, Miss Boyd had had a devotion to Richard Whiting, the last Benedictine abbot of Glastonbury (see chapter 1). Since her reception into the Church, she had become a Benedictine Oblate.

Further interest in the Slipper Chapel was generated by the publication of *Our Ladye of Walsingham* by Dom Filbert Feasey OSB in 1901.

Cardinal Bourne's pilgrimage

In 1906 Miss Boyd died, but her vision passed to the next generation and in 1934 a new National Pilgrimage was instituted by the Archbishop of Westminster, Cardinal Bourne, and the Hierarchy of England. Some nineteen thousand pilgrims accompanied them. Miss Boyd's friend, Fr Ethelbert Taunton, said of her "she is full of faith and the love of God and her heart is all gold." Dom Bede Camm (see chapter 14) described her as "a dear friend". She was buried in the Roman Catholic cemetery in Kensal Green but her vision lived on.

In 1935 the first Westminster Cathedral pilgrimage came by special train, linking at Walsingham with a party of eighteen men and women, who had walked 117 miles from London along the ancient way.

In 1938 Cardinal Hinsley led a gigantic pilgrimage of Catholic Youth, coinciding with the fourth centenary of the desecration of the Shrine.

The fourteen crosses

In 1948, at the end of World War II, as a prayer of penance, fourteen parties of priests and laymen set off on a fourteen-day journey to Walsingham carrying fourteen nine-foot crosses of solid oak. Among their number was the young Fr Derek Worlock, future Archbishop of Liverpool. They were met by Cardinal Griffin, who used the occasion to fulfil the request made at Fatima that the country be dedicated to the Immaculate Heart of Mary. In 1954, in the Marian Year, a new statue, carved by Marcel Barbeau, and mirroring the ancient representation on the priory seal, was blessed in the priory grounds by the Pope's representative in Britain, Archbishop O'Hara.

In the heart of the village of Walsingham, in Friday Market, an old pilgrims' hostelry was purchased and a priest's house and chapel were finally made available, suitably dedicated to the Annunciation of Our Lady.

Walsingham and young people

More recently, at the site of the Slipper Chapel, a vast new Chapel of Reconciliation has been constructed. At this ancient site of penance and absolution a new generation is learning again the importance of this sacrament of forgiveness. During the summer, in nearby fields, perhaps there is the greatest sign of hope. Canvas tents and caravans house hundreds of youngsters who have made Walsingham their annual destination for Catholic renewal. The Augustinian canons might not recognise their taste in music but they would certainly recognise their zeal and faith.

Today, an estimated quarter of a million pilgrims visit Walsingham each year. Erasmus described this corner of Norfolk as "a town maintained by scarcely anything else but the number of its visitors", and I suspect that little has changed. They come to pray at the two major shrines: the

Anglican shrine, built around the Holy House, and the Catholic shrine at the other end of the Holy Mile at the fourteenth-century Slipper Chapel.

Here, too, is the Greek Orthodox Chapel of St Seraphim, created in 1967 at the disused village railway station. The Russian Orthodox have a shrine by the river. The iconography points us powerfully towards the Orthodox tradition and its richness. Here also to remind us of the great Wesley brothers is the Georgian Methodist Chapel, which remains the oldest still in use in East Anglia. All of this is an ample back-drop for the enduring message of Walsingham, which is for people of all denominations and faiths. It is the message of encounter, the encounter experienced by the Lady Richeldis and which most of us desire as we search for the presence of God.

Encounter

The Rt Rev Eric Kemp, the Anglican Bishop of Chichester, developed the theme of encounter when he wrote that in Walsingham "many people find or have a fresh encounter with the Lord". He added that at Walsingham Anglicans and Catholics have re-encountered one another, not as rivals but in co-operation: "It was Martin Gillett, whose ashes now rest in the Slipper Chapel, who had the vision of Our Lady as a help rather than as a hindrance to unity and who founded the Ecumenical Society of the Blessed Virgin Mary. The story of that Society, too, is a sign of hope."

In a country where more than 40 per cent of our marriages now end in divorce and where 800,000 of our children have no contact with their fathers, Walsingham is also an encounter with a shrine that is a home, reminding us eloquently of the Holy Family. For families riven by division and facing destruction, the story of Walsingham can offer hope and healing.

A meditation

In the wracks of Walsingham
Whom should I chuse
But the Queen of Walsingham
To be my guide and muse?

Then, thou Prince of Walsingham
Graunt me to frame
Bitter plaintes to rewe thy wronge
Bitter woe for thy name.

Bitter was it, oh to see
They sely sheepe
Murdered by the ravaging wolves
While the sheepharde did sleep.

Bitter, bitter oh to behoulde
The grasse to growe
Where the walles of Walsingham
So stately did showe.

Such were the worth of Walsingham
While she did stand
Such are the wrackes as now do showe
Of that so holy lande.

Levell, levell with the ground
The Towres doe lye
Which with their golden, glittering tops
Pearsed oute to the skye.

Where weare the gates noe gates are nowe,
The waies unknowen,
Where the presse of freares did passe
While her fame far was blowen.

Oules do scrike where sweetest himnes
Lately wear songe,
Toades and serpents hold their dennes
Where the palmers did throng.

Weep, weep, O Walsingham,
Whose days are nightes,
Blessings turned to blasphemies,
Holy deedes to dispites.

Sinne is where our lady sate,
Heaven turned is to helle;
Sathan sitte where our lord did swaye,
Walsingham, oh farewell.

(Attributed to St Philip Howard
Earl of Arundel and Surrey, martyr)

Our Lady of
Haddington

8

Whitekirk, Haddington, St Andrews and other Scottish sites

ON a cold, wet February evening in the millennium year I began my pilgrimage to Haddington. Curiously, I started the journey to Scotland in Jerusalem. To be more precise, it was at a reception held in the Jerusalem Chamber of Westminster Abbey. The Dean and Chapter had made the room available to the Earl of Lauderdale, who, thirty years earlier, had the inspiration to re-establish the mediæval pilgrimage to Haddington. Before we gathered, there was the opportunity to hear choral evensong in the abbey church, surely the most wonderful of the services held in the Anglican communion.

It is said that Henry IV had always believed that he would die in Jerusalem. When his time for departing finally arrived he was taken in a semiconscious state to the abbey and when he came to he asked a retainer where he was. "Jerusalem" came the reply. And here, in the Jerusalem Chamber, where he died, we heard of another strange death, wrought by the hands of another Henry.

Haddington's history

Until the Reformation, the church of St Mary's, Haddington, fifteen miles east of Edinburgh, was one of

149

Scotland's principal places of pilgrimage. It is the county town of East Lothian and is linked to the tiny village of Whitekirk, set on a green plateau close to the East Lothian coastline.

At Whitekirk an image of the Christ child, embraced and held in his mother's arms, became the focus of pilgrimage from many parts of Europe. As many as 15,000 pilgrims came to Whitekirk annually during the twelfth, thirteenth and fourteenth centuries. In 1356, English sea-raiders destroyed the shrine and it was then moved six miles inland to Haddington.

One of the patrons of the shrine, Professor Sir Robin Barbour, says that the shrine was visited by a future Pope, Pius II. Sir Robin told the gathering in the Jerusalem Chamber that in 1435 Aeneas Sylvius Piccolomini was sent to the Scottish Court by the Council of Basle as a papal emissary. After landing at Dunbar, Piccolomini found the shrine had been destroyed and that the monks who had cared for it had departed. He wrote that "there wasn't even any food there, so we had to go to another village". This was probably Haddington, where a new church dedicated to the Virgin Mary was being built over the remains of an earlier building which had also been despoiled by the English.

In the 1540s Henry VIII tried to force his Scottish neighbours to give the infant Queen of Scots as a child bride for the young sickly Prince Edward of England. When the Scots rebuffed Henry's "rough wooing" he retaliated in his usual petulant and high-handed way. The choir and the transepts of the great church of Haddington were ripped and torn and left as a ruin without even a roof until the 1970s. In 1560, after the Scottish Reformation, the remainder of the building became a Presbyterian church. Although it is thought that there was continued devotion to Our Lady at Haddington for the remainder of the sixteenth century, it is unsurprising that in this birthplace of John Knox, the devotion and the shrine were excoriated from Scotland's collective memory.

Haddington and Walsingham

The story might have ended there if it hadn't been for an extraordinary sequence of events.

Four hundred years after the suppression of Our Lady of Haddington a conversation took place between Fr Hope-Patten, the Anglican priest who had restored the Anglican shrine at Walsingham (see chapter 7) and the Guardian of the Shrine of Walsingham, the Earl of Lauderdale.

Patrick Maitland had served as a foreign correspondent of *The Times* and the *News Chronicle* and had been a Conservative Member of the House of Commons, representing Lanark during the post-war years. Tam Dalyell, who serves as one of the Lothian MPs, describes Patrick Maitland as a "thorn in the side of the Government throughout the 1950s – not least over Suez". When he became the seventeenth Earl of Lauderdale he became custodian of the Lauderdale Aisle of the Haddington church. Here, Maitlands and Lauderdales have been buried since the sixteenth century.

The Aisle is a separate legal entity from the Church of Scotland's adjacent kirk and is only a few feet from the holy ground sanctified by thousands of pilgrims from the Middle Ages.

In what turned out to be a prophetic conversation, Fr Hope-Patten had told the Earl of Lauderdale that "One day, Patrick, you must restore devotion to Our Lady of Haddington". Now he had the opportunity to do so.

The Virgin and the three kings

The Earl of Lauderdale, the Hereditary Bearer of the National Flag of Scotland, restored the Aisle as an ecumenical chapel and, in 1978, re-dedicated the Altarage of the Blessed Virgin and the Three Kings. Painstakingly the shrine was restored. Carvings were undertaken by a former prisoner of war, Anton Wagner of Oberammergau. His three kings are in kilts, influenced by an early fifteenth-century Adoration of the Magi which is in Aberdeen. The altar is made from stones from the Lauderdale houses and Scotland's holy places, and over the altar is a figure of the Virgin with her Child seated on her lap. The three kilted kings, bearing their gifts from afar, approach her from either side.

At our Candlemas gathering in Westminster Abbey, the Earl of Lauderdale told us that his intention had always been to create a focus for ecumenism and to provide an opportunity for healing of mind and body.

He says that the dynamic impetus of the inter-church journeying in faith, an integral part of the Haddington Pilgrimage, is the most exciting event of his life: "In the evening of my life, the discovery of this pilgrimage and the event of bringing people together for healing and unity of love is the greatest thing in my life – all in the name of Christ Our Lord and his mother."

Ecumenism and sectarianism

I can vividly recall election campaigns in the 1980s in Glasgow which included sectarian stand-offs. Long after English cities like Liverpool set aside the worst of their sectarian excesses – including overt associations among football clubs and denominational allegiances – Scotland seemed prone to the hard line attitudes associated with its Ulster neighbour. At the Glasgow Hillhead by-election, in 1981, I was roundly attacked by Pastor Jack Glass, who has little time for Catholics. All the more unlikely, then, at a superficial level, that a pre-Reformation pilgrim site and a Presbyterian kirk should become the scene of a modern pilgrimage emphasising the healing power of reconciliation and forgiveness. Less surprisingly, Pastor Glass is still on hand with a few pilgrims of his own to protest at the persistent goings on at Haddington.

Yet what has happened at Haddington is truly remarkable.

On the second Saturday of May in each year since 1971, pilgrims from all the main Christian traditions – Roman Catholic, Orthodox, Anglican, Presbyterian and other Free Churches, have gathered, first at Whitekirk and then at Haddington. In 1971 the first pilgrimage attracted thirty people. Throughout the 1990s the numbers have been in their thousands, sometimes at many as 3,000 people.

The Earl of Lauderdale says: "There may not be complete unity of faith" – referring to the divided Communion – " but meantime there is great unity of love."

The reopening of the restored shrine in 1978 was probably more than the kirk in Haddington had bargained for. Lord Lauderdale admits that the original plan had simply been seen "as an ecumenical gesture. They thought it would be nice if it could be used for Christians of other traditions. They didn't really know what they were letting themselves in for."

The gathering in 1978 brought together an Eastern Orthodox priest, an ex-moderator of the Church of Scotland, the abbot of the nearby Roman Catholic Cistercian monastery, and the Most Rev Alastair Haggart, the Primus of the Scottish Episcopal Church.

At the pilgrimages, Church of Scotland, Episcopalian and Roman Catholic clergy still worship alongside one another in the main body of the restored ecumenical half of the church. Separate Communion services are held, although many pilgrims attend one another's services as a sign of respect for each other's traditions. Catholics do not see shared Communion as a step towards unity but as the culmination of the journey towards unity. Neither do Catholics wish to fudge the issue of what reception of Communion means to them. While respecting those Christians who see Communion as an act of remembrance, Catholics believe in the Real Presence of Christ under the appearance of bread and wine.

Accepting the reality of a divided Church means

accepting the impediment barring participation in the taking of Communion. Entering into the pain of this reality makes more sense than pretending that the Church is not divided and separated. Bishop Kevin Rafferty put it well when he told pilgrims that intercommunion is still not possible:

> Since as yet we have not arrived at a mutually acceptable understanding of the meaning of Jesus and his Church.
>
> It might seem desirable to share Communion as a means towards unity but this could not be done without doing violence to the consciences of many members of each of our churches.
>
> All of us need to come to a new vision. This will, with the guidance of the Holy Spirit, one day lead us to true unity.
>
> The true miracle of the Haddington Pilgrimage is this travelling side by side in the same direction.

If, one day, we are able to heal the years of division it will be because we have personally experienced the pain of division and decided to do something about it. As the Book of Lamentations says: "Restore us to yourself, O Lord, that we may be restored."

Each year the preachers at the Haddington pilgrimage rotate between the Church of Scotland, the Episcopalians and the Roman Catholics.

The late Archbishop of Glasgow, Cardinal Thomas Winning, took part as Preacher of the Day. In the morning he presided at the Catholic Mass, where the Liturgy of the Word is shared ecumenically. He concelebrated Mass with three bishops. At the Offering of the Gifts, one party, headed by a cross, leads from the credence table in the centre of the church for the High Altar at the east end; another party, headed by the Kirk Beadle, large Bible held well aloft, proceeds to the west end for a Reformed Rite celebration.

When the two services reach the recitation of the Lord's

Prayer the two congregations say the prayer together. After Holy Communion has been distributed the two churchmen exchange a public kiss of peace.

Agape

When Mass is concluded there is a pilgrims' agape, a love feast, of soup and sandwiches. One pilgrim described this as:

> Intolerably arch in prospect, it seemed the most natural thing in the world as I found myself seated on a tombstone, eating, drinking, talking with three ladies from Northumberland, a docker from Glasgow, and a Franciscan whose friary was above a fish shop and who worked in the world as a male nurse, contributing his salary to his tiny community. For the first time agape was more than an archaic technical term.

Cardinal Winning's words

Archbishop Keith O'Brien, Catholic Archbishop of Edinburgh, has been a regular pilgrim and has described it as a "wonderful experience". Cardinal Winning told the pilgrims: "we are travelling as a broken people" who need the healing which can only come from God.

He added that the modern world saw no value in suffering, regarding it as only something to be avoided – evidence of this could be seen in the public debate on euthanasia. "Through suffering, Jesus authenticated the depth of his love", he said.

Pope John Paul II has regularly emphasised the importance of inner healing and of deepening our spiritual experiences. He has repeatedly urged Christians to walk together. "Many stand close with us on our earthly pilgrimage", he once wrote.

The healing ministry of Haddington would be close to

his heart. His youthful devotion to the Black Madonna – Our Lady of Czestochowa – is well known. So is the attribution which he places on Our Lady of Fatima for protecting him from the assassin's bullet which felled him in St Peter's Square in 1981. He subsequently took the bullet to the shrine at Fatima, in Portugal, where in 1917 the Virgin appeared to local children. He laid the bullet on the altar in thanks for his own delivery. At Haddington a basket is left below the altar where pilgrims leave their own words of thanks and request.

In the Middle Ages pilgrims seeking cures would doubtless have left their crutches at Haddington, but most people, whose physical ailments continue, recognise that miraculous cures are only a small part of the equation. The preparation for death or the peace of mind which is needed to face continued suffering can be a different form of healing and no less miraculous in its own way.

The king of the place

In *The Pilgrim's Progress*, John Bunyan's pilgrim discovers no short cuts and prepares himself for the journey which all must make:

> The pilgrims then began to inquire if there was no other way to the gate? To which they answered, Yes; but there hath not any, save two – to wit, Enoch and Elijah – been permitted to tread that path since the foundation of the world, nor shall until the last trumpet shall sound. The pilgrims then, especially Christian, began to despond, and looked this way and that; but could find no way by which they might escape the river. They asked the men if the waters were all of a depth? They said, No; yet they could not help them in that case; for, said they, you shall find it deeper or shallower, as you believe in the king of the place.

Discovering the King of the place is very low on most people's agendas, but when the technological fixes come to an end and death beckons there is nothing else to fall back upon but belief, and if our pilgrimage has failed to prepare us we will fall to the depths rather than easing our way through the shallows.

The Haddington pilgrimage is an attempt to remind us of our dependence upon God. As the leaders of the different Scottish denominations stand close to one another, they pass through the church at Haddington and lay hands on the disabled and the sick, anointing them with oil. Prayer is also offered.

Redemptive healing

The rediscovery of the ministry of healing is one of the most important developments in the contemporary Church. My wife's grandfather, the Reverend Edgar Bell, would have been particularly appreciative of this.

Throughout Lent 1953 he gave several lectures as part of a Lenten series which is held at Liverpool's parish church (of Our Lady and St Nicholas). To this day, the Anglican rector, the Reverend Nicholas Frayling, has maintained this astonishingly demanding schedule of daily talks. Author of the challenging book *Pardon and Peace* (SPCK, 1996), Canon Frayling says that the phrase "forgive and forget" does not lead to healing. We need, instead to remember and forgive.

There is an echo here of something which Edgar Bell argued for fifty years ago. He said that by abandoning the oils of anointing and the ministry of healing – whether to individuals or whole communities – the church was not being faithful to Our Lord's own Ministry. He said "The healing work of the Church is the process of being made whole *by* Christ *for* Christ, *into* Christ. Because of this I have ventured to call the healing wrought by the Church

'Redemptive Healing'. It is concerned with the making whole of persons, and not only with the patching up of sick or defective bodies or minds." He argued that "the healing work of the Church is concerned with the eternal wholeness of persons and not with the production of healthy bodies only".

He quoted the Epistle of St James:

> Are any among you suffering? They should pray. Are any cheerful? They should sing songs of praise. Are any among you sick? They should call for the elders of the church and have them pray over them, anointing them with oil in the name of the Lord. The prayer of faith will save the sick, and the Lord will raise them up; and anyone who has committed sins, will be forgiven.

He goes on to record examples of healing brought about by the anointing of the sick with holy oils and by the laying on of hands.

Haddington and Healing

At Haddington the laying of hands on the sick has also brought comfort and even physical cures. A lady who was later freed from confinement to her wheelchair wrote: "We felt a great presence there at the laying-on of hands… There seems to be this warm sensation I experienced. I have never had it before."

The Earl of Lauderdale's daughter, the indefatigable Lady Olga Maitland – herself a former member of the House of Commons – described in *Time and Tide* how she felt about the laying on of hands: "While we sang, all the clergy moved among the sick, reaching out to the lame, the disabled and distressed. So powerful is the emotion that it is hardly surprising to hear accounts of remarkable recoveries."

Lady Olga tells the story of Barbara Turner, a fifty-five-year-old housewife from Cheltenham who has experienced two miracles which have restored her to perfect health: "Ever since I was eleven years old," says Mrs Turner, "I have been fighting illness." After chronic deterioration of health she began a devotion to Our Lady of Haddington. Commenting on her subsequent cure, her GP, Dr G. Peacock, says: "I have personally never come across a similar case in over thirty years of medical practice."

An Episcopalian clergyman at Haddington rightly warns against obsession with the spectacular or the extraordinary:

> What we're contributing here to the Church's life is the importance of prayer for healing. We pray for the requests left every Friday, but after that we don't inquire. There are many answers to prayer. If in fact Jesus is doing something special for his mother we can't stop that. And if she gets active in some way we can't stop that either.

Michael Beilby, in a beautifully crafted account of the pilgrimage, writes:

> The Whitekirk and Haddington Pilgrimage is about healing and is for all the churches. Healing includes the sick at heart, the sick in mind and body, healing of discord between Christians of different traditions and history, the cure of feelings of hurt and resentment – bitter memories if you like – between individuals. It is about wholeness of persons, of society and of humankind at large.

Forgiveness and the heart of wholeness

At the Candlemas meeting of Haddington supporters held at Westminster Abbey, the Catholic bishop, Charles Henderson, echoed these sentiments when he asked: "If

Jesus loved Mary, shouldn't we? If he spent thirty years of his life with her, shouldn't we spend some of our time too? She always asks us to pray for a knowledge of God, to seek peace and to do penance. Forgiveness," he said, "is at the heart of wholeness. Pilgrimage helps us to contemplate these questions."

Do as Mary asks

I am always struck by the story of the marriage feast of Cana. It is the first of Jesus' miracles recorded in the Bible. He changed the water into wine so that the festivities could continue. He told His mother that His time had not yet come, but in deference to her he nevertheless did as she asked.

A few years ago I was writing a report about human rights, abuses and persecution of the Christian minorities in Turkey. With two colleagues I took a couple of days out to go to Ephesus. My friends, who are both evangelical Christians, were deeply impressed by the Roman amphitheatre where St Paul sparked off the riot of the silversmiths, by denouncing, in his typically direct way, the paganistic materialism of the cult of Diana.

They were less sure about my determination to get them up to Marianama, the reputed house of Mary. A German nun, Catherine Emmerit (1774-1824) had a vision of this long-buried and forgotten cottage. In 1967, during his visit to Ephesus, Pope Paul VI described it as a place of pilgrimage.

My friends were even more puzzled – and slightly uncomfortable – to find that as "the mother of a great prophet" her home was also a holy place for Muslims. The small chapel within is a tranquil quiet place for prayer. What did they make of the Muslim woman who arrived while we were there? With her was her multiply handicapped daughter. The mother lit her candle, as I had done. She knelt, and laid what was on her heart before the God of Abraham, Isaac and Jacob.

As we walked down from the chapel we opened a New Testament, and there was the story of the wedding feast. Rooted in our Holy Scriptures, and in our belief in the communion of all the saints who have gone before us on their own pilgrimage to God, is all the evidence I need to believe in the power of prayer and the power of intercession. When Mary asks, surely her Son, the Son of God, will listen. Whether it is the unlikely conjunction of a Presbyterian kirk and a mediæval Catholic shrine or the convergence of Muslim and Christian prayer for the needs of a disabled girl, Mary, the mother of the Lord seems to be standing there. If Christ is the head of the Church, she will always be his mother, and it is not sentiment which reminds me that a mother's prayers will never be wasted and will always be listened to.

Elsewhere in Scotland

While at Haddington the pilgrim may care to venture farther north. Richard Trench in *Travellers in Britain – Three Centuries of Discovery* (Aurum Press, 1990) includes a chapter entitled "The Discovery of Scotland" in which he recollects the eighteenth-century travels of Samuel Johnson and James Boswell. Their journeying took them to St Andrews. They later headed west, and in Boswell's *Journal of a Tour of the Hebrides* and Johnson's *Journey to the Western Islands of Scotland* (both edited by Peter Levi and published by Penguin in 1984) they record many insights touching on the ancient faith of the more remote areas, highlighting the many traces of the old world which still survived. Eigg and Canna were still Catholic islands; so were Mull and Iona. St Kilda did not know money; there were tiny horses on Rhum; on Skye they saw an old woman by her croft, grinding oats with a quern, as the Romans used to do.

Boswell was a Catholic of sorts and Iona was for him "a sacred place" – but it was Johnson who was particularly affected by Iona: standing in the middle of the ruins he read aloud the fifth chapter of the Letter of St James and a sermon by the preacher, Ogden, and then, in the manner of the countless pilgrims who went before him, he vowed to lead a better life (see chapter 2).

St Andrews

Earlier on their travels they had been to Scotland's most noted ancient pilgrim site, the ruined cathedral and monastery of St Andrews. While undertaking a Visiting Fellowship at St Andrews University in 1997, I was fortunate enough to be shown around by Professor John Haldane, the university's Professor of Moral Philosophy. Johnson and Boswell were given their tour by one of the university's eighteenth-century academics, Dr Watson, who had bought what was left of St Leonard's College and had turned the remains into his house. It was where they stayed after supper at the Glass.

Watson showed his visitors what had once been the metropolitan See of Scotland, and at the epicentre of the Scottish Reformation. In succession, the monastery had been founded in the eleventh century, the cathedral in the twelfth, the castle in the thirteenth and the university in the fourteenth century.

St Andrew, an apostle of Christ, is Scotland's patron saint, and the Fife town and cathedral that bear his name have played a pivotal part in Scotland's history. The cross of the crucified Andrew forms the national flag of Scotland, the Saltire. The archbishopric was created on 13 August 1472 by Pope Sixtus IV.

Peace and independence

In 1320, just over a century earlier, the earls and barons of Scotland had written their famous letter to the Pope asking him to urge the kings of England to let them live in peace and independence: "For as long as one hundred of us remain alive we will never allow ourselves to fall under the domination of the English. We do not fight for glory or wealth or honours, but for liberty, which no honest man will give up while he has life." The declaration went on to make the connection between the Scots and St Andrew:

> Their true nobility and merits have been made plain, if not by other considerations, then by the fact that the King of Kings, the Lord Jesus Christ, after his passion and resurrection, brought them, the first of all, to his holy faith, though they lived in the furthest parts of the world, and he chose that they be so persuaded to faith by none other than the brother of the blessed Peter, the gentle Andrew, first-called of the apostles, though in rank the second or the third, who he wished always to be over us as our patron.

Vast numbers of pilgrims came here to the only site outside continental Europe to boast the corporeal relics of an apostle.

Pilgrim routes to St Andrews

There were several pilgrim routes to St Andrews, although the main one was the east coast route, linking with the pilgrim trails to and from the Shrine of St Cuthbert at Durham (see chapter 2).

From East Lothian the pilgrim route crossed from North Berwick to Ardross (north-east of modern Elie), Fife ,via the *passagium comitis* (the earl's ferry), and pilgrim houses existed at North Berwick and Ardross. The ferry and hostels were administered by Cistercian nuns of the convent and hospital of North Berwick.

From the west pilgrims crossed the Forth by the *passagium reginae* (the queen's ferry) founded by St Margaret. There were hostels on both sides. Travelling along the King's Road they passed through Cupar and Guardbridge. A gathering place existed by a bridge at the River Eden and from here they journeyed on to St Andrews in a group, with the protection of a guard, through the outlaw territory of Kincaple and Stathtyrum marshlands.

From the north-east pilgrims crossed the Tay by the Ferry of the Loaf from Broughty Ferry to Ferry-Port-on-Craig, or they took the ferries at Woodhaven or Balmerino, run by the monks of Arbroath Abbey and Balmerino Abbey.

The focus of the pilgrimage were the relics of St Andrew, cared for by the "dewar", or keeper of the reliquary. On the feast of St Andrew, 30 November, these would be carried down South Street and up North Street, preceded by masters and scholars from the colleges carrying flowers and leafed branches. Members of the town's guilds enacted religious tableaux and pageants.

Attack and ruin

In 1559 the cathedral was attacked by a mob, and since then it has lain in ruins, a testimony to the continuing divisions in Scottish society, the Church included. The end came when John Knox preached at Holy Trinity Church on 11 June and for three days urged those who heard him to destroy the past. John Hamilton was the last of the mediæval Archbishops of St Andrews: he was driven from his see in 1559 and executed in 1571.

All the tombs of the clergy were despoiled and looted during the Reformation. Raymond Lamont-Brown, in *The Life and Times of St Andrews* (John Donald Publishers, Edinburgh 1989) says of the mob's motives: "John Knox's rabble rightly presumed that the archbishops, bishops and priors would be buried in full canonical with personal mass sets of gold and silver, and croziers, jewelled mitres and episcopal rings."

As Johnson surveyed the ruins of the cathedral he made a gesture of mourning for what had passed by removing his hat. More recently, others have been doing more than mourning.

Restoring broken walls

During June 2000 the St Andrews Cathedral Project held a service of renewal at the site of an even earlier foundation in St Andrews, the Church of St Mary on the Rock, located on the promontory overlooking St Andrews Bay at the east end of the cathedral precincts beyond the old walls. They represent a group who are committed to rebuilding St Andrews as a centre for ecumenical prayer, celebration and fellowship.

They have taken as their text the words of Isaiah (58:12): "Your ancient ruins shall be rebuilt; you shall raise up the foundations of many generations; you shall be called the repairer of the breach, the restorer of streets to live in."

The Project Group is chaired by Professor Richard De Marco and has formulated a proposal which involves recreating a centre for Christian worship, pilgrimage, prayer, conflict resolution, mediation, celebration, information, education, evangelism and creativity. In addition to establishing a visitor centre the intention is to transfer the relics of St Andrew to the rebuilt cathedral. Perhaps they could be housed in the still-standing St Regulus's Tower, where they were once kept. Pope Paul VI gave a relic of the saint to St Mary's Catholic Cathedral in Edinburgh in 1968, and St James's Catholic Church on the Scores in St Andrews also houses a fragment of the saint's remains.

Dead fishermen and live people

St John Chrysostom, in an ancient homily on St Andrew, asked the question, "Do dead fishermen catch live people?" A question which today's pilgrim must be left to answer.

A meditation

During the laying on of hands at Haddington these words are sung:

> *Be still, for the presence of the Lord, the Holy One*
> *   is here;*
> *Come, bow before him now with reverence and fear;*
> *In him no sin is found, we stand on holy ground.*
> *Be still, for the presence of the Lord, the Holy One,*
> *   is here.*
>
> *Be still, for the glory of the Lord is shining all around;*
> *He burns with holy fire, with splendour he is crowned;*
> *How awesome is the sight, our radiant King of Light!*
> *Be still, for the glory of the Lord is shining all around.*
>
> *Be still, for the power of the Lord is moving in*
> *   this place;*
> *He comes to cleanse and heal, to minister his grace.*
> *No work too hard for him. In faith receive from him.*
> *Be still, for the power of the Lord is moving in*
> *   this place.*

Croagh
Patrick

9

Croagh Patrick,
Tochar Padraig, and
following Patrick's Path

ONE of my earliest childhood memories is of a mountain which seemed to be shaped like a pyramid, looming in the distance, dominating the skyline. For a three-year-old brought up in smog-laden streets in London's East End, the contrast with the verdant green of County Mayo could not have been greater.

Instead of trolley buses crackling along their far-flung routes, here were sprawling green acres populated by sheep and cows. Instead of terraces of two-up, two-down houses, here were tiny cottages and the ruins of many more, deserted in the massive exodus of the Irish escaping poverty, destitution or the earlier potato blight and the catastrophic famine which it left in its wake.

My mother was brought up near Tourmakeady on the Galway–Mayo border. One of eight children, her first language was Irish. She had come to England when the family broke up after the death, in quick succession, of her mother and father. My grandparents probably died of meningitis. The brothers and sisters scattered to England and America; only the youngest brother stayed, to be brought up by an uncle and aunt.

Immigrants always tend to settle in the same vicinity as other pockets of people from their homeland, and our part of the East End of London was no exception. Even my first teacher, Joan O'Neill, came from the same part of Ireland as my mother. As girls they had gone to the dances together at Balinrobe. It was a curious quirk that put her in charge of my class in the East End and an even more curious one which led to her son becoming the village schoolmaster in the one-teacher village school back where my mother and grandparents had been educated. Many years later he showed me the desks where they had sat, and the school registers.

During my years as an MP I also returned to the East End to give out prizes to the children at St Bonaventure's School. After the prize-giving they invited me to see the parish church and to examine the entry in the baptismal register recording my baptism. I asked the elderly Franciscan who had organised this what had happened to the priest who had baptised me, Fr Andrew. "That's me!" he said, with an air of mischief. Fifty years of dedicated service in a deprived neighbourhood is no mean achievement and represents the quiet pilgrimage undertaken by so many unsung men and women who give up everything for the service of God and mankind.

During the post-war years my mother occasionally took me and sometimes my cousin, Angela, back to see her remaining relatives in Mayo. From where we stayed, near Lough Carra, there was a distant view of the holy mountain. This was Croagh Patrick, the peak which the British saint scaled, and where he stayed for forty days and nights before he began the evangelisation of Ireland.

Over the years I have always been drawn back to the Reek, as it is known by the Irish. In childhood we would climb only as far as the statue of the saint, although two of my own children have made the ascent to the summit with me, accompanied by two friends from Dublin. The last part of the climb is tough, as you slither and slide across the shale, but when you reach the summit you experience a real sense of peace and quiet satisfaction, to say nothing of the stunning view over Clew Bay. In July, hundreds of pilgrims will make the climb, some in bare feet.

On one occasion, on reaching the last part of the climb I began to be deterred by the mist and was considering calling it a day. An elderly lady, probably an octogenarian, was picking her way down the slope; she must have read my mind and encouraged me to complete the climb. I felt suitably shamed by my lack of resolve. However, I was also amused by her throw-away remark that she couldn't think what Patrick had been thinking of, wanting to come all the way up here, adding, for good measure: "and heaven only knows what he did when he got here". For my part, having taken in the breath-taking views, the only mystery is why he should ever have wanted to come down again. The last time I climbed the Reek was in 1996 with my daughter Marianne and my oldest son, Padraig. Two friends from Dublin climbed with us and Denis Murphy subsequently produced some stunning photographs of our expedition. The Irish have a real love of Croagh Patrick, although even the Reek is not immune from the pressures of the world.

In the mid-1990s the Irish government had to intervene to stop a mineral company from digging up the Reek. They wanted to prospect for gold. It may not have occurred to them, but thousands of people – the old lady making her descent, the bare-footed young people and the pilgrim fighting his demons – didn't need the prospectors to tell them what they already knew. Those pilgrims discovered the gold on the Reek long ago.

Patrick prayed when he got to the summit and he literally wrestled with demons. Each of us have our different ways of dealing with our demons, and a mountain top is not a bad place to identify them. St Patrick imitated Christ's own desert experience by fasting and preparing for the coming battles for forty days and nights.

If you are really serious about making the pilgrimage to Croagh Patrick, the place to start is at Ballintubber Abbey.

Tochar Padraig

Tochar Padraig is one of the ancient pilgrimage roads that are to be found all over Ireland. Seven of these have been restored, and the longest of the surviving pilgrimage roads is Tochar Padraig. It begins at the beautiful abbey of Ballintubber, which is itself a great place of prayer and devotion.

Six of the other most notable pilgrim roads are: St Columcille's Way (Turas Cholmcille) in County Donegal; St Patrick's Way in Donegal; the Saint's Road, in County Kerry; the Pilgrim's Way in County Offaly; St Declan's Way in County Waterford; and St Kevin's Way, Sli Chaoimhin, in County Wicklow.

Ballintubber

Ballintubber and the ruins of the huge monastery at Cong, not far away, are two of the most wonderful places in the west of Ireland. Notwithstanding Oliver Cromwell's best attempts to destroy Catholic Ireland the faith persisted and survived its eviction from its churches and abbeys. Ballintubber – burnt down in 1653 – encapsulates that history in a particularly moving way.

Even when we came here as children, the buildings were largely a lifeless ruin, where Mass might occasionally be celebrated on hallowed ground. Today, after painstaking restoration, tastefully executed, this is once again a thriving centre of faithful devotion and prayer.

In the grounds, the principal events of the Passion of Jesus are commemorated. The building tells its own story of suffering. Nearby is the Informer's Tree, from which one Sean na Sagart, one of the most notorious of the priest hunters who betrayed the presence of a priest, spied out his quarry.

Helping to remind us of the antiquity of the site, and its vulnerability, are the remains of a Viking long-boat.

Fr Frank Fahey, the parish priest at Ballintubber, is a walking encyclopedia about the local history and importance of the site, and his dedicated enthusiasm is one of the main reasons why Ballintubber has so successfully risen from the ruins. This is the abbey which never died. Hearing Fr Fahey preach on a beautiful morning on Trinity Sunday was a special treat. As if to underline his erudite sermon on the Trinity, a swallow flew in and out of the rafters – something to savour and remember.

Fr Fahey wrote the introduction to *Tochar Padraig – A Pilgrim's Progress*, published 1989, in which he says: "As you walk the Tochar, whether on foot or in fantasy, you will be going not only on a spiritual pilgrimage, but on a cultural and historical journey down through the ages also. And both experiences, if fully entered into, should bring about that change of heart and insight of mind which is essential to a pilgrim's progress."

Fr Fahey says: "Do not be afraid or ashamed to walk the Tochar. To go on pilgrimage is as old as man himself. For even as we aspire to reach the stars or inhabit Mars, man more than ever seeks to find himself in that long spiritual journey inwards, symbolised by Tochar Padraig."

The abbey church marked the beginning of the road which the ancient pilgrims took to Croagh Padraig. Although the road takes you through fields and occasional bogs, it is marked by guiding stiles and by marker stones.

Dabhach an Chora

On leaving the grounds of the abbey – which is twenty miles from Croagh Patrick – the pilgrim comes across the place where returning pilgrims washed their feet. In the Irish it is known as Dancora, or possibly Dabhach an Chora, the bath of the righteous. Water flowed from a stream, filling the bath, and the water was heated by hot stones.

In the next field, the Abbey Field, is an old ecclesiastical circle, a *cashel*. The ancient track then heads off, drawing us west towards the Reek. The route is clearly marked by a series of stiles, 113 altogether, and the pocket guide is an indispensable companion for anyone wanting to understand the country in which they are travelling.

Attawalla – Lufferton Castle

Along the early part of the route lie the remains of a pre-famine village, Attawalla ("the place of the Way"). Between 1841 and 1851 the entire population was wiped out in just one decade. There are holy wells, lime kilns, thatched cottages. There are the remains of the house of Nancy Loftus, the sister of Sean na Sagart – and it was here in December 1726 that he killed the last of his cornered priests, Fr Kilger.

After crossing the main Castlebar–Galway road, the pilgrim enters Lufferton (*lubh ghortan*, or herb garden). Some of the population living here were given small-holdings by the Moores of nearby Moore Hall when the notorious Church of Ireland bishop, Bishop Plunkett, carried out mass evictions in Tourmakeady at the height of winter. His tomb is in the overgrown graveyard of the derelict church in Tourmakeady.

The pilgrim now climbs more stiles, through hazel and blackthorn woods, past a small stone circle, past Lufferton Hall and the ruins of Lufferton Castle.

Lag na hAltore to Aghagower

Further along the Tochar, close to where it crosses the roadway to Cappacharnaun, is a field known as Lag na hAltore ("the hollow of the altar") after the Mass stone which was used illegally for the celebration of the Mass during penal times.

After crossing the main Ballintubber-Westport road there is yet more evidence of pre-famine homesteads and nearby is the Well of Stringle (Cranereen Well) which is reputed to have been where St Patrick baptised the people of the area. Further on are the Ailee cliffs and caves. At the base of the cliffs is another Mass rock. It was an ideal location because Sean na Sagart and the militia could be spied from the vantage point at the top of the cliff and priest and people alerted of the imminent danger, allowing them to disperse.

Even before the persecution, believers following the Way had to face other foes. A highwayman who attacked a group of pilgrims paid with his life when he was caught by Hugh O'Connor, King of Connaught, the O'Connor chieftains having traditional responsibility for the safety of the pilgrims. Highwaymen notwithstanding, modern pilgrims continue their journey past the pretty village of Aghanmore and the hill of Cloondacon. The hill "of the two hounds" takes its name from a legend that tells of the local pagan chief setting his two vicious and starving wolfhounds on St Patrick and his followers. When the saint befriended and calmed the dogs the impressed chieftain asked to be baptised. From here the pilgrim heads towards Aghagower, and past teampall na bhFiacal, St Patrick's House, and the convent which was founded by Mathone, whose father, St Senach, was the first bishop of Aghagower. Here, too, are the ruins of the church built over the original church consecrated by St Patrick.

Aghagower – The Reek

Aghagower – meaning "field of the spring" – is said to have been beloved by Patrick.

My mother used to recall her occasional visits to relatives in Aghagower, one of whom had been a priest sent to the mission fields in China.

Here there is another ancient church dating from mediæval times (and whose bell is said to be buried in the local bog) and a beautiful round tower (built between 973 and 1013). It was restored in 1969 and leans slightly towards the north. Dabhach Padraig is a circular bath situated at the centre of the village. Next to it is an ancient tree and a place of cures for the sick.

Back on the Tochar the pilgrim should pause at the raised altar stone at Lankill, perhaps remembering how our less fortunate forebears, driven from their churches, continued to illegally celebrate the sacraments in the open fields. Tradition has it that, after Aghagower, St Patrick and his followers completed this last part of the journey to Croagh Patrick on foot, commencing the journey on Shrove Saturday, three ordinary days before Ash Wednesday, so that he could begin his forty-day fast at the beginning of Lent.

Before Patrick came to Ireland Palladius had been sent by the Pope, but his mission appears to have been short-lived. Patrick, the returning slave boy, understood the Irish people. Passing along this famous chariot road, with his own chariots and retinue of companions, the caravan must have been a colourful and impressive sight. Here, close to Lankhill, Patrick was also walking into the heart of pagan practice and Druidical authority. At Stone Park there are monuments and relics of those times, as well as the early Christian communities which followed.

Further on is a holy well dedicated to St Brendan, the Irish saint who was reputed to have journeyed to the Americas. Holy wells are a forgotten part of our Catholic heritage, but all over these islands there are wells which were dedicated to the saints, symbolising the healing power of the waters of baptism and the centrality of water to our survival (see chapter 5).

Tradition has it that as St Patrick approached the climb towards the holy mountain he remembered that he had left his missal in Aghagower. Such was the interest in his mission that the word was passed back along the road. His followers now stretched back all the way to the village, and the missal was passed forward, hand to hand.

At Behoove is a rock where Patrick probably celebrated the Mass. There are drill holes in the rock which suggest it was used by the Druids to place offerings to their gods. From here the pilgrim continues along the Tochar to the holy mountain and to where, in the Lent of 441, Patrick spent his time in prayer and fasting, beseeching God to break the power of the evil forces which held sway in that place.

Croagh Patrick

Croagh Patrick is just a few miles away from Westport, one of the loveliest towns in the west of Ireland. In pre-Christian times Croagh Patrick was used for ritual to the god Lug. As in England, at Glastonbury, and through the reclaiming of pagan festivals for Christian celebrations, the emerging Christian community in Ireland sanctified the ground and made Croagh Patrick a holy mountain and place of annual pilgrimage. A pilgrim will need to set aside at least four hours to make the climb. It is as well to check the weather conditions, to take some water, to wear a good pair of boots and to have a good walking stick. If you come by car rather than walking the Tochar, there is a car parking area at the foot of the mountain. You also need to come with the right state of mind.

Like Moses, Elijah and Christ, St Patrick is reputed to have spent forty days and nights fasting and praying. Croagh Patrick was to be his mountain top, his desert experience. Here he interceded with God on behalf of the Irish people. Each year, traditionally on the last Sunday in July, pilgrims climb the Reek carrying a stick, like the staff of their mediæval forbears. Some climb barefoot.

The Stations

The first 'Station' on the climb is known as Leacht Mionnain, or St Benin's Monument. Benin was believed to be Chieftain Sesgre's son. He became captivated by Patrick when the saint came to the court of Benin's father, following him everywhere. Ultimately he became Patrick's psalmist and his successor at Armagh. He is thought to have composed the Irish Book of Rights.

Pilgrims stop at each of the Stations and say the Lord's Prayer, the Ave and the Creed. From the first Station they ascend the steep rocky pathway – Casan Padraig – and head towards the top.

Perhaps here it is worth remembering the demons with whom Patrick wrestled on this mountain. Some in the shape of grotesque black birds, which were objects of Druid worship, attacked Patrick, leading one of his followers, Finian, to bring him a bell with which he scared them off. Each of us has our own demons with which we, too, must wrestle and confront. The bird was synonymous with pride.

As the path gets steeper and the way becomes more difficult it can be a metaphor for the things we meet in life. The early stages of this journey, through pleasant fields and the picturesque scenery around Lough Cara and Ballintubber Abbey, may have appeared deceptively tranquil, but concealed were stories of famine, destitution and betrayal, stories of endurance, restoration and faith. As the going gets tougher, the challenges and the dangers become more acute, more obvious and more pressing. The temptation to yield or to retreat becomes greater as we become wearier and less certain of our ability to complete the journey. All the more reason to give great thanks on coming finally to the summit.

(Photo: Denis Murphy)

NEXT MASS :-

LD CHURCH·   5.00

OLD CHURCH   7.30

ADORATION OF THE
BLESSED SACRAMENT·

(Photo: Denis Murphy)

Lough Derg

The Martyrs' Altar in the Shrine of the Martyrs at Tyburn Convent, showing a small replica of the Tyburn Gallows above the altar.

A Tyburn nun at adoration before the Blessed Sacrament.

The summit and beyond

The final Stations are to be found at the top of the Reek. Here there is a small chapel and a small rock pit marking the place of Patrick's bed. Here the pilgrim prays for peace and for the coming of God's kingdom.

And what of Patrick's descent? When he came down from his mountain top he felt ready for the missionary work which lay ahead. After his penitential forty days he established many churches in the nearby baronies of Murrisk and Burrishoole. There is also an extraordinary story of a swineherd who was resurrected from his grave, having been slain by soldiers many centuries before. Patrick baptised the man, heard his confession, and he returned to his tomb. From here the evangelist went next among the people of Ui Maine and founded churches in the forest of Foclut at Faragh, near Killala Bay. Near the shore at Murrisk, where there now stand the ruins of a mediæval Augustinian friary, Patrick's mission continued. From Mayo, he then journeyed eastwards through Tawney, in County Sligo, to Aghanagh, to Shanco and to Leitrim. At the River Drowes, he blessed the waters that there might be an abundance of fish and from here he went into Donegal. The mission proceeded into the northernmost part of the island, into the Donegal peninsula, through County Tyrone, across the River Bann, where he blessed a site for a church at Coleraine.

On he travelled to County Antrim, where he sat on a crag known as Patrick's Rock, and went on to found many churches in what is today the diocese of Connor.

Nostalgically, Patrick returned to Slemish, where during his seven years as a slave he had looked after Gosacht, son of Miliucc, and two of Miliucc's daughters. He gave them secret instruction in the faith, and they are often identified as the children who appeared to Patrick in a vision and called him back to Ireland to bring the faith to its people. For the remainder of his long life Patrick did just this. His extraordinary missionary zeal not only claimed Ireland for Christ but led to the Christian faith being brought back to Britain, and in later centuries to missionary territories the world over. In recent times it has become fashionable to attack the Catholic Church in Ireland, but notwithstanding its failures no-one should underestimate the seismic impact which has sprung from those early journeys of St Patrick and the gift of the Christian faith which its Catholic missionaries have taken all over the world.

In chapter 11 I have written about Lough Derg – St Patrick's Purgatory – but before going there I would recommend the pilgrim keen to walk Patrick's ways to make one other journey in Ireland – to Armagh.

Armagh

Armagh can claim to be one of the oldest ecclesiastical capitals in Europe. It was here that St Patrick founded his first bishopric in 444-445. On two of its hills stand the cathedrals of the two main Christian communities. The Church of Ireland Cathedral is the older of the two and it stands on the site of St Patrick's foundation. Elsewhere in Ulster, at Downpatrick, the relics of Patrick, Brigid and Columba were discovered in the twelfth century. St Patrick is said to have died a few miles away at Saul, perhaps in the year 461.

In September 1979 Pope John Paul II made his historic visit to Ireland, and came to Armagh. He gave twenty-four talks, which centred on the message of peace and reconciliation, justice and respect among all peoples. These were later published by the Daughters of St Paul as *Ireland: In the Footsteps of St Patrick*. (1979).

On his arrival in Ireland the Pope said, "It is with immense joy and with profound gratitude to the Most Holy Trinity that I set foot today on Irish soil. I am very happy to walk among you – in the footsteps of St Patrick and in the path of the Gospel that he left you as a great heritage – being convinced that Christ is here."

He urged the Irish to "Remember St Patrick. Remember what the fidelity of just one man has meant for Ireland and for the world. Yes, fidelity to Jesus Christ and to His Word makes all the difference in the world. Let us therefore look up to Jesus, who is for all time the faithful witness of the Father."

John Paul saw his journey to Ireland as an act of pilgrimage: "I go to Ireland as a pilgrim, just as I did first in Mexico and then in Poland, my native land. Today I express my joy at being able, by means of this pilgrimage, to find myself in those ways along which the whole people of God of the Emerald Isle have walked towards the Lord for centuries."

On his return to Rome he told a crowd of 40,000 people gathered in St Peter's Square that "the bishop who visits the communities of his Church is the true pilgrim who arrives every time at that particular shrine of the Good Pastor, which is the People of God, participating in Christ's royal priesthood. This shrine, in fact, is every man, whose mystery can be explained and solved only in the mystery of the Word incarnate."

Clonmacnois

Reflecting on his pilgrimage to Ireland, the Pope said he would never forget the time he had spent at Clonmacnois:

> The ruins of the abbey and of the church speak of the life that once pulsated there; of the Irish monks who not only implanted Christianity in the Emerald Isle but also took it from there to other countries of Europe. It is difficult to look at those ruins merely as a monument of the past; whole generations of Europe owe to them the light of the Gospel and the structural framework of their culture. Those ruins are still charged

with a great mission. They still constitute a great challenge. they still speak of that fullness of life to which Christ has called us. It is difficult for a pilgrim to arrive at those places without those traces of the apparently dead past revealing to him a permanent and everlasting dimension of life. Here is Ireland: at the heart of the perennial mission of the Church, which St Patrick started.

Drogheda

Pope John Paul went on to describe how he had followed as a pilgrim in the footsteps of Patrick, first in the direction of the primatial See of Armagh and Drogheda, where the relics of St Oliver Plunkett, bishop and martyr, had been displayed. St Oliver was dragged through the streets of London before being hanged, drawn and quartered at Tyburn, where his memory is recalled in the Tyburn chapel of the martyrs (see Cchapter 13).

The Pope's pilgrimage led him on to many liturgical celebrations and to the celebration of the Eucharist at Dublin, Galway, Knock, Maynooth and Limerick. He ended by recalling the people he had met, from Presidents to school pupils, priests, religious sisters, missionaries, married couples, parents, young people, the sick and disabled people: "Let them all remember that I was present in their midst as a pilgrim… with head bent and grateful heart, seeking together with them, the ways that lead to the future…"

For me, the most moving point during the papal visit was the appeal which John Paul made at Drogheda for peace and reconciliation.

Drogheda is in the archdiocese of Armagh: "so it is towards this foundation here in the Primatial See of Armagh that I first direct my pilgrim steps. The See of Armagh is the Primatial See because it is the See of St Patrick. The

Archbishop of Armagh is Primate of all Ireland today because he is the Comharba Padraig, the successor of St Patrick, the first bishop of Armagh."

Hill of Slane

Not far from where the Pope gave his address, on the Hill of Slane, Patrick lit, for the first time in Ireland, the Paschal Fire so that the light of Christ might shine forth on all of Ireland and unite all of its people in the love of Jesus Christ. Patrick would have used the words of the Easter liturgy, greeting Christ as the Alpha and the Omega, the beginning and the end of all things.

It was here that Pope John Paul urged his listeners to redouble their efforts to "light up the darkness of these years of trial".

Speaking directly to those engaged in terrorism he said:

I appeal to you, in language of passionate pleading. On my knees I beg you to turn away from the paths of violence and to return to the ways of peace. You may claim to seek justice. I too believe in justice and seek justice. But violence only delays the day of justice. Violence destroys the work of justice. Further violence will only drag down to ruin the land you claim to love and the values you claim to cherish. In the name of God I beg you: return to Christ, who died so that men might live in forgiveness and peace. He is waiting for you, longing for each one of you to come to him so that He may say to each of you: your sins are forgiven; go in peace.

The Pope called for pardon and for peace.

I came to Drogheda today on a great mission of peace and reconciliation. I come as a pilgrim of peace. To Catholics, to Protestants, my message is peace and love. May no Irish Protestant think that the pope is an enemy, a danger or a threat. My desire is that instead Protestants would see in me a friend and a brother in Christ. Do not lose trust that this visit of mine may be fruitful, that this voice of mine may be listened to. And even if it were not listened to, let history record that at a difficult moment in the experience of the people of Ireland, the bishop of Rome set foot in your land, that he was with you and prayed with you for peace and reconciliation, for the victory of love and justice over hatred and violence.

Subsequent events in Ireland and the beginnings of a protracted and hesitant peace process can, I think, be traced in their origins to this pilgrim's impassioned and moving prayer that a different way be found.

A meditation

"St Patrick's Breastplate" is a favourite prayer of mine. What better meditation to use in following in the footsteps of one of our great evangelists.

> *I bind unto myself this day, the name, the holy name,*
>   *of Father, Son and Holy Spirit.*
> *I arise today, through God's strength to pilot me,*
> *God's might to uphold me,*
> *God's wisdom to guide me,*
> *God's eye to look before me,*
> *God's ear to hear me,*
> *God's word to speak for me,*
> *God's hand to guard me,*
> *God's way to lie before me,*
> *God's shield to protect me,*
> *God's host to save me,*
> *From snares of devils, from temptations of vices,*
> *From everyone who shall wish me ill,*
> *Afar and near, alone and in a multitude.*

Christ be in me, Christ be beneath me, Christ be
    above me,
Christ be on my right, Christ be on my left,
Christ when I lie down, Christ when I sit down,
    Christ when I arise,
Christ in the heart of everyone who thinks of me,
Christ in the mouth of everyone who speaks of me,
Christ in every eye that sees me,
Christ in every heart that hears me.
I arise today
Through a mighty strength, the invocation of the Trinity,
Through belief in the threeness,
Through confession of the oneness
Of the Creator in creation.
I bind unto myself this day, the name, the holy name,
    of Father, Son and Holy Spirit.

Knock

10

Knock

ONE century after fifteen people, young and old, saw a vision of the Virgin Mary on the gable wall of the parish church at Knock, Pope John Paul II made the pilgrimage to Cnoc Mhuire, the Hill of Mary, Ireland's principal Marian shrine.

On the evening of 21 August 1879, the figures of St Joseph, Our Lady Crowned, and St John the Evangelist – "the disciple whom Jesus loved" – were revealed alongside a vision of the Lamb, the cross, and angels above an altar. During the century which has elapsed there has been a constant stream of pilgrims to this village, situated on the plains of east Mayo.

The church in Knock is dedicated to John the Baptist. The local bishop at the time of the apparition, John MacHale, was a redoubtable figure, well known in his own right. He established a commission of inquiry which, having evaluated all the evidence, proclaimed its belief that the apparition at Knock was genuine. In 1976, following the continuing flow of pilgrims to Knock, a huge basilica, dedicated to Our Lady, Queen of Ireland, was built and consecrated. It is capable of holding some 6,000 people. There are many fine features in this circular church, which I particularly associate with the commemorative service held to mark the one hundred and fiftieth anniversary of the Irish famine – the Great Starvation – at which Dr Michael Neary, Archbishop of Tuam, asked me to give an address.

Each of the counties in Ireland contributed one of the thirty-two pillars in the ambulatory and there are four replicas of mediæval church windows. These celebrate the four provinces of Ireland.

The Papal Pilgrim

When Pope John Paul II visited Knock, on 30 September 1979, he concelebrated Mass in the open air and an estimated crowd of 500,000 were in attendance. He entitled his homily "The Goal of my Journey to Ireland: the Shrine of Our Lady of Knock". He said that since he first learned of the centenary of the shrine "I have felt a strong desire to come here, the desire to make yet another pilgrimage to the Shrine of the Mother of Christ, the Mother of the Church, the Queen of Peace."

He told his Irish audience: "Do not be surprised at this desire of mine. It has been my custom to make pilgrimages to the shrines of Our Lady, starting with my earliest youth and in my own country. I made such pilgrimages also as a Bishop and as a Cardinal."

John Paul went on to emphasise the importance of pilgrimage in every country and in every locality: "I know very well that every people, every country, indeed every diocese, has its holy places in which the heart of the whole people of God beats, one could say, in more lively fashion: places of special encounter between God and human beings; places in which Christ dwells in a special way in our midst."

He saw pilgrimage as an unthreatening way in which Christians from many and varied backgrounds could stand alongside one another. He also rooted the tradition of pilgrimage into the Old and New Testaments, into the experiences of the wandering Jewish people, and into the pilgrim guides that both Moses and Jesus became:

Do we not confess with all our brethren, even with those with whom we are not yet linked in full unity, that we are a pilgrim people? As once this people travelled on its pilgrimage under the guidance of Moses, so we, the People of God of the New Covenant, are travelling on our pilgrim way under the guidance of Christ.

The Pope said that he was in Knock as a pilgrim, "a sign of the pilgrim church throughout the world participating, through my presence as Peter's successor, in a very special way".

He felt it was not surprising that many of these special places of pilgrimage have traditionally been dedicated to the Mother of Christ, and he said that his devotion to Mary united him in a very special way with the people of Ireland. Earlier pastoral visits had taken him to the shrines of Mary at Guadeloupe, in Mexico, to the shrine of the Black Madonna in his homeland of Poland, to the shrine of Our Lady of Loreto, in Italy. Most famously, he subsequently took the bullet which had been intended to kill him during the assassination attempt in St Peter's Square and placed it at the shrine of Our Lady of Fatima, whose protection he believed had saved his life (see also chapter 6).

In Ireland the veneration of Mary is interwoven in the earliest experiences of the Christian faith. Today, the traveller in Ireland will still see roadside shrines dedicated to the Mother of God, and devotions to Mary in the ordinary homes and farm houses where they stay for bed and breakfast.

Monsignor James Horan

Thanks to an extraordinary parish priest in Knock, Canon James Horan, the town now boasts a successful airport allowing today's pilgrims to fly direct to Knock Airport. Father Horan's interest in developing an airport for Connaught and for the shrine at Knock began in 1963 when he arrived there as a curate. Born in Tooree, a hamlet lying on the shore of Lough Mask (not far from Partry, near Ballinrobe), he was brought up in the Gaeltacht (Irish-speaking area) of County Mayo, one of seven children. He said that "from the sixties until 1979 I was so busy preparing the shrine and the village for the centenary celebrations that I forgot about an airport". He subsequently contacted Jim Ryan and his brother Peter, the pioneers of Castlebar Airport. When it proved to be impossible to extend the airport at Castlebar they examined the possibility of developing an airport at Knock. The feasibility study was sent to the Taoisach, Charles Haughey.

Having received outline planning permission in 1981, the canny Fr Horan got Albert Reynolds, then Minister of Transport, and Padraig Flynn – later to be an EC Commissioner – to turn the first sod. The Minister promised £8.5 million at 1980 prices towards the completion of the airport. Fr Horan later remarked: "Promises are made to be broken and history will prove that this promise was not kept by other administrations." It wasn't long before the project was being lambasted as a white elephant and the site being accused of being "foggy-boggy". Fr Horan nevertheless persevered and raised national subscriptions while persisting in his lobbying. By 30th of May 1986 the airport was ready to be officially opened. Fr Horan's dream has since proved to be an invaluable asset to the West of Ireland. Fr Horan put the project under the patronage of Mary and the airport has certainly proved to be another of Knock's little miracles.

The Virgin's silence

Of the original apparition Fr Horan said that the Virgin's silence:

> ...is one of the greatest proofs of the sincerity and good faith of the fifteen people or more who witnessed it. Surely, if they wanted to perpetrate a fraud, it would

have been the easiest thing in the world to put words into Our Lady's mouth but never did they attempt to do so. Their reaction at the scene of the apparition varied from feelings of great delight to prayers of tears and joy. They all felt that they were in the presence of a heavenly scene which stirred their very hearts and souls.

He asked:

Should the silence of Our Lady of Knock make us wonder when in the history of the Gospels she only spoke six short sentences? One of the reasons why she came to Knock was to console people in great sorrow and affliction and words often fail to convey such deep feelings. The apparition is a beautiful picture to behold and we all know very well that every picture tells a story. No words are necessary! The liturgical significance of the apparition speaks louder than words."

Knock and the famine: comfort in suffering

Suffering there certainly had been. The famine had claimed a million lives, and the mass exodus of millions more had fractured every family. By 1879, Ireland was inhabited by propertyless rural farm workers whose lives were literally at the behest of their employers. They lived on the verge of starvation.

For most of the previous 300 years Irish Catholics had been denied the right to hold public office, even the right to vote. Their church had been persecuted, their bishops outlawed, priests dispersed, monasteries dissolved and pillaged and chapels closed. Yet 1879 was also a time of change. It was the year the Land League was born. Building on the Emancipation Act, passed fifty years earlier, the struggle against rapacious landlords and iniquitous laws was underway. If ever there was a moment when a people needed encouragement in their endurance and consolation in their suffering, this was it. The effect of the apparition in affirming individual and national faithfulness was incalculable.

Dominick Byrne, one of the visionaries, in his evidence before the Commission of Inquiry, said: "I was filled with wonder at the sight I saw; I was so affected that I shed tears."

Patrick Hill said that the Virgin was:

>...clothed in white robes, which were fastened at her neck, her hands were raised to the height of her shoulders. She appeared to be praying, her eyes were turned towards heaven, she wore a brilliant crown on her head, and over the forehead where the crown fitted the brow, a beautiful rose... On the altar stood a lamb, behind the lamb a large cross was placed around the lamb. I saw angels hovering during the whole time, for the space of 90 minutes or longer.

Brigid Trench, another visionary, said: "I continued to repeat the rosary on my beads while there, and I felt a great delight and pleasure in looking at the Blessed Virgin. I could think of nothing else while there but giving thanks to God repeating my prayers." For Brigid Trench the apparition was so real that she actually approached the Virgin and tried to grasp her feet, but as she said herself, in her native tongue: "Nior mhothaios tada i mo bharroig seachas an balla. (I felt nothing in my grasp except the wall)"

Mary: guide to Jesus

In Irish speech the names of God, Jesus and Mary are linked with one another. An eighth-century Irish poem describes Mary as "Sun of our race" and a litany from that period honours her as "Mother of the heavenly and earthly Church".

Knock is simply an extension of that long tradition of

devotion. It has become hallowed over the past century by the sick and suffering, by the disabled people and those troubled in their minds who have come here for comfort and healing.

It is to misunderstand the nature of pilgrimage to places like Knock to imagine that everyone who comes is looking for a spectacular physical healing. Often it is simply to seek renewal of faith, strengthening of conscience, or healing of some deep and personal anguish. Mary guides us to Jesus. At Cana, at the marriage feast, she told the disciples "do whatever he tells you" and she is still saying that to our world today.

In her "the Word was made flesh", and through her God became man so that we might find our way to God and learn how to live authentically human lives. Traditionally, Irish Catholics have revered Mary as the Seat of Wisdom, recalling the old Irish homily used on the feast of the Epiphany and taken from Leabhar Breac, which states that as the Magi found Jesus on the lap of his mother, so we today find Christ on the lap of his Church.

At Knock, the Pope singled out the disabled people and the sick people – and those who care for them and work for them – with words of special encouragement. He told them that his visit "…brings back many happy memories of the many pilgrimages in which I took part in my homeland at the shrine of Jasna Gora, the Bright Mountain, in Czestochowa and at the other sites throughout Poland; it also recalls my visits to the Shrine of Our Lady of Guadeloupe in Mexico." These places, he said, underlined the importance of learning how to serve others and to put their needs first.

The Gospel, he said, is full of instances where Jesus showed his love and concern for those who are sick or in pain. He loved those who suffered – and that attitude was one which the Church, too, must strike: "To love the sick is something that the Church has learnt from Christ."

John Paul said he was in Knock to give witness to

Christ's love for the sick, and to tell them that the Church and the Pope loved them too. "They reverence and esteem you. They are convinced that there is something very special about your mission in the Church."

Suffering and strength

Christians believe that by his suffering Jesus took on himself all human suffering and gave it a new value. By linking pain and suffering with his own suffering and death, and to his sacrifice on the cross, Christ makes some sense of what for most people is one of the biggest stumbling blocks in coming to faith: what C.S. Lewis called "the problem of pain". John Paul did not try to sentimentalise pain or explain it away in cosy language. He told his audience that: "Your call to suffering requires strong faith and patience. Yes, it means that you are called to love with a special intensity. But remember that Our Blessed Mother Mary is close to you, just as she was close to Jesus at the foot of the cross. And she will never leave you alone."

While they are in Knock, the modern pilgrim, perhaps carrying the burden of a disability or pain, may find it useful to make the traditional Stations of the Cross, a journey of faith that St Francis of Assisi first mapped out for us nearly 800 years ago.

The Stations are an underused resource in the Church's spiritual armoury and are a beautiful discipline for drawing together, by yourself or in a group, to study the most intense passages of Scripture and to offer prayer. Many texts have been published to accompany the pilgrim through the story of the Passion of Christ. One of the loveliest is *On the Way of the Cross – with the Disabled* by Elizabeth Greeley (St Pauls, Slough 1989). Another is *A More Perfect Way* by Richard Hobbs, with illustrations by the Benedictine nuns of Turvey Abbey, which sees the events mapped out by the Stations through the eyes of Christ (Hilltop Publishing, 1998).

Statue of Oscar Romero, Westminster Abbey

DOMINE·JESU·REX·ET·REDEMPTOR
PER·SANGUINEM·TUUM·SALA·NOS

(Photo: Oremus, Westminster Cathedral)

Cardinal Murphy-O'Connor in Westminster Cathedral

The illustrations in Elizabeth Greeley's booklet are taken from the Stations designed and executed by the sculptress Imogen Stuart for Ballintubber Abbey – the traditional starting point for the pilgrimage along Tochar Padraig to Croagh Patrick (see chapter 9).

In my preface to Elizabeth Greeley's pamphlet I wrote that:

> To meditate and pray on Our Saviour's death on the cross is one way of coming to terms with a difficult situation, imagining how desolate the early Christians must have felt on that first Good Friday, worried about Roman persecution now that their guide seemed to be gone and how great their joy must have been with the news of the resurrection.

Making the Pilgrim Stations

The Stations recall the humiliation, the trial and the death of Jesus, but they simultaneously give comfort and hope. Even as Jesus carried his cross he was comforted by the women along the way, and on the cross He gave the good thief the promise of heaven. This comfort is there for all who carry the pain of disability, and for those with the responsibility for caring for them.

Elizabeth Greeley is a disabled person herself. She says that:

> Jesus' suffering and death touches me very deeply. If I am struggling with an aspect of my disability – I have a swallowing problem that makes it very hard for me to have a drink – it is helpful for me to look at the cross and ask Jesus to help me to swallow a few mouthfuls, thanking him when I can and asking him to help me persevere when I can't.

Other people's disabilities will, she says, be different from hers, "but my thoughts may help them to think about their own problem in the sight of Christ's sufferings and death". I have attempted to summarise some of her thoughts below. They can be used to make the Stations at the Basilica in Knock – or, for that matter at any location.

STATION ONE: *Pilate condemns Our Lord to death*

Pilate did not want to get involved.

- It's easy to condemn.
- We need grace to act with compassion and tact when dealing with other people. We need to be willing to pay a price when we do what is right.

STATION TWO: *Jesus Receives the Cross*

Mocked, scourged and spat upon, Jesus takes up his Cross – for us.

- We need grace to carry our own cross.
- We need wisdom to see the difference between struggling with a disability and with our sinfulness.

STATION THREE: *Jesus falls for the first time*

In his physical weakness Jesus fell – and the soldiers simply dragged him to his feet and offered no help in forcing and rushing him on his way.

- Are we patient with those who are weak, or those who fall?
- Do we simply want to rush people on their way?

STATION FOUR: *Jesus meets his mother*

Knowing what was in her heart Jesus comforted his mother – despite his pain and suffering.

- Words of comfort are useless unless they come from the heart.

- How many mothers gaze at their disabled child and feel discouraged but yearn to give comfort?

STATION FIVE: *Simon helps Jesus carry his cross*

Simon was a stranger and was pressed – perhaps reluctantly – into becoming involved.

- How often do we stand back?
- Do we help others to carry their cross?
- Do we, like Simon, open ourselves and learn from the suffering of those we encounter?

STATION SIX: *Veronica wipes the face of Jesus*

Veronica risked stepping forward to wipe the blood and sweat from Jesus's face.

- Do we stand back when we see the beggar, the homeless or the sick?
- Do we instinctively want to be of service to others?

STATION SEVEN: *Jesus falls the second time*

Falling again, under the weight of the cross, Jesus is scorned again by the soldiers.

- How do we react when we face a setback?
- Do we pray for the grace to get back onto our feet again?

STATION EIGHT: *The women of Jerusalem mourn for Our Lord*

Perhaps the women wept because they knew that this condemnation to death was unjust.

- Without self-pity, Jesus told them to weep for themselves and for their children.

— When we weep it should be with dignity and not through preoccupation with self.

STATION NINE: *Jesus falls the third time*

Close to the end of his journey, to the Place of the Skull, Jesus falls again.

- When we fall repeatedly do we summon the courage to turn again to the Father?
- Do we seek his help or simply rely on ourselves?
- Do we give up?

STATION TEN: *Jesus is stripped of his garments.*

Without a single act of kindness from his tormentors, Jesus is humiliated in public.

- How often is human dignity belittled or ignored?
- Do we strip away self-seeking attitudes?
- Are our physical or mental aliments a way of being stripped back to the essentials in life?

STATION ELEVEN: *Jesus is nailed to the cross*

Jesus did not resist the Cross – but accepted it for our sake.

- Even as the pain intensified and the isolation and desolation increased, Jesus accepted every cruelty which was thrown at him.
- Can we summon the strength to endure unto the end?

STATION TWELVE: *Jesus dies on the cross*

Even as he died Jesus cried out, "Father, forgive them, for they know not what they do."

- Are we able to forgive – others and ourselves?
- Even in torment, are we able to reach out to others and see our disabilities as a gift for others?

STATION THIRTEEN: *Jesus is taken down from the cross*

What did the huddled group – his mother and a few friends – make of the broken body?

- In our brokenness can we provide a healing for others?
- In our desolation do we despair?

STATION FOURTEEN: *Jesus is laid In the tomb*

Joseph of Arimathea gave his tomb for Jesus' body.

- We will all face death – and want our remains honoured and attended to.
- But is the tomb the end?
- Will all things be made perfect and whole?
- Do we believe in the resurrection that heals all pain and ends all suffering?

These Stations were used in Parliament during Lent 2000 when a group of parliamentarians, led by their Spiritual director, the Franciscan priest, Fr Michael Seed, gathered each Wednesday evening. The crypt chapel does not have illustrated Stations and the makeshift numbers, simply placed on seats, around which the group stood, added to the simplicity of the occasion.

Many commented on how helpful they found Elizabeth Greeley's accompanying text. Whether it is at a place of pilgrimage, such as Knock, in a parish church, or in the home, the many variations on the Stations can be a deeply enriching spiritual experience.

The great starvation

Before leaving Knock, it is worth considering another question – the long-term effect of communal suffering. Knock, and the surrounding county of Mayo, was grievously affected by the Irish famine. Over the intervening 150 years memories of a collective trauma, which reduced the population of Ireland from eight million to four million and left one million dead, have contributed to the enmity and mistrust between the Irish and British people. Before there can be healing and renewal, the first steps are surely to remember and to repent. Only then can there be renewal and reconstructed relationships. Knock is a place to remember these things.

Remember – repent – renew

As an inquisitive little boy, brought back to the west of Ireland on occasional holidays, I remember asking my mother about the ruined cottages and deserted homes which littered the countryside. The vestiges of broken walls, bushes and trees protruding from broken hearthstones, and sheep grazing among the stones which had once been homes are the tell-tale clues which stir a thousand questions.

Like many another child with an Irish parent, that was how I first learnt the bare outline of the terrible famine years: years that swept away whole families and communities; years that devastated and ravaged the countryside; years that rang out the death knell for a million souls and which, through an enforced exodus, decimated the native Irish population.

Famine took the land by the throat; the foul-smelling breath of plague rose over the little patches of fields as the people's humble cabins became death-ridden hovels. The rotting stems of potato stalks, the stench from decayed tubers, were the foreshadowing of the stench of death which would shortly follow.

The famine has no need for cenotaphs; every scattered stone tells its own story.

Being brought up in a British–Irish family can lead many people to choose one country against another. My father fought as a soldier in the British Army in World War II. A Desert Rat, he followed his father, who had fought in World War I. Their family home in London's East End was blitzed into oblivion. My father's younger brother, Ted, served in the RAF and was killed. But love of one country – and a willingness to die for it – need not imply a hatred of another country. It would have been easy to forget my Irish antecedents. That my mother had to leave the country with most of her young brothers and sisters after the death of her parents has been a crucially important formative experience, perhaps giving me a particular affinity with refugees and asylum seekers who are disengenuously dismissed as scroungers and economic migrants.

Lessons for today: history is a great teacher

Like me, my four children have Irish as well as British passports. I want them to understand and love both countries. Central to that understanding must be to learn the lessons of the Irish famine. Any pilgrim coming to Knock and to the west of Ireland needs to reflect on the history of those times and ask what lessons it holds for today.

The genesis of the great hunger, the greatest calamity to ever befall the Irish people, is to be found in England in the false economic and political creeds of Malthus, Bentham, Trevelyan and Ricardo. It is to be found in the callous indifference of political leaders such as Peel and Russell.

It is instructive to consider how cold intellectual rationalism provided a thin veneer of respectability for the policies so assiduously and unquestioningly pursued by the politicians.

Malthus, in particular, argued that Ireland's population would be tempted to emigrate to Britain in search of higher wages and that the population could not be sustained. In a cynical attempt to protect narrow economic interests, and to prevent the proliferation of Irish Catholic voters in English constituencies, Malthus said that the population of Ireland – especially in the agricultural sector, which was particularly impoverished – should be reduced.

In a widely quoted comment to Ricardo, Malthus spelt out what had to be done in Ireland: "The land in Ireland is infinitely more peopled than England; and to give effect to the natural resources of the country, a great part of the country should be swept from the soil." In case this did not work he also argued that any child born within a year or two of the abolition of the Corn Laws should simply be ineligible for relief.

Population, not poverty

Malthus argued that the population should be attacked – not poverty. His twenty-first-century followers continue to promote these theories through the British-funded coercive one-child policy in China, and aid programmes which only deliver if population targets set by the West are being achieved.

One hundred and fifty years ago Peel repealed the Corn Laws as Malthus wished, but, in an act of discrimination which would become all too familiar, he did not apply the new law in Ireland. There would be cheap corn for the English, but no corn for the Irish poor. For them, Peel offered a new Coercion Bill.

Daniel O'Connell begged Dublin Castle to open the Port, to stop the export of Irish wheat, to stop distilling, to give employment on railways, to use the Crown rents on the Irish woods to repay a loan for the relief of the hungry. The pleas fell on deaf ears, and through political inertia and indifference Ireland became a country of corpses and walking skeletons. What questions are there here for us on our pilgrim way as we consider the situation in parts of Africa, Asia and Latin America, not least the continuing impoverishment caused through indebtedness?

The hungry are in our hands

In February 1847, knowing what was happening to the people living in areas such as Knock, a sick and tottering O'Connell spoke in the British Parliament. It was his last speech in the Commons: "Ireland is in your hands... She is in your power... If you do not save her, she can't save herself. And I solemnly call on you to recollect that I predict with the sincerest conviction that one quarter of her population will perish unless you come to her relief."

O'Connell's challenging words resonate down the pages of history, speaking prophetically to the indifference and hardened hearts that characterise these times.

Culture of death

Pope John Paul has called this "the culture of death". It is a culture which in the past chaotic century led to more people dying in wars than in all previous history. Millions die through recreational use of drugs, drink and tobacco. A baby born in an American city has a statistically greater chance of being murdered than an American soldier had of dying in battle during World War II. Our civilisation is saturated with violence.

The culture of death begins before birth. Six million unborn babies have died through abortion in the past thirty years; over the last decade, half a million human embryos have been destroyed or experimented upon. Now Parliament has permitted the creation and destruction of human embryos for cloning. In Ireland (both north and south) a concerted campaign is underway to introduce the same values into a country which has thus far resolutely insisted on the upholding of human dignity and on the sanctity of human life. If it does so it will have forgotten all of the hard lessons of the famine years.

The culture of death begins at fertilisation, but it does not end at birth. One-hundred-million children die every year of readily treatable diseases and 1.3 billion people live on less than 70p a day; a further three billion people live on under £1.50.

Through laws which permit the sale of arms or which allow for the killing of the disabled or terminally ill we entrench the very values which 150 years ago led to such human misery. The old mistakes are simply dressed up as new ideas. I wrote about these issues in *Life After Death* (Christian Democrat Press, 1997).

These are all questions which involve human dignity. They are all questions which involve the sanctity of human life. During the Irish famine the political classes and the powerful turned their backs on their brothers and sisters who were suffering. At Knock the modern pilgrim has the chance to reflect on these momentous questions, and to ask: Who is my brother and my sister; do I use my opportunity to speak out for those who are without a voice? Through Mary, the Word may have become flesh but what do I care about the creation and sustenance of life today?

A meditation

The words of Mother Teresa of Calcutta:

> *Only God can decide life and death…*
> *That is why abortion is such a terrible sin.*

You are not only killing life but putting self before
    God…
People want to make themselves God Almighty.
They want to take the power of God in their hands.
They want to say,
"I can do without God. I can decide."
To me, the nations which have legalised abortion are the
    poorest nations.
The greatest destroyer of peace today is the crime against
    the unborn child.
We are destroying love,
Destroying the image of God in the world.

Lough
Derg

Lough Derg and
some other Irish sites

THE National Association of Catholic Families publishes an excellent newspaper known as *Catholic Family*. In their first edition for the third Christian millennium they carried an interesting insight by Michael Willis, who suggested Lough Derg as the ideal location for a family pilgrimage.

After returning from a visit in 1992 Michael captivated his four daughters and son with enthralling stories about the place and its history.

He told them how the Druids are reputed to have offered human sacrifice on the Lough's island and that St Patrick drove them out with a forty-day fast. Since those early times a religious community has flourished on the Lough and pilgrims from all over Europe have come to do the spiritual exercises associated with Lough Derg – Patrick's Purgatory. These consist of a fast, a night vigil and the stations.

The pilgrim site gets its name from an incident which occurred when a crusader knight came here in the Middle Ages; while he was undertaking a vigil he had a vision of purgatory. The story was related to Dante, who incorporated the vision into his *Divina Commedia*.

Michael Willis has undertaken the pilgrimage six times, and his wife four times. Their twenty-year-old daughter, Anne-Marie, has been twice and in 1999 their fifteen-year-old daughter, Sophie, went for the first time.

Pilgrims need to be able to walk unaided and recognise that this is a tough and gruelling programme. It involves fasting on bread and water for three days, being deprived of sleep for twenty-four hours, and praying barefoot on the penitential "beds" in a cycle of nine stations. The "beds" are rings of stone at the water's edge which formed the monastic caves and are named after the local Irish saints who were living out their lives on the very edge of the then known world.

Purging Sin

The sacrament of Confession – Reconciliation – has always been an essential part of pilgrimage. In the run-up to the millennium one of the better initiatives was the Clean Slate Campaign, through which people were invited to use the Jubilee Year as a time to wipe the slate clean; a time to put right old enmities, longstanding feuds, unresolved conflicts and buried pain. As far as it goes, such confession of past failings can no doubt be a cleansing experience. What the Church has always offered is something deeper than this: Christ's promise of absolution, that He can wash away the iniquity. When we become confident that this is truly so, the pilgrim really can contemplate renewal of life and strive to make a fresh start.

Pilgrimage takes a person out of a familiar environment. In the context of confession this may be particularly liberating. Sometimes in a parish setting it is acutely difficult to speak honestly and candidly. For many people, being in a different setting makes the process easier and more accessible. There is little doubt that the spiritual experience of visiting a great shrine, in the knowledge that thousands have been this way before, all carrying the same baggage, stirs up deep and unresolved issues.

Youth 2000, who used the Jubilee year to focus in on renewal of Spiritual life in young people, highlighted the role of confession as a central part of their message. My generation were brought up to see the point of regular confession, but undoubtedly the concept became a casualty of the heady days of self-sufficient individualism. This present generation are rediscovering many of the old treasures and reminding the rest of us of some of the things which we have lost. I was intrigued to learn during the Jubilee Pilgrimage of Parliamentarians to Rome in November 2000 that one of the significant features of the year in Italy had been a return to this sacrament. Confession and purgation of the soul are an indispensable part of the pilgrim way.

In 1932 Shane Leslie, in *Saint Patrick's Purgatory* (Burns Oates & Washbourne) captured the atmosphere at the end of purgation:

> Lastly when the twenty-four hours are expired, for now we are come to the last Act, they are revisited by the overseer of the pilgrims, by whom they are brought to the waterside where they duck themselves overhead in the water and by their expiation they are purged as new soldiers of Christ and by the bath of repentance being born again, they go into the Church, according to the custom being thereby renewed to go forward boldly in their Christian warfare and courageously to carry the Cross of Christ. And thus is the great work finished.

There may be up to 800 pilgrims bound together in penance at any one time at Lough Derg. There are few material comforts and the whole emphasis is on performing penance for sins committed and for the sins of others. Here is the sentiment expressed in Bunyan's seventeenth-century *Pilgrim's Progress:*

> *Thus far did I come laden with my sin,*
> *Nor could aught ease the grief that I was in,*
> *Till I came hither. What a place is this!*
> *Must here be the beginning of my bliss?*
> *Must here the burden fall off my back?*

Must here the strings that bound it to me crack?
Blest Cross! Blest sepulchure! Blest, rather, be
The Man that there was put to shame for me!

Michael Willis says that, as well as being a place for the shedding of burdens, the pilgrimage has brought his family "many blessings". Over the years it has provided "the opportunity to walk with Our Lord and to share in His Calvary. Just as we share the symbolic locking into the tomb as the night vigil begins, so we share the electrifying joy of the symbolic sharing in Our Lord's Resurrection as the sun comes up the next morning."

I was struck by this family's testimony, along with that of others who have experienced the rigours of this pilgrimage, that the intensive denial of comfort allied to the physical form of prayer brought huge personal spiritual rewards. Perhaps it is the ultimate antidote to a world which measures us by what we own rather than who we are. Materialism and consumerism – "I shop, therefore I am" – have tended to become a new religion.

Lough Derg is a penitential pilgrimage; a shaking off of all the things which the world holds dear and which too frequently capture and hold us. On this pilgrimage we take stock of our inner life and perform penance, even if the penance is not explicitly linked to a particular act of wrongdoing.

Perhaps we begin to appreciate that a filled Filofax doesn't represent a fulfilled life, and that no man, on his death bed, was ever heard to utter the despairing cry that he wished that he had spent more time at the office.

The Celtic saints linked pilgrimage to an examination of priorities and with a renewal of the inner spiritual life and took as their text the words from the letter to the Hebrews (11:13) which depict the Jews as "strangers and pilgrims on the earth". This imagery of exile led to rugged asceticism which manifested itself in the spiritual pilgrimage typified at Lough Derg. It also led to these men and women going into permanent exile on extended missionary journeys – which would sometimes lead to the pilgrim–missioner taking to their coracle and letting God take them where He wanted them to be. These remarkable journeys of faith, peregrinations *pro Christo*, took the pilgrims to countless destinations. Many never returned to their homeland, but this pilgrim journey was always just a metaphor for the journey within, the journey into the interior life, the journey towards God and heaven.

Laurence of Pasz

Lough Derg appeals to that part of us which we dislike intensely and would seek to amend. The man or woman who has never made a mistake has never made anything. The only issue which arises is what we are going to do about the mistakes of our lives. That, in essence, is the challenge of Lough Derg.

Pilgrims come here for a variety of reasons, and they have always come from far and wide. Laurence of Pasz recorded his reasons:

> I, Laurence, Knight of Hungary, have visited Ireland for three reasons. Firstly and chiefly, because I had heard through reports by word of mouth and in writing that if any one had a doubt in the matter of the Catholic faith, and entered the Purgatory of St Patrick in the prescribed manner, he could there satisfy all doubts either severally or as a whole… The second reason was that I might say to the serene prince, my Lord the King of the Hungarians, that I had visited the place of purgatory referred to… The third reason was that I might see the marvels and miracles of the saints of Ireland, for I had heard much of these marvels and miracles, the great diversity of which I had learned from many sources.

Like the climb up Croagh Patrick, the encounter of pilgrims with faithful old Irish farmers in their Sunday best suits, as a mark of their respect, also has a telling impact on those who travel to Lough Derg. There is a simplicity in their faith and love of God ,which we always seek to make more complicated than it needs to be. There is a "take-it-in-your-stride" approach which stands in stark contrast with our business. Why is it that when we are materially better off than ever, all the indicators suggest that the nation has never been less happy?

Michael Willis describes his fellow pilgrims as salt of the earth and their faith "hardened in the furnace of devotion; it appears almost indestructible."

Seamus Heaney

The young Seamus Heaney, Ireland's Nobel Prize-winning and best-known contemporary poet, made the pilgrimage to Lough Derg three times. The eldest of nine children, he was brought up in County Derry in a warm and loving home. Catholicism was central to his upbringing – Mass, confession, family rosary, the catechism, and a host of pieties. Their family would have lived out the familiar words of the west of Ireland priest, that "the family which prays together, stays together". Heaney was shaped by a rich religious tradition which coloured the years in the bright raiment of May processions in honour of the Virgin, the plaiting of Brigid's Crosses, and the Easter, Whitsun and Christmas liturgies. Faith and culture were inextricably linked, leading Heaney to comment in his essay *The Poet as a Christian* that "we never felt ourselves alone in the universe for a second". He was also scarred by sectarian divisions and hatred which he experienced on a daily basis, but remarkably he refused to use his magnificent poetic talent to give succour or encouragement to those who fuelled the furnaces of Northern Ireland's divisions.

Station Island

In 1984 Heaney published Station Island (Faber & Faber), an anthology of some of his most powerful work. Station Island, or St Patrick's Purgatory, has inspired a wealth of popular legend and literature – much spawned by the eighteenth-century suppression of the pilgrimage under the anti-Catholic Penal Laws.

Seamus Heaney follows a long and distinguished cast of writers who have taken Station Island for their inspiration. In 1828 William Carleton wrote mockingly but with fascination in *The Lough Derg Pilgrim*; in 1942 Patrick Kavanagh penned his "Lough Derg: A Poem". Denis Devlin's poem, "Lough Derg", appeared in 1946; and Sean O'Faolain's short story, *The Lovers of the Lake*, was published in 1958.

Heaney takes Dante's encounter with ghosts in the Purgatorio as the model for *Station Island*. The pilgrims from the other world gather in the way of pilgrims:

I turned
at another sound:
a crowd of shawled women

were wading the young corn,
their skirts brushing softly.
Their motion saddened morning,
it whispered to the silence,
"Pray for us, pray for us,"

it conjured through the air
until the field was full
of half remembered faces,
a loosed congregation
that straggled past and on.

As I drew behind them
I was a fasted pilgrim,
light-headed, leaving home
to face into my station.

As he makes his ethereal pilgrimage, Heaney recounts a series of dream meetings at each of the pilgrim stations; one is with "a bleeding, pale-faced boy, plastered in mud", Heaney's cousin, Colum McCartney, who was shot through the head by Loyalist paramilitary terrorists while driving home one Sunday in County Armagh. Yet this does not drive Heaney into the expression of blood-curdling imagery or call to arms, but into an encounter – at the end of the poem – with the Irish writer James Joyce, who warns against the solution of tribalistic tit-for-tat vengeance: "You are raking at dead fires, a waste of time for somebody your age. That subject people stuff is a cod's game, infantile, like your peasant pilgrimage. You lose more of yourself than you redeem doing the decent thing." Joyce also wants the poet to take an isolated secularised road away from the orthodox Catholic pilgrim path:

> *You are fasted now, light-headed, dangerous*
> *Take off from here. And don't be so earnest.*
> *Let others wear the sackcloth and the ashes.*
> *Let go, let fly, forget.*

Forgetting is not in the Irish character nor, I daresay, are most people inclined to simply forget. Our ghosts have a habit of appearing out of the shadows when they are least expected. Heaney chooses to recall figures from his personal past whose memories had grown dim. For instance, in Section IV of the poem, Heaney encounters a priest called Terry Keenan, who was a seminarian when Heaney first knew him and who died on the foreign missions shortly after ordination. Then come ghosts of teachers, mentors, friends who have died, and a hunger-striker who died at Long Kesh in 1981.

Through the medium of his poetry and his ghosts Heaney takes us through the introspective process of soul-searching and examination of conscience. Everything is here, from the youthful pangs of guilt over fatal sexual attractions to the agonising over whether unwillingness to bear arms was conscionable in the face of the death of friends and family; and the deep urge which we all have to be forgiven:

"Forgive the way I have lived indifferent –
forgive my timid circumspect involvement,"

I surprised myself by saying. "Forgive
my eye," he said, "all that's above my head."
And then a stun of pain seemed to go through him
and he trembled like a heat-wave and faded.

In Section XI he meets a monk who once heard his confession and who set him the penance of translating some of the work of the sixteenth-century Spanish mystic, St John of the Cross; he chooses the "Song of the soul that is glad to know God by faith", a hymn to the "fountain" of the Trinity which is to be found in the sacrament of Holy Communion, the bread of life:

And from these two a third current proceeds
which neither of these two, I know, precedes
although it is the night.

This eternal fountain hides and splashes
within this living bread that is life to us
although it is the night.

Hear it calling out to every creature.
And they drink these waters, although it is dark here
because it is the night.

I am repining for this living fountain.
Within this bread of life I see it plain
although it is the night.

The pilgrim field – full of folk

Station Island begins with an echo of William Langland's *The Vision of Piers the Plowman* invoking the familiar

213

"field full of folk" preparing for their pilgrimage. In a real sense pilgrimage is about dealing with dysfunctional relationships and about learning to see Christ in the people we encounter. It is also about confronting personal ghosts and laying them to rest.

Heaney collects his vaporised assembly and hopes to profit by it, maybe being able to say at the conclusion, like Piers Plowman, that "I have walked full widely, in wet and in dry, And sought out good saints for the health of my soul." Meeting his ghosts may help him come to terms with himself and with his many regrets. Heaney invites us to share his richly sensuous world but leaves us guessing about the painful conclusion of the baring of his soul. His ambiguous thoughts about religion and culture are a long way from the simple pilgrimages of his youth, but it is self-evident that this magnificent poem would not have been possible without that early formation.

Becoming more fully human

Over the three days of fasting at Lough Derg, a meal of dry toast and black coffee or tea is all the pilgrim takes. There is no cacophony of noise or distractions. Radios, TVs and all the other paraphernalia of modern living do not exist on the island. Instead there is the Angelus, Mass, Confession, Stations of the Cross, Benediction and constant prayer. All this, says Michael Willis, "helps us to become more fully human."

It continues to have significant appeal. In July 2000 Monsignor Richard Mohan, the prior, said that the number of pilgrims had increased by 34 per cent on the previous year, with more than 4,500 people enduring the rigorous retreat (*Universe*, 9 July 2000).

One in seven of those making the three-day pilgrimage were there for the first time, with 70 per cent stating that they had gone there "for personal and spiritual renewal".

This included high-powered business managers and executives.

The pilgrim season ends each year on the feast of the Assumption (15 August). The cost, including the boat trip from the mainland to the island, is £20. The cost covers sustenance and accommodation, including a comfortable bed on the final night. A one-day retreat, including the boat ride, a light lunch and tea or coffee, has also been recently introduced.

Other places of Christian pilgrimage in Ireland

In addition to Croagh Patrick, Lough Derg and Knock (see chapters 9 and 10), Ireland is a country brimming over with sacred places. In 1999 the Dublin Diocesan Jubilee Committee produced an excellent guide to encourage pilgrimage in Ireland: *A Pilgrim's Handbook* (Columba Press).

In a foreword, the Archbishop of Dublin, Cardinal Desmond Connell, says, "When we travel on a pilgrimage we are going to meet Christ… it is an image of life itself." The organisers of the handbook hope that making a pilgrimage will be a part of the Jubilee celebrations and they include much practical and spiritual guidance on how to organise and structure a pilgrimage. One day: 21 May 2000, was designated as national Pilgrimage Day for Ireland, and families, friends, neighbourhood groups or parishes were encouraged to prepare and organise an event, especially on ecumenical lines. They suggested the formation of Christian heritage groups within parishes, set up to identify local saints, holy places, the creation of a sacred space, and the organisation of pilgrimages. Jubilee Office is based at Clonliffe College, Dublin 9 (see appendix for details).

Pilgrim destinations

Among the locations in Ireland which the handbook lists are Ulster: Armagh, Downpatrick, Lough Derg, and

Devenish; Connaught: Croagh Patrick, Ballintubber Abbey, Knock, the Arran Islands, Clonfert and Kilmacduagh; Munster: Ennis, Dysert O'Dea, Killeedy, Sceilg Mhichil, Ballyvourney and Holly Cross Abbey in County Tipperary; and Leinster: Clonmacnois, Graiguenamanagh, Jerpoint Abbey, St Canice's Cathedral, Moone, Kildare Town, Foughart, Lady's Island, Kells, Monasterboice and Drogheda.

Dublin: three pilgrim routes

Glendalough is the principal place of pilgrimage for the archdiocese of Dublin, but the handbook also lists three pilgrimage routes in the city centre. It takes approximately three hours to walk each route.

The first route is in the west inner city and takes in Christ Church Cathedral, High Street; the Franciscan Church of the Immaculate Conception in Merchants' Quay; St Audoen's Church of Ireland and Catholic churches in the High Street, and the Martyrs' Graveyard; the Church of St Augustine and St John the Baptist, Thomas Street; St Catherine's, Thomas Street; St Nicholas of Myra, Francis Street; the church ruins and graveyard of St Kevin, Camden Row; the Church of Our Lady of Mount Carmel and the Shrine of Our Lady of Dublin, both in Whitefriar Street.

The second route is in the east inner city and begins at St Stephen's Green, where there are the University Church and a Unitarian church; the Carmelite church in Clarendon Street; St Anne's Church, Dawson Street; early Christian art, National Museum, Kildare Street; the Huguenot Graveyard, Merrion Row; *The Flight Into Egypt* (Rembrandt),and *The Taking of Christ* (Carravaggio), to be seen at the National Art Gallery; Archbishop Ryan Park, Merion Square; St Andrew's Church, Westland Row; and the Book of Kells, Trinity College.

The third route is in the north inner city and consists of

the Blessed Sacrament Chapel, Bachelor's Walk; statues of Daniel O'Connell, O'Connell Street; the Pro-Cathedral, Marlborough Street; Our Lady of Lourdes Church: the body of Matt Talbot, Sean McDermott Street; St Francis Xavier Church: the body of Fr John Sullivan, Gardiner Street; Garden of Remembrance, Parnell Square; St Saviour's, Dominick Street; St Mary's Abbey, Meeting House Lane; St Michan's Catholic Church, Halston Street; St Mary of the Angels, Capuchin Church, Church Street; and St Michan's Church of Ireland, Church Street.

Other pilgrimage sites in Dublin include the Mercy Centre, Catherine MacAuley's grave, Baggot Street; and Cardinal Cullen's tomb at Clonliffe College Chapel. Around Dublin the pilgrim may also want to visit the papal cross in Phoenix Park; St Bridget's Well, Castleknock; St Patrick's Well, Finglas; St Margaret's Well, Finglas; Rathfarnham Abbey; the Mass Rock at Ballinascorney; St Begnet's Well and churches, Dalkey; the Round Tower at Lusk; St Laurence O'Toole's birthplace in County Kildare; the ruins of the Franciscan friary, Kilee, Castledermot, and St Patrick's College and museum at Maynooth.

Meditation

"The Pilgrim"

> *I fasted for some forty days on bread and buttermilk,*
> *For passing round the bottle with girls in rags and silk,*
> *In country shawl or Paris cloak, had put my wits astray,*
> *And what's the good of women, for all they can say*
> *Is fol de rol de rolly O.*
>
> *Round Lough Derg's holy island I went upon the stones.*
> *I prayed at all the Stations upon my marrow-bones,*
> *And there I found an old man, and though I prayed*
>   *all day*
> *And that old man beside me, nothing would he say*
> *But fol de rol de rolly O.*

All know that the dead in the world about the place
    are stuck,
And that should mother seek her son she'd have but little
    luck
Because the fires of Purgatory have ate their shape away;
I swear to God I questioned them, and all they had
    to say
Was fol de rol de rolly O.

A great black ragged bird appeared when I was in
    the boat;
Some twenty feet from tip to tip it stretched right out,
With flopping and with flapping it made a great display,
But I never stopped to question, what could the boatman
    say
But fol de rol de rolly O.

Now I am in the public-house and lean upon the wall,
So come in rags or come in silk, in cloak or country
    shawl,
And come with learned lovers or with what men
    you may,
For I can put the whole lot down, and all I have to say
Is fol de rol de rolly O.

(W.B. Yeats, from *The Collected Poems of W.B. Yeats*,
                                    Macmillan, 1965).

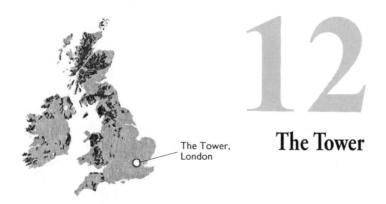

The Tower, London

12

The Tower

DURING parliamentary "term time" hardly a day has gone by over the last twenty years without my passing the spot where St Thomas More stood trial. Westminster Hall is the oldest and grandest of the parliamentary buildings which make up the Westminster estate. Standing at the heart of the Palace of Westminster this is where, in 1265, Simon de Montfort and the barons first challenged the supremacy of the king and began the long tortuous process of creating a parliamentary democracy. The battles which followed were real enough, reaching their climax in the Civil War. It was in 1648 in Westminster Hall that Charles I stood trial and from here that he was taken away for execution. In 1649 the House of Lords and the monarchy were abolished, and for eleven years England experimented with republicanism.

The rupture in the relationship between the universal Church and the English State – and the beginning of the destruction of life-long marriage – was an even messier revolution with far more disastrous long term consequences. That revolution began when Thomas More stood trial at Westminster and was committed to the Tower of London, via the Traitors' Gate, on 17 April 1534. He was executed on 6 July in the following year.

A Man for All Seasons

Before embarking on their journey to discover More and his legacy, modern pilgrims could do worse that watch Fred Zinnemann's celebrated movie of Robert Boult's play, made in 1966, *A Man for All Seasons*. Paul Scofield, as More, and Robert Shaw, as Henry VIII, graphically bring to life the high drama of More's dilemma and his trial. He wanted, in his own words, to be "the king's good servant, but God's first" – echoing, in this famous dictum, Our Lord's challenge to "Render unto Caesar the things that are Caesar's but unto God the things that are God's." More's stand for conscience also created a new standard for believers.

In coming to terms with the implications of trying to be dutiful to both the king and God, More's struggle is at one with the struggle many people face today in reconciling their faith with the great contemporary battles of secular Britain. Thomas More stands at the head of the tradition of Catholic lay involvement in public and political life.

Near to Westminster Hall is the St Stephen's entrance. Most people passing through this long corridor which leads to the Central Lobby – where any citizen may seek out their MP – will be unaware that this is the historic church of St Stephen, and that to this day the crypt chapel of Our Lady Undercroft (below St Stephen's) is in regular use as a place of worship.

On the wall of St Stephen's, in close proximity to the brass studs which mark the place where the High Altar stood and the place where the abbot's chair was situated, is a painting of More and Cardinal Wolsey. If More stands for everything the lay Catholic should be in public and political life, Wolsey stands for everything that the clerical Church should not be.

Westminster Hall

If these walls and those of Westminster Hall could speak, they could tell us most things that we need to know about English history, and about the difficult relationship between Faith and politics.

A succession of Catholics were to stand here in More's place. Most notably, the Hall also saw the trial of St Edmund Campion and the unravelling of the conspiracy to attack Parliament by force, documented so admirably by Antonia Fraser in *The Gunpowder Plot* (Mandarin, 1997). Having survived pillage, plunder, arson and the Luftwaffe, Westminster Hall has been the focus of surges of national emotion. It was here that the masses came to pay their last respects to prime ministers such as Gladstone and Churchill, and to the kings and queens they served. Westminster Hall is where visiting statesmen have been invited by both Houses of Parliament to address commoners and peers, as the greatest honour that Parliament can confer. Most memorable in recent times was the visit of South Africa's President Nelson Mandela, particularly poignant for those of us who had supported him during his long years in prison and throughout his steadfast campaign to end the evil of apartheid.

But for me it is More, the greatest of Englishmen, who occupies the place of precedence in the history of this most significant of English buildings. Perhaps it is suitably ironic that a plaque commemorates this former Lord Chancellor and Speaker of the House of Commons, the author of *Utopia*, although there is nothing here to commemorate his principal adversary, Henry VIII. It was this plaque which Mother Teresa of Calcutta knelt down to kiss during her visit to Parliament in 1989.

More's cell

After his trial More was taken to the Tower of London. The modern pilgrim can now, since January 2000, visit the cell in the lower part of the Bell Tower which is said to be the cell where More was detained.

Perhaps this was one of the most significant gestures of the coming of the third millennium, that 465 years after he was beheaded on Tower Hill, we can at last stand where More languished and prepared himself for death. Over the distance this will be a more enduring sign of the millennium than the Greenwich Dome, full of materialistic trinkets and worthless artifacts.

Today's pilgrims visiting More's cell will see only a bare stone floor and the handsomely vaulted ceilings. There are none of the hangings and furniture which Henry's former Lord Chancellor would have been permitted to bring there.

The Tower's curator, Anna Keay, says that More was "a high status prisoner. He was allowed visitors and writing materials and would have been allowed to furnish the cell more or less as he wished ." She adds that "we know very little about what was there so to put anything in the cell at all would have been based on total conjecture and the room itself is architecturally very interesting."

The Catholic pilgrim to the Tower is likely to be less interested in the architecture than in the exhibition, "Thomas More, Man and Martyr", which Miss Keay has assembled in an adjacent ante-room. This puts flesh on the dry bones. Here is the now ragged and tattered transcript of the conversation between More and the Solicitor General, Richard Rich. It is Rich who finally undoes More by perjuring himself during the trial. His pay-off is a sinecure in Wales. The treachery is brought vividly to life in Zinnemann's film, with More asking Rich whether this was the best price he could extract: was his life to be paid for by a minor political post in the principality? Rich's evidence was to lead directly to More's conviction on the charge of treason.

Also in the exhibition is a relic of More's hair shirt, loaned by the diocese of Portsmouth, which he frequently wore as a penance for his own sinfulness. The modern pilgrim feels distinctly uncomfortable when confronted with the fight which such a self-evidently holy man was prepared to put up against the temptations which beset us all.

Here, too, are the transcripts of some of his letters, including the final letter which he composed to one of his daughters before his execution.

More's pilgrimage to the Tower

More was detained here for fifteen months, along with his fellow martyr, Bishop John Fisher. He had been educated at Oxford and was regarded as one of the greatest scholars of his age. He was a close friend of Erasmus and Holbein. His exploration of what an egalitarian society might be like, *Utopia*, still remains well read and influential.

Initially he considered becoming a Carthusian monk, and remained close to that Order throughout his life. Ultimately, it was marriage, his family, the law and politics, which became his vocation.

His refusal to swear an oath of succession which implicitly repudiated Rome's authority was followed by the charge that he had treasonously refused to acknowledge Henry VIII as head of the Church in England, rather than the Pope, and culminated in the famous trial at Westminster and More's subsequent execution at the Tower.

This clash had been sparked off by the monarch's decision to abandon the first of six wives, Catherine of Aragon, in favour of the young Ann Boleyn (who would, herself, be subsequently held at the Tower). When the Pope refused to grant Henry a 'divorce' from Catherine, the king launched the English Reformation and declared himself as the new head of the English Church. When he proceeded to marry his mistress, Sir Thomas More was appalled. But More was no insignificant rebellious nuisance. He was the king's principal political advisor and had held the highest offices of state.

More resigned the Chancellorship in May 1532. Henry married Anne Boleyn in April 1533. More continued to wrestle with his conscience; although he was willing to swear political fidelity to Henry, he could not take an oath which impugned the Spiritual authority of the Church and inevitably threatened the unity of the universal Church.

Thomas More told the Tower's executioner: "Pluck up thy spirits, man. My neck is very short."

More's body was buried in a chapel at the Tower. His head was fixed to a spike on nearby London Bridge. Tradition has it that Margaret, his loving and devoted daughter, arranged for his head to be taken to Canterbury, where it was buried.

In 1935, in recognition of his life's work and his martyr's death, Pope Pius XI canonised him and his fellow prisoner, Bishop Fisher. In the Bull of Canonisation which was presented by Pope Pius XI, Thomas More is presented as a model of proven moral integrity for all Christians, defined him as "*laicorum hominum deus et ornamentum*".

With the passing of time St Thomas More's appeal becomes more vivid and even greater. He is particularly potent as a symbol of what John Paul II has described as "unity of life". In another telling phrase the Pope calls on modern Christians to be "signs of contradiction". Thomas More was most certainly these things.

In *Christifideles laici*, Pope John Paul II wrote that

> …the laity's unity of life is enormously important: for indeed they must sanctify themselves in their ordinary professional and social life. In order to be able to respond to their calling, then, the laity should look upon the activity of daily life as an opportunity for unity with God and the fulfillment of His will and for the service of their fellow man.

The Second Vatican Council declared, in *Gaudium et Spes*, that the breaking of this unity of life, splitting faith from culture and splitting daily living from the principles of faith, is "among the gravest error of our time". For Thomas More there was no dichotomy, no double personality offering one face to the world and keeping another face for his private life.

A personal portrait will also inevitably have some darker shades. More was no exception. Someone rightly said that we mustn't make him a saint too soon. He was not an easy man; he undoubtedly persecuted; he was fearfully hostile to and abusive of (in language) England's first Protestants, and personally secured the death, by burning, of at least three, having examined them for himself in his own house while he was Lord Chancellor. In this context, Professor Scarisbrick has said of him: "More was, one might say, a man of his times as well as for all seasons. Not at all cuddly. Often enigmatic."

Yet by the end of his pilgrimage, More was a man ready to lay down his life for his beliefs – and his friends. He was a man whose powerful intellect continues to challenge us today.

Christian humanism

In his astute observations about the world in which he lived, in his thirst for truth, and in his pursuit of Christian humanism, More never sacrificed his allegiance to God. This "unity of life" was also to be found in his dealings as a lawyer and as a judge, much to the frustration of his opponents, who wanted to undo him by pinning false charges of judicial malpractice and corruption to him. In the end, they abandoned this approach because More's reputation stood so high that they assumed that no-one would believe them.

Thomas More is considered to be one of the greatest

protagonists of Common Law, and he passionately believed that it was through the formulation and interpretation of just laws that true social justice might best be established and peaceful relations created within and between nations. He reconciled his advocacy of the common good through a fair and transparent judicial system with the constant practice of charity. Contemporaries called this sworn enemy of favouritism, and implacable opponent of the grotesque creation of disproportionate privileges for the powerful, "the patron of the poor".

These same contemporaries described More's family as a "Christian academy", in which the cultivation of learning and the consideration of morality and ethics were daily fare. He was a much imitated educator and a champion of women's education. Despite holding high office he maintained a simplicity of life in his own household and insisted to those closest to him that they must not become infatuated with the baubles of office and the trappings of power.

More's handling of high office and his subsequent martyrdom strikes a discordant note in the world of modern politics. Collaboration and conformism have become hallmarks of the sophisticated world of career politics. Take your cue from the electronic instruction of a pager or a mobile phone, tailor your remarks to the on-message demands of party managers or whips, and never mind your conscience; just think about your preferment and the patronage which awaits you. They say that for the pearl to emerge from the oyster a bit of grit has to enter in. For thirty years in British politics I have despaired at the sometimes ruthless attempts to prevent the bits of grit from entering in. I have despaired at the feeble excuse that "I won't cause problems now but if I get just one more rung up the ladder, then I'll change things." Invariably the only thing which changes are the politicians who, by the time they come tumbling back down the ladder, belatedly realise that they missed their opportunity and that the moment when they might have made a difference has passed.

Protector of politicians

Contrast all of this with Thomas More, who at the end of October 2000 was proclaimed by Pope John Paul II as the protector of politicians and all those in government. Contrast More with the bitter partisans reduced to paying off old scores. Throughout his extraordinary trials he preserved a sense of serenity and good humour. He held firm to his convictions while refusing to vilify those with whom he disagreed. And, at the block, at the very end, there was no valedictory speech denouncing others with hatred and venom; instead, there was forgiveness and understanding.

Political life is so often about personal aggrandisement and advantage. Its participants fall into two camps – the be-ers and the doers. The doers prefer public service to personal status. They pursue causes rather than careers. It is often instructive to simply ask the questions: What are a politician's causes? What are a politician's convictions? If they have none, you probably know all that you need to know about them.

Politics for Thomas More was never a matter of personal advantage or the accumulation of personal power. Instead it was rooted in the desire to serve. It was informed by the deepest impulses of citizenship: a sense of duty and an understanding of every person's responsibility to strive for the common good. Any understanding of More's rigorous intellectual approach to the study of law, history, theology, philosophy and the culture of his country reveals his abiding belief in the importance of formation: the formation of the mind and spirit as prerequisites for public service and high political office. The cultivation of virtue was, for More, an indispensable requirement for good governance.

Two centuries after his death, Jonathan Swift extolled More as "a person of the greatest virtue this kingdom ever produced", while the poet John Donne said he was a "man of the most tender and delicate conscience that the world saw since Augustine".

What is especially appealing about More is that he is not an icon of pietism. His inner conflicts often loom darker than some of his modern admirers may care to admit. It was Erasmus who famously called him a man for all seasons; he was undoubtedly a man with flaws as well as virtues. His final jousts with his accusers and his determination to find some way out of the death he sees before him present us with a man who knew all the ways of politics and law. What makes him a saint is that, having seen all those doors close before him, he embraced inevitable death with courage and acceptance. We often say there are beliefs for which we would be prepared to die, but in our private moments many of us must wonder what would really happen if the question were ever to arise.

Politics, for More, had to be informed by knowledge and truth. The primacy of truth over power and the supremacy of goodness over utility were More's enduring tests for decision-making. Decisions which might lead to short-term popularity or personal gain were merely expediency, and More was not to be found standing on these shifting sands.

The true freedom fighter

Thomas More is the greatest of the true freedom fighters. His struggle against those who sought to commandeer his conscience and to subvert his convictions was a remarkable stand against tyranny. The history of the twentieth century is a history of States subverting conscience and violently suppressing political and religious belief. It is a history indelibly marked by collaboration and acquiescence in ideologies based on racial purity, class warfare, eugenics and other evils. Through this din, More's voice reminds us of the crucial role of conscience, the eternal quest for truth, our personal responsibility for our decisions, and our ultimate accountability for our actions.

At the request of Senator Cossiga, a former president of Italy, statesmen and politicians throughout the democratic world petitioned the Holy See to declare Thomas More as the patron of all those who are engaged today in these endless political struggles. In their petition they said that the fundamental lesson which Thomas More offers all statesmen is "the lesson of flight from success and easy compromises in the name of fidelity to irrevocable principles, upon which depend the dignity of man and the justice of civil society – a lesson truly inspiring for all who feel themselves called to expose and eradicate the snares laid by the new and hidden tyrannies".

There are many excellent biographies of Thomas More, to enable the pilgrim to learn more of the life and times of this exceptional man. Most recently, Peter Ackroyd has published a biography which is as sharp as Holbein's famous drawing (*The Life of Thomas More*, Chatto and Windus, 1998). In 1995 Gerard Wegemer published *Thomas More, A Portrait of Courage* (Scepter Publishers, Princeton), and in 1984 Richard Marius published *Thomas More: A Biography* (Collins Fount Paperbacks). There is a Thomas More web site which contains the Works of Thomas More.

The Tower's other martyrs

While in the vicinity of the Tower, the pilgrim might also wish to recall some of the others who were held there and who suffered grievously for their faith. Following Thomas More, John Fisher and the Carthusian martyrs (St John Houghton; St Augustine Webster; and St Robert Lawrence) came a succession of people who suffered for their religion and a variety of associated causes. The trickle grew to a flood during Elizabeth's reign. Edmund Campion SJ and many of the seminary priests who had trained in continental Europe returned to a bloody death (many at Tyburn and Lancaster, see chapters 13 to 15).

More and Fisher were occupants of the Bell Tower. So, too, was John Leslie, Bishop of Ross (1527–96),who had been a member of Mary Stuart's Privy Council and was her chief ecclesiastical adviser.

Passing from the Bell Tower to the Traitors' Gate, the pilgrim can stand at the place where the prisoners were brought from Westminster following trial and sentence. It was here that St Thomas More was brought from Lambeth Palace after he declined to swear that the marriage between Henry and Anne Boleyn was true and lawful, that her progeny were the true heirs to the throne..

The Traitor's Gate is also where More bid farewell to his oldest daughter, Margaret Roper, on 1 July 1534. Others who also passed this way included Anne Boleyn, Katherine Howard, Thomas Cromwell, and the Earl of Essex.

The Bloody Tower

To the left of the Traitor's Gate is the Bloody Tower, originally known as the Garden Tower. This is said to be the scene of the murder at the behest of Henry VII (or Richard III? – the jury is still out) of Edward V and his brother, Richard, Duke of York, the young sons of Edward IV. Here, too, the Jesuits, Garnet and Oldcorne, executed in connection with the Gunpowder Plot, were kept.

Nearby is the White Tower, standing at the centre of the enclosure. Built in about 1078 by Gandulf, Bishop of Rochester, for William the Conqueror, the White Tower was designed to signify the supremacy of the king over his city. It was traditional for monarchs to be lodged there before going to Westminster Abbey for their coronation. The surrounding buildings were gradually extended over the centuries. Among them is St Thomas's Tower and an oratory dedicated to St Thomas Becket.

The Horse Armoury, situated within the White Tower, was the room from which prisoners would be taken after interrogation and led down to the torture chamber. In the Catholic Truth Society pamphlet *The Tower of London* (1979), J.J. Dwyer says that here "in that subterranean hell, far from all human aid or sympathy, was obtained the 'evidence' by which the agonized sufferers convicted themselves and any other people whose names might come into their minds".

Little ease, great suffering

Next to this is a dungeon which was known as the "Little Ease". There was insufficient room to stand upright or to lie down. Guy Fawkes was kept here, chained to a ring in the floor. Other frequently used forms of torture included the rack and, in the case of Fr John Gerard for instance, hanging by the wrists. When he entered the torture chamber he saw "ranged divers sorts of racks and other instruments of torture. Some of these were displayed before me, and told me that I should have to taste them." Fr Gerard's hands were screwed into two iron rings and he was then suspended from a height which ensured that his feet did not touch the ground. When he fainted they poured vinegar down his throat. Through the intervention of the lieutenant the tortures were suspended after about twenty days and he was transferred to the Salt Tower. While he was here a Catholic gentleman, Francis Arden, was also held prisoner. He is thought to have been one of the Warwickshire Ardens, who suffered greatly for their faith. One of their number, Mary Arden, was the mother of William Shakespeare (see chapter 16). Francis Arden's wife managed to smuggle in some bread and wine, and on the feast of Our Lady's Nativity Fr Gerard was able to visit his fellow prisoner and to say a clandestine Mass in his cell.

Subsequently, Fr Gerard was moved to the Cradle Tower. One night in 1579 two Jesuit lay brothers, John Lily and Richard Fulwood, came to the Tower wharf in a boat. A rope was thrown and Fr Gerard and Francis Arden made good their escape.

The Salt Tower

Another Catholic held in the Salt Tower was St Henry Walpole who, while observing the execution of St Edmund Campion at Tyburn, had famously been sprinkled by the priest's blood. He followed in Campion's footsteps and was hanged, drawn and quartered at York on 7 April 1597. St Henry was tortured in the Tower fourteen times, and the large room on the first floor of the Tower bears three inscriptions of his name. One appears under a drawing of a heart marked with a cross and the letters IHS. Elsewhere his name appears: "Henry Walpole, Societatis Jesu Presbiter". The pilgrim will also see a hand with a mark at the centre, capturing the five wounds of Christ In the upper room of the Salt Tower is an inscription of a heart and the legend: "Blessed are they that suffer persecution for righteousness."

St Nicholas Owen, a Jesuit lay brother, was also held in the Salt Tower and died here under torture. St Nicholas was responsible for constructing the hiding places in Catholic homes which saved the lives of countless priests during penal times. His knowledge of where these hiding holes were located made him a special prize. He refused to give any information and was literally torn to pieces. Beatified in 1929, he was canonized in 1970 as one of the Forty Martyrs of England and Wales.

Apart from the subterranean cave known as "The Pit"

and "Little Ease", the Tower specialised in any number of other cruel barbarities. It was at the base of the White Tower, in one of the cells there, that St Robert Southwell SJ was examined thirteen times and "experienced new tortures worse than the rack". Fr John Hart SJ compiled his *Index, or Diary, of the Transactions which occurred in the Tower of London, an Account of the Catholic Religion*, detailing some of the enormities which were experienced by priests and lay people.

Campion and the rack

The White Tower is also the location of the chapel of St John the Evangelist. It was here that St Edmund Campion was taken after he had been tortured on the rack and subjected to the Little Ease. Without any time to recover he was forced to take part in a theological disputation with his accusers, including the Deans of St Paul and Windsor. Campion and Fr Ralph Sherwin, a classical scholar of distinction born in Rodsley in Derbyshire, were ridiculed and taunted. St Ralph was held in the Martin Tower. One unexpected consequence was that Philip, Earl of Arundel and Surrey, who was present, became a convert.

St Philip Howard and the Tower

St Philip reappeared in the Tower, as a prisoner in the Beauchamp Tower, in 1585, and was fined £10,000 for his Catholic activities. Under an Elizabethan Act of 1581 he was found guilty of high treason for being reconciled to the ancient faith and he lived under a sentence of death until 1595. He died in captivity and is numbered among the martyrs. Over the fireplace in the Beauchamp Tower is an inscription which he cut into the stone: "The more affliction we endure for Christ in this world, the more glory we shall obtain with Christ in the next." Elsewhere, up the stairs of the Tower, appears another Latin inscription carved into the stone by Philip Howard: "As it is a disgrace to be bound on account of sin, so, on the contrary to sustain the bonds of prison for Christ's sake is the greatest glory" (see also chapter 6).

Thomas Peverel, Blessed John Story (a professor of civil law at Oxford), Thomas Roper (grandson of Thomas More), Fr John Prine and the Venerable Francis Page (executed at Tyburn in 1602) are just some of those who were detained in the Beauchamp Tower and whose inscriptions appear there. Under the name of Fr Page appear the words: "In God is my hope."

St Ralph Sherwin and the Martin Tower

The Martin Tower is where Ralph Sherwin was confined. Executed along with Edmund Campion and Alexander Briant SJ, on 1 December 1581, they were followed in May 1582 by seven other priests, William Filby, St Luke Kirby, Laurence Richardson, and Thomas Cottam SJ, Thomas Ford, John Skert and Robert Johnson. Five more were sent to Tyburn from the Tower in 1584: George Haydock, James Fenn, Thomas Hemerford, John Munden and John Nutter. The roll call is enormous.

Public Record Office

A record of the fate of the 1,506 prisoners who were committed to the Tower between 1101 and 1941 may be viewed at the Public Record Office and at the library of the British Museum. The authorities at the Tower produce their own excellent guide books and material. Their educational unit produces a question sheet for children which they complete as they make their way around. My nine-year-old thoroughly enjoyed working his way through this, but it would be a shame if Catholic parents allowed their children to leave this daunting building thinking that it was simply a place of pageant and Beefeaters and home to the Crown Jewels. The memories of More and Fisher, Campion, Owen, Howard and the rest should ring down through the centuries, for was not Tertullian right when he observed of the Roman martyrs that their blood was the seed of the Church?

Perhaps a good place to end the day is a journey down to Chelsea, where, on the Embankment, close to the Catholic seminary of Allen Hall and at the site of More's Chelsea home, the modern pilgrim may sit by the statue of Thomas More which gazes out over the River Thames.

Meditation

Some words of St Thomas More

> *If you love your health;*
> *if you desire to be secure from the snares of the devil;*
> *from the storms of this world;*
> *from the hands of your enemies;*
> *if you long to be acceptable to God;*
> *if you covet everlasting happiness – then let no day pass*
> *without at least once presenting yourself to God in*
> *prayer… not merely from your lips, but from the*
> *innermost recess of your heart…*

> *Give me the grace, good Lord, to set the world at naught;*
> *To set my mind fast upon Thee*
> *And not to hang upon the blast of men's mouths.*
> *To be content to be solitary.*
> *Not to long for worldly company*
> *But utterly to cast off the world*
> *And rid my mind of the business thereof.*

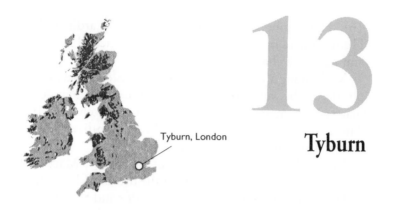

Tyburn, London

13

Tyburn

IN 1910 Catholics decided to mark the execution of more than a hundred Catholic martyrs at London's Tyburn Tree by inaugurating an annual walk. The nuns at Tyburn Convent continue this tradition with a walk organised each summer and there is an annual Tyburn lecture. In addition to these annual events a walk of witness can be undertaken at any time by individuals, small groups or by parishes.

In this chapter I suggest an outline for such a walk of witness, and in the next, some other locations which capture the spirit of the recusant families who refused to conform and were prepared to sacrifice everything, including their very lives, for the right to hold firm in their religious faith. The culmination of the pilgrimage – in every sense – is Tyburn Convent, home to a congregation of cloistered Benedictine nuns.

Westminster Cathedral and Abbey

My starting point would be Westminster Cathedral and the Chapel of the Martyrs – where a glass case contains the remains of the Lancashire martyr, St John Southworth, who died at Tyburn on 28 June 1654 (see chapters 15 and

237

16). Here, too, is the tomb of the late Cardinal Basil Hume, where many people visiting the cathedral now stop and pray (see chapter 16).

Walk along Victoria Street to Westminster Abbey, where plinths on the western entrance house the statues of modern martyrs drawn from all denominations (see chapter 16). These include Oscar Romero, St Maximilian Kolbe, Dietrich Bonhoeffer and Martin Luther King.

Inside the abbey is the tomb of the sisters, Mary and Elizabeth, responsible for many of the deaths of Protestant and Catholic martyrs alike. During Tudor and Stuart times about 350 martyrs from both traditions died for their beliefs. Protestants died as heretics, and many were burnt at Smithfield under the Catholic Queen Mary. Her father, Henry VIII, as well as executing Catholics who stayed loyal to the papacy and disputed his divorce, also executed Nonconformists, and many others died under Elizabeth, James I, Charles I and Charles II.

Under Elizabeth and the Stuarts, and during the Commonwealth, Catholics were executed for being illegal priests, for sheltering or helping priests, or for participating at Mass or persisting in Catholic beliefs.

In the Abbey an inscription appears on the tomb of the two sisters which reads: "Consorts both in throne and grave, here we rest, two sisters, Elizabeth and Mary, in the hope of one resurrection."

Perhaps that can be our own hope, today, as we consider the themes of suffering and penance which spring from these stories of religious intolerance and persecution: the hope of one resurrection.

The word "martyr" has Greek roots and originally meant "witness". Predominantly the word has been used to describe a willingness to surrender life itself rather than disown faith in Christ. A walk of witness associated with the martyrs might usefully challenge us to consider what price we might be prepared to pay in upholding our faith today. The true witness has to learn how to walk the pilgrim's way in a spirit of tolerance and humility while steadfastly holding onto the central tenets of faith.

In *Life After Death*, (Christian Democrat Press, 1997), I illustrate the willingness of some of our contemporaries to pay a real price for their beliefs: Barbara Janaway, a secretary at a medical practice who lost her job for "gross misconduct" because she refused to process a form requesting an abortion; Stephen Clark, an environmental scientist, who suffered a similar fate for refusing to monitor the stack of a hospital in Salford where the remains of unborn babies were being burnt; Patrick McCrystal, who lost his job as a pharmacist for refusing to dispense the morning-after pill; Simon Caldwell, whose employment as a journalist ended when he refused to rewrite a story about abortion; or Tracy Anderson, a Liverpool woman, who went ahead with the birth of her child after doctors had wrongly told her, on three separate occasions, that her child would be multiply handicapped, and social workers had tried to bully her into ending the life of her child. These are all modern witnesses for their faith.

Westminster Abbey to Westminster Hall

Across the road from the abbey is Westminster Hall, where St Thomas More and St Edmund Campion both stood trial. In *Signs of Contradiction* (Hodder & Stoughton, 1996) I tell Campion's story, and in chapter 12 of this book, the central events of More's life are recorded. As Lord Chancellor and Speaker of the House of Commons, he would have known these buildings well.

Westminster to the Tower

The option now is to take the London Underground from Westminster to Tower Hill or to walk the distance along the Embankment of the River Thames.

From the window of Thomas More's cell at the Tower it is possible to see, as he did, where three Carthusian priors, a Bridgettine priest and the vicar of Isleworth were taken from the Tower to meet their deaths as the first martyrs, executed at Tyburn on 4 May 1535. More said to his wife, Meg, that they went "as gladly as to a marriage feast".

The Tower to Charterhouse

In following their footsteps and passing Tower Hill, where More and St John Fisher, Bishop of Rochester and Cardinal, would in turn be executed, we head west towards Holborn Viaduct (close to Canon Street and Blackfriars, whose names tell us something of their past). Adjacent to Holborn Viaduct tube station is the Old Bailey. This stands on the site of what was Newgate Prison. Here and at other notorious Tudor and Stuart prisons, such as the Marshalsea and the Clink, many of the martyrs were held prisoner, and many died in captivity. The Old Bailey is today synonymous with the scales of justice: an appropriate theme to ponder here.

Turning left into Holborn Viaduct, the pilgrim comes to the junction of Charterhouse Street, Holborn and Ely Place.

The very first of the martyrs, St John Houghton, was Carthusian prior of the London Charterhouse. Born in Essex, he studied at Cambridge. He was cut down from the Tyburn Tree – a wooden triangle where ten people could be hanged together – still alive. As he bore the butchery which followed and his organs were cut from his body he cried out, "Good Jesu! what wilt Thou do with my heart?" as his executioners tore it from his body.

St Ethedreda's, Ely Place

The Church of St Etheldreda, in Ely Place, is a good place at which to stop and consider the cruelties which mankind is capable of committing.

The Catholic Writers Guild, the Keys, uses this church for its monthly meetings. Undoubtedly it is the combination of good speakers and this evocative venue which has acted as a powerful attraction to so many who attend.

The parish priest of St Etheldreda's is Fr Kit Cunningham, who is also chaplain to the Keys. Its eclectic gatherings are presided over by the Master of the Keys, Antony Tyler OBE.

The story of St Etheldreda's is itself a powerful invocation of Catholic heritage and culture, but it also serves to remind those of us who take our liberties of free association and free speech so much for granted just how different life was for our forbears not so many generations ago.

The Catholic journalist and broadcaster, Mary Kenny put it characteristically well when she said that the intimacy and charm of St Etheldreda's make it "different from almost any other church building I know: above the altar, the brilliantly lit stained glass window, and on the side walls, looking down on the congregation, those Elizabethan and Stuart figurines. The sense of history is resonant."

Most Catholic congregations used to be all too well aware of the breaking of the tradition and the discontinuity of worship which led to the underground years and ultimately to early nineteenth-century emancipation. Their parish churches are, therefore, by necessity of fairly recent creation. St Etheldreda's is a rare exception and is a good place to begin for the Catholic pilgrim trying to piece together a lost past.

In about the year 1250 the then Bishop of Ely built the first oratory on this site and dedicated it to Saint Etheldreda, who at one time was the most popular of Anglo-Saxon women saints. A native of Suffolk, she was daughter of King Anna of East Anglia and sister to Saints Sexburga, Ethelburga, and Withburga. Twice married, she remained a virgin. She took the veil at Coldingham under St Ebba, migrated to Ely and was chosen as abbess of the double monastery, where, despite its sumptuous wealth, she lived a life of simplicity and great holiness. Her body remained incorrupt after death.

Her shrine, in what is now Ely Cathedral, became one of the most popular centres of pilgrimage until its destruction under Henry VIII in 1541. Her hand is preserved in the Catholic church at Ely. Catholics celebrate her feast on 23 June and usually depict her as an abbess wearing a crown, holding a crozier and a budding rod or lily.

The oratory of Saint Etheldreda named in her honour grew rapidly and became the nucleus of a palace used by Bishops of Ely when they attended Parliament or held high office in London. The palace was used by John of Gaunt after the Peasant's Revolt of 1381 led to Wat Tyler's mob burning down his home at the Savoy. Kings and queens regularly frequented the palace, and Elizabeth I pressurised the Anglican Bishop Cox into leasing some of the property to one of her favoured courtiers, Sir Christopher Hatton. The chapel and buildings then began their decline.

For a while, in the seventeenth century, the Spanish ambassador to James I used the property as his official residence and Mass was again celebrated here, but Cromwell subsequently demolished many of the buildings. The church passed through a number of hands, including Welsh Episcopalians, until it was put up for auction in 1874. Fr Lockhart, of the Rosminian Order, made a successful bid, and by 1879, on the feast of Etheldreda, the upper church was once again used for the celebration of Mass.

Around the walls of the church are plinths commemorating some of those who were executed for their faith. The pilgrim may wish to sit and think about the sacrifice made by their countrymen for their religious beliefs. Clockwise, from the altar, are St Edmund Gennings, a seminary priest executed at Gray's Inn in 1591 for his priesthood; St Swithun Wells, a schoolmaster, executed at Gray's Inn in 1591 for sheltering Fr Gennings; St Margaret Ward, a lady-in-waiting, executed at Tyburn in 1588 for helping the escape of a priest; Blessed John Forest, a

Franciscan friar, executed at Smithfield in 1538 for refusing to take the Oath of Supremacy; Blessed Edward Jones, a secular priest, executed at Fleet Street in 1590 for his priesthood; Blessed John Roche, a Thames water-man, executed in 1588 for helping the escape of a priest; St Anne Line, a seamstress, executed at Tyburn in 1601 for sheltering a priest; and St John Houghton, Carthusian prior of the London Charterhouse, executed at Tyburn in 1535 for refusing to take the Oath of Supremacy. This Charterhouse was where Thomas More had once tested his own contemplative vocation. If Houghton, and other Carthusian priors – St Robert Lawrence of Beauvale in Nottinghamshire and St Augustine Webster of Axholme in Lincolnshire – had taken the oath accepting Henry VIII as head of the Church of England, and had rejected the spiritual authority of the Pope, their lives would have been spared.

Willingness to die for belief is perhaps best summed up in the words of St Margaret Ward who, at her trial, offered no apologies for helping a priest to avoid capture but rejoiced "in having delivered an innocent lamb from the hands of those bloody wolves". John Roche was hanged with her.

Before leaving St Etheldreda's, the west window should catch the visitor's eye. A detail in the window depicts the Tyburn Tree. As they made their last pilgrimage on this earth, dragged on wooden pallets, this terrible procession would take them past St Etheldreda's and on towards Tyburn.

Holborn to Soho

Walking along Holborn and High Holborn we come to St Giles' (the great patron saint of people with leprosy and disabilities in the Middle Ages) and to the church of St Anselm and St Cecilia, in Kingsway. This was built in 1909 to replace the old church of St Cecilia which had served as the chapel of the Sardinian Embassy and during the reign of Charles II had been the first chapel to be opened in London after the Reformation.

The first patron of the church is St Anselm, who was a highly learned man, and as Archbishop of Canterbury, despite his gentle spirit, stood firm against King William Rufus and Henry I.

The other patron, St Cecilia, patron saint of music, was one of the most famous Roman martyrs. Perhaps this is an appropriate place to consider how we reconcile our duties to church and state, and how faith and culture – learning, literature, music, and media – inform one another.

Crossing Tottenham Court Road and entering Oxford Street, we pass the old churchyard of St Giles, the ancient parish church of Tyburn, where several martyrs were buried. A short detour takes the walker into Soho Square, where the church of St Patrick is situated. Following the passage of the Catholic Relief Act, this was built in 1792 on the site of the first Catholic church publicly opened in London. Given its location in Soho this is a good place to consider the children who suffer today through exploitation in the sex industry. In countries such as the Philippines and Thailand, men such as Fr Shay Cullen, an Irish Columban priest, and women like Sr Laurence Pautinet – Sr Love– have devoted the whole of their lives to countering the way in which waves of foreigners, who often book their "holidays" via firms in London's Soho, abuse children as young as seven and eight years of age.

Oxford Circus to Tyburn

Crossing Oxford Circus, the remaining walk along Oxford Street, takes us to our destination of Marble Arch.

Many of those who were martyred at Tyburn came from Newgate Prison (now known only from a plaque in the wall) and they were drawn from Newgate Street by

St Paul's, through High Holborn and Oxford Street to Marble Arch.

This is the site of Tyburn Field, which stood two miles outside of the city. For five hundred years it was a place of execution. The first took place in 1196 and the last in 1683. Of the religious martyrs who died here almost all were Catholics. This is because they were sentenced to die as traitors, to be hanged, drawn and quartered. Protestant martyrs died as heretics, at the stake, very few at this traditional place of execution of felons.

The site of the gallows is shown today by a circular slab of Portland stone which lies on the traffic island at the entrance of Edgeware Road. Inscribed on the stone is a cross surrounded by the legend: "The site of Tyburn Tree".

Between 1535 and 1681 more than a hundred Catholics died here and, not surprisingly, it became a secret place of pilgrimage. For instance, Queen Henrietta Maria, the Catholic wife of Charles I, came to pray and sent her French chaplain to observe events and to gather relics by which the memory of the dead might be recalled.

It was these relics which were eventually to be brought from safe-keeping in France to the religious house established in 1901 by a group of French Benedictine nuns who had fled from anti-religious laws in France and settled in London. Their house, at 8 Hyde Park Place, is now the permanent home of the relics collected by Dom Bede Camm (author of *The Forgotten Shrines*, 1910, see chapter 14) and of an exhibition setting out the history of the persecution. This is the culmination of the Tyburn pilgrimage.

A day in the life of Tyburn

A typical day in the convent consists of a 5.30 am start with Nocturns (liturgy of the hours); 6.30 am *Lectio Divina* (study); 7.15 am Lauds (liturgy of the hours); 8.30 am

Mixte (simple breakfast); 9.15 am Terce (liturgy of the hours); 9.30 am Conference/choir practice; 10.00–noon, work; 12.15 pm Sext (liturgy of the hours); 12.30 pm Midday meal; 1.30 pm Recollection hour (free time); 2.45 pm, Mixte, cup of tea; 3.15 pm None (liturgy of the hours); 3.30 pm Recreation; 4.30 pm Vespers (liturgy of the hours); 5.00 pm work; 6.30 pm Evening meal; 7.00pm, *Lectio Divina* (a form of prayer leading to contemplation}; 8.15 pm Compline, (liturgy of the hours).

I was fortunate, indeed, to be able to spend a couple of hours talking to the community and being shown around the crypt chapel by the learned Mother John Baptist. Each day Sisters are on hand, at 10.30 am, 3.30 pm and at 5.30 pm to take around individuals or groups, and they have several excellent pamphlets, including *The Forty Four* (martyrs of the Venerable English College, Rome), *They Died at Tyburn, Guide to the Crypt of the Martyrs*, as well as copies of their regular magazine, *The Tyburner*.

A replica of the triple tress gallows stands in the crypt. On the beams of the gallows are inscribed the last words of Henry Heath, born in Peterborough, a convert who became a Franciscan priest: "Jesus, convert England, Jesus, have mercy on this country." Here also is the last prayer of St Ralph Sherwin, who kissed the blood of Edmund Campion as it dripped from the hands of the executioner, before going to his own death: "*Jesu, Jesu, Jesu, esto mihi Jesus*" (to me be a Jesus, i.e. a Saviour).

Under the replica of the Tyburn Tree is a small altar and reredos. Seven niches contain carved figures of Thomas Sherwood, a twenty-six-year-old seminarian from London executed in 1578; St Edmund Campion, the Oxford academic and leading Jesuit missionary who died in 1581; St John Houghton (see above) who died in 1535; the Virgin Mary, depicted with her Son's crown of thorns close to her heart; Sebastian Newdigate, son of the lord of Harefield Manor, Middlesex, and a Carthusian monk, fettered in an upright position for fifteen days in the Marshalsea Prison before dying at Tyburn in 1535; St Richard Reynolds, a Devonian, Cambridge graduate and Bridgettine monk of Syon Abbey, executed in 1535; and St Ralph Sherwin, protomartyr of the English College, Rome, and executed with Campion in 1581. Each year on 1 December (feast day of Campion, Sherwin and their Jesuit companions), High Mass is celebrated by the Jesuit chaplain at Stonyhurst College, Lancashire, honouring their memory.

Tyburn lessons

Here are any number of contemporary lessons: lessons about intolerance, persecution, fortitude, endurance and courage. In all the controversy about what should and should not be in the new religious education syllabus to be used in Catholic schools, a visit to the Tyburn crypt exhibition should take place at some stage in every Catholic child's education – perhaps ideally at the time of Confirmation. I took a non-Catholic friend with me when I met the Tyburn community. He candidly admitted that he had no idea of the horrors which had taken place here. Everyone can learn something from a pilgrimage to Tyburn.

Above the crypt is a chapel which is open twenty-four hours a day. It is a beautiful oasis in the heart of turbulent, frenetic London. There is perpetual adoration of the Blessed Sacrament and a nun will be seen kneeling at her prie-dieu, praying for people who contact the Tyburn community from all over the world. An internet site and e-mail address providing the community with a state-of-the-art means of receiving prayer requests from all over the world is in regular receipt of requests for help. What a travesty it would be if, as prayer requests and requests for information pour in from all over the world, we in the country of their birth allowed the deaths of these men and women to be forgotten.

Meditation

The Tyburn Benedictine: an offer of life

Trinitarian worship and praise, with, in and through the Heart of Christ, our one, only Mediator between God and Man, sharing his Eucharistic sacrifice to become with him a continual offering to the Father in the Spirit, for the salvation of the whole human family.

Tyburn martyrs hallowed this spot, and we with them in this holy place yearn for the coming of Christ's Kingdom, pledging ourselves to him in the mystery of faith, the Blessed Sacrament, his greatest gift of love to his Church, uniting with him in perpetual prayer and adoration; urged on by the zeal of the martyrs to sacrifice ourselves in prayer and penance for the Church, the Roman Pontiff, all bishops, priests, religious, Christ's faithful and our separated brethren, never will we cease our prayer and sacrifice till God grants full unity of faith and worship to his Church.

Benedict, our Father, left us his Rule of Monastic Living; Evangelical; hearkening to Christ; its precepts are:

Never forget the presence of God and his holy angels;
Ever remember all the commandments of God;
Deny oneself to do always the Will of the Father;
In compunction and purity of heart to offer prayer
  to God;
Contentment and peace of mind in the midst of
  affliction;
To prefer absolutely nothing to Christ;
In the joy of the Holy Spirit to do penance and to practise
  virtue;
Never to despair of God's mercy;
Ever to desire eternal life with all spiritual longing;
Seek first the Kingdom of God; and serve one another
with humble and pure love, and so glorify the Father,
Son and Holy Spirit, the Creator and Redeemer of all.

14

The recusants

"RECUSANTS" were those people found guilty of refusing to attend Church of England Services. It is thanks to the Tyburn nuns and to men like Dom Bede Camm, who worked tirelessly to bring artefacts and martyrs' relics to Tyburn, that we have access to so much invaluable information about these martyrs and their families.

Dom Bede, who was born in 1864 and died in 1942, was painstaking in the research he undertook for *Forgotten Shrines*. For today's pilgrim wanting to trace the footsteps of the Catholic martyrs back to their homes and to their local communities this Edwardian publication still remains one of the best sources of material available. A pilgrimage to the recusant sites might follow the footsteps of the Benedictine historian as he brought back to Erdington Abbey the material which he had gathered.

Dom Bede: modern pilgrim

Dom Bede passionately believed that through the act of pilgrimage something of the holy and the sacred would rub off on the inquirer. Of the recusant homes he wrote: "The air of mystery and romance which seems to exhale from the crumbling walls of these old houses, irresistibly moves those who come across them to curiosity if not to reverence."

He believed that at the dawn of the twentieth century

"we are beginning to understand the extraordinary loyalty of these recusants, so faithful to the sovereign who persecuted them just because they were so true to the religion of their fathers."

The son of an Anglican clergyman, and himself ordained for the Anglican ministry, Dom Bede was not only a Catholic but also a priest and Benedictine monk. In 1903 he had met Marie-Adele Garnier, the foundress of the Tyburn Convent, a meeting which would profoundly affect the course of his life. Dom Bede loved the martyrs of England and Wales and he venerated the foundress of Tyburn, so he gave himself tirelessly to the task of telling the story of the martyrs and to developing the shrine at Tyburn. He gave retreats to the sisters, preached at many celebrations in honour of the martyrs or the conversion of England and Wales, and he worked tirelessly to raise funds to establish Tyburn and to help the emerging community of monks on Caldey Island (see also chapter 3).

In 1913 he transferred his membership of the community at Maredsous in Belgium to the English Benedictine community at Downside. In 1993 another monk of Downside, Dom Aidan Bellenger, published a memoir commemorating Dom Bede's work.

Dom Bede was born at Sunbury Park in Middlesex. His father had served in the Twelfth Lancers and he had been educated at Westminster School and Keble College, Oxford. He became a Catholic in 1890 and became well known as an exponent of the cause of the English martyrs. His early books included *A Benedictine Martyr in England, In the Brave Days of Old* and *Blessed Sebastian Newdigate.* They were followed by his two-volume *Lives of the English Martyrs Declared Blessed By Pope Leo XIII in 1886 and 1895* and *A Birthday Book of the English Martyrs. Forgotten Shrines* was perhaps his most memorable and accomplished piece of writing, recording as it does the mystery and romance which so moved him to "curiosity and reverence". He described his book as "an attempt to satisfy such legitimate curiosity".

Dom Aidan says that Dom Bede may have drawn on the writings of Fletcher Moss, whose *Pilgrimage to Old Houses* appeared, privately printed, between 1903 and 1906. He was also influenced by Dom Odo Blundell, a Benedictine monk at Fort Augustus Abbey who wrote *Ancient Catholic Homes of Scotland* (1907) and *The Catholic Highlands of Scotland* (1907). *Forgotten Shrines* ushered in a new perspective on English Catholicism which clearly influenced Robert Benson's *Come Rack, Come Rope* (1912). It would later affect Evelyn Waugh as he painted his picture of "great-families" Catholicism in *Brideshead Revisited* (1945).

Dom Aidan says that "making the martyrs known was at the centre of Camm's apostolate."

The monk was instrumental in obtaining many relics, reliquaries, the stained glass windows and embellishments for the martyrs' altar in the Shrine of the Martyrs. In his diary he recorded, on 26 June 1912: "I have a brilliant idea for decorating the Oratory of the Martyrs at Tyburn. The new altar will be put within a model of the Tyburn tree, which will form a sort of baldacchino for it. I sketched out my idea and took it to Dom Sebastian, who is very pleased with it and will work it out." This is the altar which stands at Tyburn today.

Dom Bede was able to use a legacy from his father to build the novitiate at St Benedict's Priory, Royston. He celebrated the funeral Mass and burial of Marie-Adele Garnier at Royston in 1924, and twice gave the annual Tyburn retreat as well as writing numerous accounts of the life of the convent's foundress and the martyrs whose lives are commemorated there. He later published a sequel to *Forgotten Shrines* entitled *Pilgrim Paths in Latin Lands* (1923) and *Nine Martyr Monks: The Lives of the English Benedictine Martyrs Beatified in 1929* (published 1931). Undoubtedly the beatification of a further eighty-five martyrs in 1987 owes much to the work which he undertook.

In *Forgotten Shrines*, Dom Bede takes us to the homes of some of the great families of England; but first and foremost these were Catholic families. He recounts their deeds and the terrible toll which they paid.

Padley, Derbyshire

His pilgrimage begins with the Fitzherberts of Norbury Hall, in Derbyshire. Then he introduces us to the martyrs of Padley, at the other end of the county. Here, he says,

> the secluded parish of Hathersgate has ever been a stronghold of the faith, and there has never been a time when the holy Mass has not been said in some secret corner of the district. To the little flock, hidden away in the heart of the Peak District, Padley Chapel has always been a sacred shrine, and of late years it has become the goal of an annual pilgrimage under the auspices of the Guild of Our Lady of Ransom.

Among the martyrs of Padley was the Venerable Nicholas Garlick, who in 1588, was caught celebrating Mass in Padley Chapel. He was hanged, drawn and quartered, with two other priests, at Derby and interred at Tideswell.

Warblington Castle

Dom Bede then takes us to the border of Hampshire and Sussex and to the ruins of Warblington Castle. This was the favourite home of Blessed Margaret Pole. She was the last surviving member of the royal house of Plantagenet, the niece of Edward IV. Having supported Catherine of Aragon against her husband, Henry VIII, she became protector of Princess Mary. She was also mother of Reginald Cardinal Pole, who in his book, *De Unitate Ecclesiae*, had vigorously denounced the king's iniquities. The Cardinal opted for a life of exile but Henry exacted a terrible price on the Pole family. Lord Montague, the Cardinal's brother, was executed. His little nephew was thrown into the Tower. In 1539 Cardinal Pole's mother was also sent to the Tower and two years later she was executed at East Smithfield Green in the precincts of the Tower. Her last words were, "Blessed are they who suffer persecution for justice' sake." Warblington remained for many years afterwards a constant place of hospice, known as the common refuge, open to priests and to persecuted Catholics from all walks of life. Reginald Pole survived and may be remembered as the last Catholic Archbishop of Canterbury.

Stonor

Next, Dom Bede takes us to Stonor Park, the seat of Lord Camoys. Situated five miles north of Henley-on-Thames, in Oxfordshire, Stonor holds a unique place in the collective memory of English Catholics, and the collection housed under its roof still makes it a destination which will both captivate and inspire.

Stonor was home to the printing presses, hidden under the gables, which St Edmund Campion relied upon to disseminate his tracts in defence of faith.

Stonor's little church of the Most Holy Trinity, the secret hiding places, the privations and sufferings of the Stonor family, are all a moving experience for the modern pilgrim whose faith often inspires indifference in others rather than open hostility.

Markenfield

Returning north, Dom Bede bids us to Markenfield Hall, three miles away from St Wilfrid's city of Ripon. Here the faithful planned their desperate rebellion beneath the banner of the Five Wounds of Christ and rode out "for God, Our Lady and the Catholic Faith". Wordsworth captures the moment in *The White Doe of Rylstone*:

> *It was the time when England's queen*
> *Twelve years had reigned, a sovereign dread;*
> *Nor yet the restless crown had been*
> *Disturbed upon her virgin head;*
> *But now the inly-working North*
> *Was ripe to send its thousands forth,*
> *A potent vassalage, to fight*
> *In Percy's and in Neville's right,*
> *Two earls fast leagued in discontent,*
> *Who gave their wishes open vent;*
> *And boldly urged a general plea,*
> *The rites of ancient piety*
> *To be triumphantly restored,*
> *By the stern justice of the sword!*

The rebellion was ruthlessly crushed. Sir George Bowes, the Provost-Marshall, wrote that in Richmondshire, Allertonshire, Cleveland, Ripon and Weatherby, "there is of them executed six hundred and odd".

Ripley Castle and York

From Markenfield Hall, Dom Bede takes us to Ripley Castle, four miles from Knaresborough and Harrogate. Here he recounts the story of the Ingleby family. Five miles away from Fountains Abbey (the Cistercian house of Our Lady of the Fountains (see chapter 3), this family seat retains many of the monastery's illuminated books and manuscripts. Then a devout Catholic family, the Inglebys produced a martyr, Francis Ingleby, who was born here in 1557. In 1582, he joined the English seminary which had been established at Rheims. Two years later he returned to Yorkshire as a priest Among his great supporters and friends was Margaret Clitherow (see chapter 15), who sheltered him in her own house at the Shambles, in York. In 1586 York's sheriffs searched her house and she was arrested . She was executed by being pressed to death in the Tollbooth on Ousebridge.

She was stripped, laid on the ground and her hands tied – outstretched in the form of a cross – to two stakes. A door was laid on her and stones heaped on to a weight of six hundredweight. As she died she was heard to say: "Jesu, Jesu, help me. Blessed Jesu, I suffer this for thy sake." A relic from her body is venerated at St Mary's Convent in York.

On 3 June Francis Ingleby followed Margaret Clitherow to his death. He was executed at York's Tyburn, Knavesmire; this was about a mile and a half beyond Micklegate Bar, on the London road, near the York race course. Margaret Clitherow had come here on secret pilgrimages, some at midnight and made barefoot from her home, praying that like those already executed for their faith, she too would gain a martyr's crown.

As Francis Ingleby was taken to his death a young man, Robert Bickerdyke, was walking nearby; when he heard Ingleby described as a traitor he said, "No, no thief, but as true as thou art." For this, Bickerdyke, who was born at Low Hall, near Scotton, also paid with his life.

Oxford

Dom Bede's epic pilgrimage then moves on to Oxford, where he reminds us of the three Anglican bishops – Latimer, Cranmer and Ridley – who were executed by Queen Mary. Here he traces the ancient Manor of Holywell, where Oxford recusants secretly heard Mass. The Manor took its name from a well which was dedicated to St Winifrid and St Margaret and which drew many pilgrims. They continued to come secretly under the favour of the

Napier family who owned the manor, and this family would in due course, give a son, George Napier, as a martyr for the faith.

Brindle and Hoghton Tower

In Lancashire, Dom Bede's quest for the forgotten shrines takes him to the triangle formed by Blackburn, Chorley and Preston, commencing at Brindle and Hoghton Tower (see chapter 15). He takes us to Winnick, where St Edmund Arrowsmith, the Jesuit martyr, was born; and to Gregson Lane, in Brindle, where tradition has it that Fr Arrowsmith said his last Mass. At the turn of the last century, the then occupant of the house, a Mr Walmesley, claimed that a cross of light appeared at intervals on the wall of the room where that last Mass was said. In 1628, at the age of forty-three, Edmund Arrowsmith was apprehended and was executed at Lancaster.

Mawdsley

Elsewhere in Lancashire, Dom Bede is keen that we visit the village of Mawdsley "at the very heart of that blessed land where the faith still flourishes". Here is Harrock Hall, birthplace of St John Rigby, celebrated for his youthful courage and purity. John Rigby's feast day is celebrated on 26 June.

Nearby was Lane End House, home to the family which produced John Finch, a young layman executed at Lancaster in 1584. Through marriage they were connected with the Haydocks of Cottam Hall (who also produced a martyr, George Haydock, executed at Tyburn in 1583).

Mawdsley is the birthplace of James Mawdsley, the young Catholic layman sentenced in 1999 to seventeen years' imprisonment in Burma for protesting against the atrocities committed by the Burmese military regime. His is a modern form of witness. Appropriately enough, a vigil marking his imprisonment was held in Westminster Cathedral's Chapel of the Martyrs, where Lancashire's St John Southworth is buried. James Mawdsley was released in the autumn of 2000, having served fourteen months in solitary confinement.

Wardley Hall

Dom Bede now travels to the Salford diocese and to Wardley Hall, home today to the Bishop of Salford. Situated in Worsley, about six miles from Manchester, the hall is known as Skull House after the skull enshrined on the staircase wall. The skull is that of the Manchester Benedictine martyr, St Ambrose Barlow, who was brought up at Barlow Hall, near Didsbury. It was brought to Wardley Hall after the priest's execution at Lancaster in 1641. His head had been impaled on a spike outside what is now Manchester Cathedral.

Harvington Hall

Heading south, the meticulous Benedictine takes his readers to Worcestershire's Harvington Hall, home to the leading Catholic recusant family, the Throckmortons (also of Coughton Court, Warwickshire). In the churchyard stands a cross commemorating the Franciscan martyr, St John Wall (executed at Worcester in 1679), "who, obeying God, rather than man, for twelve years ministered the sacraments to the faithful in this and other parts of Worcestershire in daily peril of death". During penal times, Harvington, Chaddesley Corbett, Purshall Hall, Badgecourt and Rushock (where Fr Wall was captured) were the centres of Catholicism in north Worcestershire. For more than two hundred years the upper room at Purshall Hall, where Mass was secretly said, was kept sacred by successive occupants:

When a man pent up his brother men,
Like brutes within an iron den,
Proud of Persecution's rage,
Their belief with blood have sealed.

A copy of Fr Wall's last speech, given at Red Hill, overlooking Worcester, is held at the library of the Catholic Seminary of St Mary's College, Oscott, near Birmingham. It concludes with the words: "I beseech God to bless all that suffer under the Persecution and to turn our captivity into Joy: that they that sow in tears may reap in Joy."

To enable an exhibition of photographs depicting the story of Harvington to be staged in 2000, a grant was awarded by the Heritage Lottery Fund. The photographs, taken by pioneer photographers Benjamin Stone and Thomas Lewis between 1896 and 1910, were used by Dom Bede Camm in *Forgotten Shrines*.

Those photographs and Dom Bede's account stimulated significant interest in Harvington. After World War I, following a period of decline and neglect, when the house was put up for auction the property was acquired and given to the archdiocese of Birmingham. They restored it and have cared for it ever since. Some of the walls still have their original Elizabethan wall paintings and the hall contains the finest series of priest-holes anywhere in the country. Some of them are almost certainly the work of the great Jesuit brother, St Nicholas Owen (alias Little John), who was finally captured at Hindlip House, near Worcester in 1606 and taken to the Tower (see chapter 12).

In 1743 the Throckmortons built a Georgian chapel which has been restored with an eighteenth-century altar, rails, and organ. It is decorated with red and white drops for the blood and water of the Passion of Christ.

Throughout the Reformation many religious paintings

were whitewashed. In 1936, those at Harvington were discovered and revealed. The modern pilgrim can visit and spend time here. Harvington Hall is open on several days each week from 11.30 am until 5.00 pm. Further details appear in the Appendix.

Pembridge Castle

In Herefordshire, we are taken to Pembridge Castle and to the one-time home of the Herefordshire martyr, Fr John Kemble. His dismembered body lies in the churchyard at Welsh Newton, about three miles away (where an annual pilgrimage took place and at which Dom Bede preached in 1909).

Fr Kemble was born in 1599 at Rhydyar Farm, in the parish of St Weonard's, and was ordained a priest in 1625. The shires of Hereford and Monmouth had clung tenaciously to their Catholic faith and significant nobles, such as the Marquis of Worcester at Raglan Castle, and most of the land-owning gentry – such as the Vaughans, Blounts, Wigmores, Pritchards, Bodenhams, Moningtons and Berringtons – gave shelter and succour to clandestine priests.

In 1610 John Kemble's friend and Spiritual father, Roger Cadwallader, was martyred at Leominster, when John was just eleven. On returning to Pembridge, where he lived with his nephew, he must have had a clear understanding of the dangers which would lie in store for him.

When Dom Bede visited the Castle it had been converted into a farmer's home but he said that "the pilgrim was kindly welcomed... though they do not share his faith, are proud of Father Kemble and anxious to tell all they know of him".

An old seat, known as "Fr Kemble's seat", was the usual resting place of this elderly priest, who was seventy-nine when he was arrested and dragged off to prison. At the top of the house is the old chapel, and the altar which was used here is today preserved at the Catholic church at Monmouth.

Several Jesuits – including the martyr St David Lewis SJ – stayed nearby at Raglan Castle, where they founded a school. Raglan was the last castle to hold out for Charles I and when it fell some forty priests were found within its walls.

In 1678 Father Kemble was arrested. In April of the following year, the House of Lords ordered that he be brought to London. He suffered terribly during this period before being sent back to Hereford. Here, he was sentenced to a barbaric death, and was strapped to a hurdle and dragged out to the public race course called Wigmarsh, or Widemarsh Common, just outside the city. The old man's last utterance was: "I die only for professing the old Roman Catholic religion which was the religion that first made this kingdom Christian; and whoever intends to be saved must die in that religion… I do heartily forgive all those that have been instrumental in my death."

To the hangman he said this: "Honest Anthony, my friend Anthony, be not afraid; do thy office; I forgive thee with all my heart. Thou wilt do me a greater kindness than discourtesy." His last words were those of Jesus: "*In manus tuas, Domine, commendo spiritum meum.*"

Baddesley Clinton

In Warwickshire, Baddesley Clinton, the home of the Ferrers family, is another house of chapels and hiding places. The tenacious struggle of a clandestine faith is summed up in the legend inscribed over the door: "*Transit gloria mundi: fides Catholica manet*". The diary of Henry Ferrers (1533–49) is preserved in the Bodleian and it provides minute detail of the life of a typical Catholic country squire during the bleak days of persecution. A modern pilgrim enjoying the tranquillity of this idyllic setting should perhaps remember the subterranean passage under the moat in which six Jesuits, including John Southwell and John Gerard (virtually the whole of the young Jesuit community in England), hid for three days, knee-deep in water. This was an event of very great significance for English Catholicism. Had these men been caught at what had become the Jesuit headquarters, some historians, including Professor Scarisbrick, believe that the Jesuit general would probably have withdrawn the Society from this country. The abandonment of the English mission would have had incalculable consequences.

Washingley Hall

In Huntingdonshire another Jesuit, St Edmund Campion, stayed at Washingley Hall. This was also the birthplace of the martyr Robert Price, who was a layman. He was imprisoned at Ely for being a recusant, and his sons were also gaoled for helping three priests to make good their escape from Wisbech Prison (two of them, Robert Nutter and Thomas Hunt, would be martyred in due course). In 1644 he was executed at Lincoln. Washingley Hall is situated six miles from Oundle, where St Wilfred died, and thirteen miles from Kimbolton Castle. Dom Bede recorded that each year at the beginning of the twentieth century, during the month of May, a small group of pilgrims made an annual pilgrimage to Washingley.

East Hendred

In Berkshire, Dom Bede visited the chapel of St Amand and St John the Baptist at East Hendred. The chapel stands in the Manor of Arches and the sanctuary lamp burnt there for more than six hundred years. The house was first occupied by the Turbervilles, then by the Arches and then by the Eystons. In the stained glass window in the north lancet appears the monogram HF, and the crozier of Hugh Cook (or Farringdon) last Abbot of Reading, martyred by Henry VIII. The abbey had a grange, or monastic cell, in the village.

The Eystons are descended from Thomas More and own the famous Holbein portrait of More. They also have his drinking cup and the stick on which St John Fisher, Cardinal Bishop of Rochester, leaned as he made his way to the Tower, just two weeks before More (see chapter 12).

From Berkshire, Dom Bede's search for our recusant past took him north to Yorkshire: first to Doncaster and then to the moors.

Burghwallis Hall

Burghwallis Hall, near Doncaster, the Yorkshire home of the Annes, is where John Anne (also called Amyas) is remembered. Born at nearby Frickley Hall (now disappeared) he was executed at York on 15 March 1588. The family were leading recusants and the missals, breviaries, portraits and books of leading Catholics, as well as secret hiding places, bear testimony to its role in servicing the faithful who lived in these parts.

Kirkdale House

Next Dom Bede traces the story of Nicholas Postgate, martyred at York at the age of eighty-two; and this will bring us to the end of this pilgrimage of recusant sites.

Fr Postgate was born at Kirkdale House in Egton, near Whitby. Many Catholics lived in these inaccessible parts of Yorkshire. In 1604 Egton parish recorded the presence of more than sixty known recusants. After secret ordination

Fr Postgate returned to his native county and made his first home at Saxton, near Tadcaster, with the Hungate family. He then served as chaplain at Burton Constable, Kilvington Castle and Hall (near Thirsk), and later lived among the poor in a thatched cottage at Ugthorpe, in the middle of a wild moor known as Cleveland Blackamoor. In his poem, "England's Reformation", Thomas Ward wrote that Fr Postgate was:

> *A reverend priest, devout and good,*
> *Whose spotless life, in length was spun,*
> *To eighty years and three times one.*
> *Sweet his behavior, grave his speech,*
> *He did by good example teach…*
> *His sanctity to that degree,*
> *As angels live, so liveth he.*

In 1678 he was arrested at a house in Littlebeck, near Whitby, while he was baptising a baby. At the Lenten Assizes in York in March 1679 Fr Postgate denied any involvement in the fictitious plot of Titus Oates (the aftermath of which had led to anti-Catholic agitation and a new wave of persecution). He was found guilty of his priesthood and was sentenced to death. In his dying speech he said: "I die in the Catholic religion, out of which there is no salvation… I die not for the plot, but for my religion… I forgive all who have wronged me, and brought me to this death, and I desire forgiveness of all people." Fr Postgate's body was quartered by his executioners. His hands are each preserved as relics at Ampleforth Abbey, near York, and at St Cuthbert's, Old Elvet, Durham. At St Mary's Convent, York, they preserve a piece of the rope from which he was hanged. His memory is treasured by the people of Yorkshire and is still fresh among his own people in the moorland parishes of Egton Bridge and Ugthorpe.

Dom Bede Camm's work in undertaking his pilgrimage of love has ensured that this generation has a meticulous record, scrupulously documented and authenticated, an excellent basis on which to begin a pilgrimage to the recusant sites. In choosing the name Bede as the name of his religious profession, Fr Camm's Edwardian testament makes him a worthy successor of a much earlier Benedictine monk to whom we are also indebted for shedding light on pages of history which would otherwise have remained forever closed.

A meditation

A hymn attributed to Fr Nicholas Postgate, Yorkshire martyr

> *O gracious God, O Saviour sweet,*
> *O Jesus, think of me;*
> *And suffer me to kiss Thy feet*
> *Though late I come to Thee.*

> *Behold, dear Lord, I come to Thee*
> *With sorrow and with shame*
> *For when Thy bitter Wounds I see,*
> *I know I caused the same.*

> *O sweetest Lord, lend me the wings*
> *Of faith and perfect love,*
> *That I may fly from earthly things*
> *And mount to those above.*

> *For there is joy both true and fast,*
> *And no cause to lament,*
> *But here is toil both first and last,*
> *And cause oft to repent.*

> *But now my soul doth hate the things*
> *In which she took delight,*
> *And unto Thee, the King of Kings,*
> *Would fly with all her might.*

> *But oh, the weight of flesh and blood*
> *Doth sore my soul detain;*
> *Unless Thy grace doth work, O God!*
> *I rise but fall again.*

And thus, dear Lord, I fly about
In weak and weary case,
And like the dove that Noah sent
I find no resting place.

My wearied wings, sweet Jesus, mark,
And when Thou thinkest best,
Stretch forth Thy hand out of the ark,
And take me to Thy rest!

Lancashire
and Liverpool

15

Lancashire
and Liverpool

NOWHERE in England can lay greater claim to be Catholicism's "sacred heartland" than Lancashire. The seeds of faith were planted fifteen hundred years ago and, despite the attempts to eradicate all trace during penal times, it clung on with extraordinary tenacity. Partly this was due to the county's remote location but it was also to do with the nature of the people and the social structures. They were not people easily swayed by fad or fashion and had a quiet resolution which bred a dogged and even stubborn courage. Later they were bolstered in numbers and resolve by the influx of Irish Catholics fleeing the famine. One of the best accounts of the people of Lancashire and their faith is J.A. Hilton's admirable work, *Catholic Lancashire: From Reformation to Renewal* (Phillimore, 1994).

A survey conducted in 1578 set out to establish how many people were recusants – that is, people found guilty of refusing to attend Church of England services. In Lancashire these numbered 304 with a further 29 attending Anglican services but refusing to participate in Communion. There were many more who secretly held on to the ancient faith. By 1601 the number of known recusants had doubled to 754, and during this period about 56 recusant priests were working in the county. Leading recusant figures such as Lawrence Vaux, Cardinal William Allen and Edmund Campion all had connections with the county.

Lancashire, Shakespeare and Hoghton Tower

Professor Richard Wilson, Professor of Renaissance Studies at Lancaster University, in a memorable address given in May 2000 to the Catholic Writers Guild, pointed to the probable links between Campion, Allen and William Shakespeare, and suggested that the young Shakespeare may even have been contemplating a vocation as an underground priest, living as a "subseminarian" for a time at the heart of recusant Lancashire in Hoghton Tower.

Building on Ernst Honigmann's work, *Shakespeare: The Lost Years* (Manchester University Press, 1985), published ten years ago, and on a theory first proposed in 1937 by Oliver Baker and restated in 1944 by E.K. Chambers, Professor Wilson argues that the long-standing myth that "we know nothing about Shakespeare's upbringing and personal beliefs" has been shattered by the uncovering of substantial new evidence. He argues that Shakespeare grew up in a powerful Catholic counter-culture in Warwickshire's Stratford-upon-Avon, which Antonia Fraser has described as the epicentre of Catholic England: "the town which lay at the centre of the recusant map."

In 1999 I took my children to visit Shakespeare's home and the adjacent exhibition at Stratford, but we could find no reference to the family's faith. There was no reference to the faith of Mary Arden, the poet's mother, whose family remained conspicuously Catholic throughout Elizabeth's reign. Nor was there any reference to John Shakespeare's *Spiritual Testament*, of 1577, presented to Jesuits in Milan by St Carlo Borromeo and discovered in the roof of the house by workmen. This document would not have appeared in the ownership of any casual acquaintance of the Jesuit mission and marks out John Shakespeare as a key player.

John passed on his faith to his son, and evidence shows how his education and formation was entrusted to Lancashire Catholic teachers (four out of his five likely masters in Stratford were linked to the Jesuits), to the Hoghtons (who had provided the funds to establish the illegal seminary at Douai), and to the dazzling Edmund Campion. The Anglican clergyman, Archdeacon Davies, had no doubt of Shakespeare's beliefs, for he wrote: "He dyed a Papyst".

Rather than having a narrowing or stifling influence, it was precisely the effect of Lancashire's great houses – with their links to the Continent and the Catholic world – that stimulated Shakespeare and created the unique environment in which he crafted his work.

Campion's arrest on 16 July 1581 led to his imprisonment in the Tower, where he was racked. The information which his torturers extracted was like a smoking gun which would be held at the heads of the great Lancashire Catholic families – the Hoghtons, the Heskeths and the Derbys – and, indeed, many of their homes were raided and leading figures were arrested . On 3 August, it triggered the hasty writing of a will in which Alexander Hoghton, the owner of Hoghton Tower, devolved his estate and made arrangements for "William Shakeshaft to be taken into the protection of Sir Thomas Hesketh", his neighbour, in Rufford. He was subsequently passed to Lord Strange who brought the player to London in 1590.

Richard Wilson argues that Shakespeare remained a part of the underground recusant Church, secretly believing and secretly practising his faith, and using his verse subtly to challenge the new religious settlement. Here is the hope of a second spring, nostalgia for the Catholic England which has been lost, an embodiment of tragic figures who suffer but do not reveal the secrets of their hearts, and the description of a world of aliases and double identities.

Sonnet 73, he says, is "a sonnet for lost Catholicism":

That time of year thou mayst in me behold
When yellow leaves, or none, or few, do hang
Upon those boughs which shake against the cold,
Bare ruin'd choirs where late the sweet birds sang.

In me thou seest the twilight of such day
As after sunset fadeth in the west,
Which by and by black night doth take away,
Death's second self, that seals up all in rest.
In me thou seest the glowing of such fire
That on the ashes of his youth doth lie...

In *The Winter's Tale*, Wilson points to the statue scene where Hermione steps down from her pedestal and weeps. He asks us to read the Histories in relation to the claims made in *Conference on Succession* (1595), written by Father Robert Parsons, head of the Jesuit mission, advocating the Catholic claims of the House of Lancaster. He cites references to the Catholic belief in purgatory and the last sacraments in *Hamlet* and points us to the plays written at the end of his career, the supernatural and magical plays which seek to restore a lost world, with Prospero, in *The Tempest*, pleading for something like religious toleration.

Unlike virtually all of his contemporaries Shakespeare does not denigrate priests and friars, women in the religious life, or the Church; quite the reverse. In *The Comedy of Errors*, for example, an abbess appears to prevent tragedy and through "her holy prayers" brings resolution and harmony. Conversely, in Falstaff he parodies the new hypocrisies, which quote endlessly from the Bible to support their sins. The Shakespearean texts were, then, recusant themselves, using a secret encoded language of maimed rights and rights suppressed. Richard Wilson says: "It's all there, all the way through" and that the secularisation and metropolitanisation of Shakespeare has been a travesty. In re-reading the texts – Cordelia, for instance, declaring how much she loves the king or John of Gaunt's "sceptred isle" speech – we can see pleas for the right to believe in return for Catholic loyalty to the Crown; and we can read a memorialisation of a lost Catholic England.

Certainly Shakespeare's own contemporaries had no doubt about his faith. In 1611, the historian John Speed linked him with Fr Robert Parsons as "this Papist and his Poet", and he was vilified by Puritans for "prelatical trash".

The present owners of Hoghton Tower, Sir Bernard and Lady Rosanna Hoghton, hope to see their home become a centre of study for the lost legacy of Shakespearean Catholicism and this, linked to the development of the nearby Stonyhurst College with its outstanding collection of Jesuit artefacts and manuscripts from the period, will offer the Catholic pilgrim a deep understanding of their history and heritage.

The clash and the consequences of loyalty forcing the Hoghtons to choose between the Catholic faith and the state, were well summed up in a ballad penned by Thomas Hoghton, entitled "The Blessed Conscience":

At Hoghton hygh, which is a bower
Of sports and lordly pleasure,
I wept, and lefte that loftie tower
Wich was my chiefest treasure.
To save my soul and lose ye reste
Yt was my trew pretence:
Lyke fryghted bird, I lefte my neste
To kepe my conscyence.

At Hoghton where I used to reste
Of men I had great store,
Ful twentie gentlemen att least,
Of yeomen gode three score.
And of them all, I brought but twoe
Wyth mee, when I cam thence.
I left them all, ye world knows how,
To kepe my conscyence.

Fayr England! now ten tymes adieu,
And frendes that theryn dwel;
Fayrwel my broder Richard trewe,
Whom I did love soe wel.
Fayrwel, fayrwel, gode people all,
And learn experience;

271

Love not too much ye golden ball,
But kepe your conscyence.

Underground church of Lancashire

Lancashire produced many of those who put conscience first and provided leadership to the underground church. Within the county many of the Lancashire gentry stayed loyal to the faith, suffering huge personal consequences. One fifth of those who had entered Douai by 1584 came from Lancashire and nine of the twenty-one Catholic school-masters executed by Elizabeth were Lancastrians.

The lists of dissenters also reveal the crucial role played by the county's Catholic women in holding onto their faith – some travelling to the Continent to enter religious houses there (over thirty between 1603 and 1642). The daughter of Robert Dalton, of Aldcliffe, summed up her defiance on a stone carved with the words *"Catholicae Virgines no summus: Mutare vel tempore Spernimus Ano Dni 1674* – We are Catholic virgins who scorn to change with the times."* The stone was later removed to Thurnham Hall.

The Jesuit Order, the Benedictine Order and the seminary priests trained at Douai were the principal influences, with eight Lancastrians joining the Jesuits during Elizabeth's reign alone. By 1642 some forty Lancastrians had joined the Benedictines. Missionary centres were organised by both Orders, and some of the churches in the county still administered by them have their antecedents from this period.

Lancaster

Edward Smith and Anselm Beech were both born near Manchester and after ordination on the continent became

Benedictines. In 1607 they returned to England and sought out Dom Sigebert Buckley, the last remaining member of the old English Benedictine Congregation (he was a monk of Westminster Abbey); they were received by him in his cell, thus ensuring the survival of the historic Congregation. One of the county's most famous martyrs, Ambrose Barlow, was born in Manchester, ordained a Benedictine in 1617, and was arrested on Easter Sunday 1641, while saying Mass. He was hanged at Lancaster on 18 September 1641. Today's pilgrim visiting Lancaster Castle will see the only castle still in use as a working prison but will also see the cells where the Catholic priests were held. They will also find, in towns such as Warrington, parishes still administered by Benedictine priests.

Chaigley

Dom Bede Camm, in *Forgotten Shrines* (see chapter 14), tells many stories of individual acts of heroism and endurance. In one chapter he records " the secret treasure of Chaigley".

Chaigley – or Chadgley – is named for the Mercian missionary saint, St Chad. It is a small village near Stonyhurst College. The Holden family lived here at Chaigley Hall until 1637. The story has it that Cromwell's troops burst into the old chapel of St Chad at Chapel House, Chaigley, and killed the priest who was celebrating Mass, severing his head from his body. The priest's mother took the head in her apron, and throughout the centuries which followed, the family secretly treasured the relic. The family tradition held that the martyred priest was of their family; and, indeed, when Dom Bede came to write his account he recorded that it had been a special blessing on this family that since the penal era there had never been a time when the Holdens had not given a young man to the Church for priestly service.

The Ribble to the Mersey

The pockets of these enduringly faithful people were concentrated in the coastal areas, in the deaneries of Warrington, Leyland and Amounderness, and in pockets in the Ribble Valley and around Blackburn. The Catholic area was described in an old rhyme:

> *When all England is aloft*
> *Where so safe as in Christ's croft?*
> *Where do you think that Christ's croft to be*
> *But between Ribble and Mersey?*

The old Roman road running from Warrington to Wigan, Preston and Lancaster and the track running south from Morecambe Bay at Heysham, through Lancaster and Preston and then south to Ormskirk, Liverpool and Chester, marked the extremities of the enclave.

Furness

Anne Parkinson in her booklet *Catholicism in the Furness Peninsula*, 1127–1997 (Centre for North West Regional Studies, University of Lancaster, 1998) eloquently gives the lie to the misrepresentation that the old faith completely died out north of Lancaster. She points the pilgrim towards the ruins of Furness Abbey (near Barrow) and Cartmel Priory (see chapter 3), to the history of recusancy at Bardsey Hall, Kirkby Hall and Rampside Hall in Yarleside, and the role of Stonyhurst in securing priests for the Manor Mission for Furness (who lodged initially at Titeup Hall) and for the people in Ulverston (where the first church was finally opened in the early nineteenth century).

Homes of the gentry

The Catholic gentry – whose homes often still exist and are open to the public – included John Towneley of Towneley,

Burnley (who spent most of his time in prison from 1568 until his death in 1608), the Blundells of Crosby, the Gerards of Bryn (who held the manors of Aston, Garswood and Windle) and the Shireburns of Stonyhurst. The report of a spy attending the 1629 pilgrimage to St Winifrid's Well (see chapter 5) lists some of the county's most significant names among those who were there. By 1639, of eighty-two Mass centres in the county seventy-five were provided by the gentry, although one quarter were ordinary husbandmen and 62 per cent were women. William Blundell described the new divisions in these words:

The time hath been we had one faith
And strode aright one ancient path.
The time is now that each man may
See new religions coined each day.

They kept up their faith and provided a priest to minister to their tenants. Each year, their children used flowers to decorate the crosses at Ince Blundell and Great Crosby at midsummer, maintaining an ancient and hallowed Catholic custom.

At Speke Hall, in Liverpool, Sir William Norris came to blows with the magistrate in 1631, for putting undue pressure on him to attend a local Anglican service against his will. Today's pilgrim will still see the system of mirrors which the occupants of Speke used as part of an early warning system to see who was calling on them, and the house, which is beautifully cared for by the National Trust, also boasts a priest's hiding hole.

Preston to Wigan

In the urban areas recusants began to make their presence felt by the beginning of the seventeenth century. By 1605 a secret chapel had been established in Chapel Yard off Friargate, Preston, and Wigan soon followed.

A major mission centre was at Birchley Hall, Billinge, near Wigan, where a secret printing press was established by Roger Anderton (cousin to Laurence Anderton, the Jesuit superior).

By the time of the Civil War, in 1642, in the hundreds of Amounderness, Blackburn, Leyland , Salford and West Derby some 11 per cent of a population of about 30,000 were openly refusing to take an oath of loyalty to the Protestant religion, with some pockets of particular opposition: Broughton , 43 per cent; St Michael's,

29 per cent, Woodplumpton, 20 per cent, Chipping, 17 per cent, Brindle, 54 per cent, Mawdsley and Rufford, 67 per cent, Bispham and Croston, 69 per cent and Wigan, 14 per cent. The defeat of Charles I left Lancashire's Catholics open to retaliation by the Puritans, and in 1646 three priests were executed at Lancaster (Edward Bamber of Blackpool, Thomas Whittaker of Burnley, who was arrested at Goosnargh, and John Woodcock, a Franciscan who was born at Clayton-le-Woods, Leyland, and arrested at Bamber Bridge).

Eight years later, John Southworth, of Samlesbury Hall (which remains open to the public), joined the ranks of the Lancashire martyrs when he was executed in London (see chapter 16). His feast day is celebrated on 28 June.

In 1987, Michael Mullett and Leo Warren published their excellent account of the martyrs of the diocese of Lancaster (to coincide with their beatification on the feast of Christ the King). This would be an invaluable guide for anyone wishing to make a pilgrimage in the footsteps of the Lancashire martyrs.

Homes of martyrs

There are still many marker stones to be found recalling this turbulent period of sacrifice and valour.

In 1566, for instance, George Haydock, was born into the family of gentry at Cottam Hall, near Preston. Today, the home is in the present parish of St Andrew's, Cottam (established in 1793). In 1584, aged twenty-eight, George Haydock was executed.

Christopher Robinson was born at Woodside, a few miles south-east of Carlisle, and in the present parish of St Margaret Mary. In 1592 he was ordained to minister in Cumbria. In 1594 he travelled to Durham to witness the martyrdom of John Boste. As he was inspired by Boste's faithfulness and witness, three years later his own execution at Carlisle would inspire many others.

In 1571, Thomas Sprott was born at Skelsmergh, near Kendal, in the present parish of Sts Alice and Robert. Secretly ordained on the Continent, he returned to England. In 1600, he was executed at Lincoln.

Edward Bamber was born around 1600 at "The Moor", Carlton, in the parish of Poulton-le-Fylde, near Blackpool. At sixteen he was ordained in Spain at the Abbey of Santa Maria in Cadiz. In 1646, he was executed at Lancaster, where he threw some coins to the onlookers, declaring that God loved a cheerful giver.

Lancaster ballad

In 1615 a ballad was published and sung to the tune of "Daintie Come Thou to Me". It was the song of four priests who suffered death at Lancaster:

> *In this our English Coast much blood is shed*
> *Two hundred priests almost in our time martered*
> *And manie lay men dye with joyfull sufferance*
> *Manie moe in prison lye Gods cause to advance.*

> *Amongst this gratious troupe that follow Christ*
> *   his traine*
> *To casue the Devill stoupe four preists were latlie slaine*
> *Nutters boulde constancie with his sweet fellow*
> *   Thwinge*

Of whose most meeke modestie Angells and saints
    may singe.

Huntes hawtie corage stout with goldlie zeale soe true
Myld Middleton o what tonge can halfe thy virtue shew
At Lancaster lovingly these marters tooke their end
In glorious victorie true faith for to defende.

And thus hath Lancashyre offered her sacrifice
To daunt theyre lewde desyre and please our
    Saviours eies
For by this meanes I trust shall have victorie
When as that number just of such saints compleat bee.

Whose sacred members rent and quarters set on hye
Caused more to be content in the same cause to dye
Whose lyves whyle they did live whose blessed
    deaths also
Doe admonition give what waie we ouht to goe.

Praise be to Gods good wil whoe doth his truth defende
Lord to thy vineyard still such worthie workmen send
And good lord graunt us grace that we may constant bee
With our crosse in each place to please thy majestie.

Titus Oates and the Jacobites

It was not yet time for Lancashire Catholics to lay down
their cross.

In 1678 further anti-Catholic feeling was whipped up
by the so-called discovery, by Titus Oates, of an anti-
government Catholic plot. Attacks were made on Catholic
centres, such as Fernyhalgh (see chapter 6), but quiet
confidence was leading to the creation of more private
chapels and even small schools. This received a massive jolt
when, in 1688, William of Orange invaded England and
the Jacobite sympathies of Catholics loyal to King James
inevitably once again put them on the receiving end of

repression. Among those who suffered was Charles Townley, a Jacobite colonel who was executed in 1746. The chapel at Liverpool was destroyed, and at Lee House, Chipping, Fr Germanus Helme, a Franciscan, was seized and taken to Lancaster, where he died in the castle, probably becoming the last Catholic recusant to die there.

A rich harvest was ready to be gathered from all this adversity. Within twenty years, the community had made substantial growth, even in the urban areas. The Manchester community, at Rook Street, grew from 300 in 1767 to 4,000 in 1793.

Stonyhurst

Throughout this time, Stonyhurst had been at the centre of resistance. In 1700 Sir Nicholas Shireburn had given £140 to poor Catholics, £100 to defray debts of the Lancashire Jesuits, £100 to a Franciscan house at Douay, £23 towards vestments and altar hangings, a guinea towards the release from prison of a convert, a guinea to a poor travelling priest and a guinea for a Requiem Mass of a servant.

In 1794 the Weld family gave Stonyhurst to the Jesuits and it became the corner-stone of the Society's central educational role in preparing young Catholics to play their part in secular society, becoming "men and women for others". The buildings are open to visitors during the summer months and plans are in hand for the creation of a cultural centre, which will be a huge asset for the Catholic pilgrim in Lancashire. The story of Stonyhurst is best told by T.E. Muir in *Stonyhurst College (1593–1993)*, published in 1992 by the College.

Stonyhurst was where Hopkins wrote some of his poems; it was where Arthur Conan Doyle was educated; and it was where J.R.R. Tolkien's son taught after entering the Jesuit Order. His father stayed at the College from time to time and perhaps drew some inspiration from Ribble Valley's outstanding countryside. Are there not echoes here of Rivendell in Ribblesdale; and across the two rivers, a shimmering of Mordor's looming darkness on the heights of Pendle Hill; in the remnant of hobbits, something of the remnant of recusant people who lived on in these parts; and in the people of the Shire some of the characteristics of Stonyhurst's Shireburn family? Walk down Shire Lane in Stonyhurst's village of Hurst Green and you come to something very like the Hobbit hole.

Stonyhurst to Mitton and Whalley

From Stonyhurst many of the places mentioned in this and other chapters are within easy striking distance. *Where Shall we Go in Ribble Valley?* by Edward Popham, was published in 1993 by the Salford Diocese Catholic Truth Society, and sets out some of the key sites of Catholic interest. A logical route might take the pilgrim first, from Stonyhurst, across the River Hodder, passing the old bridge used by Oliver Cromwell on his visit to Stonyhurst Hall in 1648. Then, on to Mitton Church, built by Sir Richard Shireburn, and where his family are buried. From Mitton it is a short journey into Whalley where there are the remains of a Cistercian abbey. The monks arrived in about 1330 having previously erected the smaller abbey of Sawley, eight miles to the east. The last abbot, Abbot Paslew, was hanged outside the monastery gates in March 1537, having been charged with high treason for refusing to recognise the claims of Henry VIII to be accepted as head of the Church of England.

Whalley was also the birthplace of the martyr John Thules. Baptised in the parish church just over thirty years after the suppression of the abbey, John was just fifteen when he followed his older brother, Christopher, to Rheims, to become a priest. Ordained at twenty-four, he immediately headed home to the English mission field. He was arrested in 1615 with Roger Wrenno, a weaver from Chorley, who was sheltering him. They were both executed the following year at Lancaster. Fr Thules' quarters were put on public display in Wigan, Warrington, Lancaster and (on the church steeple) at Preston, as a dire warning to others.

Stonyhurst to Dutton and Knowle Green

Seven miles east of Clitheroe and two miles west of Longridge is the hamlet of Knowle Green. It includes parts of the civil parishes of Dutton, Dilworth and Ribchester (see below). Two Roman roads weaved their way north through this little hamlet. In the millennium year, Mavis Earnshaw published a short appraisal of Knowle Green's history, *Knowle Green Through 2000 Years*.

Local families, such as the Seeds, the Towneleys, the Crumbleholmes and the Cottams, refused to give up their Catholic faith and suffered accordingly.

Thomas Cottam was born in 1549, son of Lawrence and Ann Cottam, of Knowle Green. Graduating from Oxford in 1568 he taught in London before studying theology at Douay. A Jesuit priest, he returned to England and, in 1582, for refusing to confess his sins "for his priestly character" was dragged on a hurdle from Newgate to Tyburn where he was hanged, drawn and quartered. He was thirty-three years of age.

The Cottams had homes on the old Clitheroe Road (the High House), and in Knowle Green (Cottam Hall). Cottam House Farm is also visible on the current Ordnance Survey map.

Another priest, William Crumbleholme, was arrested as a Papist in 1584. His family home, Huntingdon Hall, which was rebuilt in 1619 and which has recently been renovated, is situated in Huntingdon Hall Lane. There are conflicting reports of his life but, like Thomas Cottam, he appears to have spent a spell in the Tower of London (see chapter 12).

The parish church of St Wilfred, in Ribchester, has records from 1598. Among the early entries are the christening, on 25 February 1602, of Richard Cottam, son of another Thomas Cottam, of the High House; in 1611, the marriage of John Cottam and Grace Byrley; and, in 1602, the burial of the wife of Henry Towneley of Dutton Hall. The Towneleys, like the Stonyhurst Shireburnes (a branch of which lived in Knowle Green at Buckley Hall) were leading Lancashire recusant families, who paid heavy fines and risked imprisonment for their refusal to comply. However, as becomes evident from further examination of the arrangements at the parish church of St Wilfred at Ribchester, the Reformation line was capable of being blurred and even ignored in the more remote parts of the country.

Stonyhurst to Ribchester and Stydd

To the west of Stonyhurst, and two miles to the south of Knowle Green, lies the small town of Ribchester, once a Roman garrison. St Wilfred's Church lies by the River Ribble in Ribchester. Crosses in the graveyard show evidence of Christian worship here in Saxon times. The Norman arch in the north wall dates from 1193, the chancel from 1220. The building suffered at the hands of the Cromwellian Puritans in the seventeenth century. Next to the church is a small museum tracing the town's origins as the meeting place of the northern roads from Manchester, Lancaster and Carlisle.

To the east of the town is the tiny settlement of Stydd. Here, cheek by jowl, are the 200-year-old Catholic church and the ancient chapel of St Saviour's, Stydd. The church of St Peter and St Paul was constructed during penal times and designed to appear inconspicuous. The mandatory eighteenth-century simplicity has a particular appeal in our over-embellished age. St Saviour's is equally simple and is reputed to be the oldest ecclesiastical building in Lancashire, having been built in the reign of King Stephen.

Stydd was originally the setting of a small priory of the Knights Hospitallers of St John, where shelter was given to pilgrims. On the chapel wall is a small reminder of this period, a commemoration of the work of the St John Ambulance Brigade.

Since Queen Elizabeth I prohibited its use by Catholics, the chapel has been administered by the Anglican authorities in Ribchester, who occasionally hold ecumenical services there. The present rector, the Rev John Francis, told me that he had guessed that there must have been a holy well nearby and after consulting local farmers duly uncovered a well which was identified by another farmer as St John's Well.

Father Francis has two interesting stories to tell about the chapel.

After Margaret Clitherow was crushed to death in York for harbouring a Catholic priest (1586), her body was thrown on a dung heap. When it was recovered six weeks later it was still incorrupt. Her right hand was removed and is preserved at the Bar Convent in York (see chapter 14). It was assumed that her body was buried in the grounds of the home of a sympathetic Catholic, who later conformed and wanted the body removed. Parish records list a mysterious internment at around this time. Two hundred years later it is where a Jesuit, Sir Walter Vavasour, who died in 1740, chose to be buried; and, even more extraordinarily, it is where Bishop Petre, the Pope's Vicar Apostolic to England in the eighteenth century, is also buried. They clearly believed this to be greatly hallowed ground.

Bishop Petre's tomb in Stydd chapel bears the inscription: "Here lies the most illustrious and Reverend Lord Francis Petre – he died in the Lord on December

24th of the year 1817, at his age the 84th. May he rest in peace."

An ecumenical carol service is held by candlelight at Christmas time, and on the last Sunday of the month, throughout the summer, evensong is held at 6.30 pm.

Stonyhurst to Towneley Hall

To the south-west of Stonyhurst, in Burnley, is the home of the Towneley family. There were once some eight priests' hiding holes in Towneley Hall; two remain open to public view. The Hall was an important secret Mass centre and was used to shelter priests, especially those travelling between Lancashire and Yorkshire. The secret altar, disguised to appear like part of the furniture, is now at Ladyewell House, Fernyhalgh, but many of the original artefacts may still be viewed. The official guided tour takes about ninety minutes.

Robert Nutter was born in Burnley around 1557, and was the younger brother of the martyred priest, Blessed John Nutter, who died in 1584. Educated at Blackburn Grammar School, he was ordained in 1581. Captured in 1584, he was tortured in the Tower and banished. He risked all and returned to the missions, was duly arrested, and in 1600 he was executed with Edward Thwing, a priest born at Heyworth, near York.

Stonyhurst to Dunsop Bridge, Chaigley, Chipping and the Hill Chapel

Travelling north from Stonyhurst towards the Trough of Bowland takes the pilgrim into remote recusant country. At Dunsop Bridge is the church of St Hubert, built by Burnley's Towneley family in 1864 (when their racehorse, Kettledrum, won the Derby and they used some of the winnings for the building costs). The water stoop came from the abandoned pre-reformation church at Burrholme, near Whitewell. On the road back from Dunsop Bridge, the pilgrim can visit Chaigley (see above) and the Vale of Chipping.

To the north of the village of Chipping is Leagram Hall, which was a remote bastion of recusancy owned by the Welds. The local martyr, William Marsden, came from nearby. During a visitation by Bishop Matthew Gibson in 1784, 42 were Confirmed and 120 received Holy Communion.

In 1828 the last resident priest moved to the new church in Chipping, where the side chapel was built for the private use of the Weld family.

On the road from Chipping to Longridge the pilgrim should look for Lee House and Hill Chapel. Lee House is the oldest established parish in Salford Diocese, founded in 1738. Mass had been celebrated for many years before that in the adjacent farmhouse. A local yeoman farmer, Thomas Eccles, gave the land to the Franciscans.

The first priest, Fr Germain Helmes, was arrested at Hill Chapel, near Goosnargh, after the Jacobite rebellion in 1745 (see above).

After the Reformation, Mass was secretly celebrated in local homes, most notably those of the Keighleys of Whitelea and the Threlfalls of the Ashes, near Whitechapel. Gradually the celebration of Mass was tolerated and in 1671 the chapel at White Hill was established by the Franciscans and dedicated to St Francis of Assisi. The first church was destroyed and a second one was built in 1715. It was at this time that Fr Helmes was thrown into Lancaster Gaol, where he died in 1746. His subsequent "appearances" at Hill Chapel are part of the parish legend.

In about 1755 the present Hill Chapel was built at the end of the house which is now the presbytery. The house was privately owned by the Blackburne family. Baptismal registers began in 1770 and the chapel was extended in 1802.

In 1834 the Franciscans passed the care of the parish to the Benedictines, and they remained until 1983 when the Lancaster Diocese began to provide secular priests for the parish. The parish tercentenary in 1987 included visits from Lancaster's Bishop John Brewer and Cardinal Basil Hume.

This was also the year in which Blessed George Beesley was beatified. Born in what is now the presbytery at Hill Chapel, he was ordained on the Continent and was executed on 2 July 1591 at Tyburn after working secretly as a priest for three years. The Beesley inscription is one of seventeen which may be seen on the wall of the Martin Tower at the Tower of London. Carved in Latin, alongside the cross-keys and under a cross and chalice, appear the words from Psalm 41: "As the hart longs for flowing streams, so longs my soul for thee, O God."

Fr Patrick McMahon, the parish priest at the Hill Chapel, tells me that the inscription is also to be seen in their garden and that there is a glass panel in Beesley's memory in the church. The garden also contains a unique sculpture depicting the life of Christ which was commissioned to mark the new millennium, and which was unveiled on 1 January.

The Hill Chapel may be reached by car from exit 31 on the M6 motorway and is situated just five miles away from the roundabout at Broughton.

Stonyhurst to Blackburn and Pleasington

On another journey from Stonyhurst into Catholic Lancashire, the pilgrim can head south to Blackburn. The town's cathedral stands on the site of the former mediæval Catholic church. On the Preston New Road is a Carmelite convent – with a shrine to the Virgin – and on the road to Pleasington is Hoghton Tower (see above). At Pleasington the pilgrim may visit Pleasington Priory and the ruins of

Pleasington Old Hall, which was a Mass centre in penal times. Nearby is the village of Tockholes, where the graveyard boasts a former Saxon preaching cross, from which the Gospel was proclaimed in Lancashire in 687. Off the road towards Belmont and Bolton there is a rough track which leads to St Leonard's Well, formerly known as Ladywell.

Stonyhurst to Salmesbury and Fernyhalgh

The last of these six suggested forays will take the pilgrim south-west from Stonyhurst towards Preston. In addition to the already mentioned Mass centres which were secretly used by local Catholics, others operated at Chaigley, Bailey, Osbaldestone, Hothersall, Salesbury, Showley, Wiswell, Bolton, Clayton, Dunkenhalgh, Samlesbury Upper Hall and Samlesbury Lower Hall. The martyr, John Southworth, was born at Samlesbury (see chapter 16) and over the large fireplace there is a carving of his head. The chapel still exists, and over the priest's room is a hiding hole. The armorial bearings of the Southworths may be seen in the nave of the nearby St Leonard's Church. The Catholic church of St Mary built in 1818 is also in the same vicinity.

A short journey leads to the shrine of Our Lady of Fernyhalgh (see chapter 6). The name is thought to mean "ancient shrine" or "ancient saint" and, like Marsden's Well, near Samlesbury, is thought to have been used for baptisms in Saxon times. Access to Ladyewell is by foot. The well is about half a mile away from Fernyhalgh Church (where, in the sanctuary, Our Lady of Fernyhalgh is depicted holding the Christ Child). Ladyewell House has been developed as a pilgrimage centre, with seats, an outside altar, and Rosary Way. In a modern chapel each of the names of the Catholic martyrs is inscribed on a role call, the names themselves a reminder that the same faith was once held by all the people of these islands. Like the ancient pilgrims who recited the Jesus Psalter and had a great love of the Virgin, today's pilgrims will find peace here.

Liverpool and Irish influences

The ancient faith celebrated at Fernyhalgh refused to die despite the war of attrition that sought to destroy it. Thanks to the heroic labours of the Jesuit priests and the Lancashire faithful (after the restoration of the English Hierarchy, in 1850), the 1851 census showed that Lancashire was still the most Catholic county in England, with 102,812 (42 per cent) of the 241,000 English Catholics living there. By 1910 the Catholic population in Lancashire had increased six-fold, and at the heart of the influx of new Catholics was Liverpool and the Irish immigrant community (although the Irish also settled in many other parts of the county). As the Catholic pilgrim journeys into a city which was forged on the back of the slave trade and populated by the forced exodus from the Irish Famine (see chapter 10), a good starting point in the journey is Liverpool's Maritime Museum, which graphically tells the story of those double tragedies.

St Patrick's, Dingle

Not far away, in the Dingle, is St Patrick's Catholic Church. The Park Lane church was one of the first churches which I visited when I first went to Liverpool as a student in 1969. I had some teaching experience in the parish school, which in those days was housed in a former Victorian warehouse. It was explained to me that the church was one of the very last to be built before the Emancipation of Catholics in 1829 and had, therefore, to be constructed in the form of a tithe barn as pre-Emancipation Catholics were not permitted to erect buildings which looked like churches.

Within twenty years the Catholic population of Liverpool multiplied exponentially as Irish refugees fled the great famine which was gripping Ireland (see chapter 10). Many headed to America via Liverpool, and those unable to get any further remained in the burgeoning sea port. St Patrick's parish could no longer accommodate the numbers and another church was built nearby. St Vincent's was constructed with a spire and with all the Gothic beauty which Pugin, its architect, could muster.

The conditions in which the émigrés were living were indescribably awful. It is little wonder that typhoid and cholera were soon sweeping the overcrowded cellars and courts where the people were sheltering. Ten priests died ministering to the sick and they are buried in St Patrick's Church. The pilgrim visiting the church will see the stone marking their sacrifice with the words "The good shepherd lays down his life for his sheep."

Famine memorial

Before making their way from St Patrick's to St Luke's Gardens in Hardman Street, where, since 1999, there has been a memorial commemorating the famine dead, the pilgrim may care to ponder on these facts:

- In 1847 no fewer that 17,280 mainly Irish people died in Liverpool.
- There were 20,000 street children.
- Dr Duncan, the city's pioneering public health officer, estimated that some 100,000 people were living in abject conditions.
- The workhouse, which stood on the site of today's Catholic Cathedral of Christ the King, was crammed with 3,000 people, and there was room for no more.

- Fever sheds were erected and two ships were moored in the Mersey as lazarettos, that is, hospitals for the diseased poor.

The Metropolitan Cathedral: site of the workhouse

The cathedral's crypt (part of the original design by Lutchens, see chapter 4) and the chapel of St Columba are two appropriate stopping places for today's pilgrim tracing these events. The former takes you to the place of holocaust where so many Irish people died, while the latter is a quiet corner of the 1960s cathedral dedicated to the Irish saint who brought the gift of Christianity back to these isles.

St Mary's parish

The city coroner at the time of the famine recorded that one woman died after eating only one scrap of bread in three days. Sarah Burns died two days before Christmas 1846, after complaining of pains in her head and in her chest.

The coroner wrote of her Liverpool home: "The floor was composed of mud; in that hovel there were seventeen human beings crowded together without even so much as a bit of straw to lie down on."

The first typhus victim in the city's St Mary's parish was twelve-year-old Catherine Joyce. In one week in that parish alone there were 166 burials of Catholics; 105 of them were children.

Typhus was compounded by hunger. In May 1847, eight-year-old Luke Brothers died. His post-mortem report stated that there "was not the least particle of food in his stomach". With thousands dead, the typhus passed, but in 1849 it was followed by cholera.

St John's Gardens

As the authorities largely ignored the tragedy, Canon Major Lestor, Fr James Nugent (whose statue stands in St John's Gardens behind St George's Hall, and after whom Liverpool's Catholic Social Services are named) and, later, the Rathbone family organised basic care. But the record and the memory is mainly one of callous indifference. The modern pilgrim will want to ponder on these events and see them as a backdrop when considering the continued sectarian divisions in Northern Ireland and the response to contemporary appeals to help the starving and destitute.

Jospice and the Lazarus Walk

A worthy heir to the tradition of Fr Nugent is Fr Francis O'Leary, MBE, MA, founder and director of St Joseph's Hospice Association: Jospice International, who died in the autumn of 2000.

Fr O'Leary was a Mill Hill Missionary priest born in the Crosby parish of St Peter and Paul, in whose graveyard he is now buried.

While working on the Indian sub-continent he came across a dying man whom he cradled in his arms while the man died. He vowed to try and ensure more dignity for the dying, and on his return to Britain Fr O'Leary founded Jospice. It now has hospices caring for the dying and sick in Britain and in several other parts of the world, including the Indian sub-continent and Latin America. Jospice has its headquarters and an Academy of Life at Ince Blundell, near Crosby.

Each year the indefatigable Pat Murphy organises a sponsored walk for Jospice, which usually takes place around the second Saturday of May, between Crosby's coastguard station and the northern perimeter of the Port of Liverpool and back again. Pat's mother was one of Fr O'Leary's first hospice patients. She lived for many more years and died on the same day as Fr O'Leary, on 4 October 2000.

I have usually tried to take part in this six-mile trek and my children come along, too. In 2000 we were accompanied by their dog, Isaac. Striking up conversation with one of the other walkers I discovered that Mr Charles Evans had a special reason for walking for Jospice. He described it as his "Lazarus Walk". A year earlier he had been told that he was close to death. He undertook a pilgrimage to Walsingham, and having experienced a restoration to full health he promised that in return he would walk for Jospice. His efforts had generated nearly £3,000 of sponsorship.

Charles Evans' first pilgrimage to Walsingham had been in 1948 as part of the restored national pilgrimage (see chapter 7). He had walked over 200 miles from Liverpool. Just married, he had undertaken that pilgrimage and prayed that his wife would come to share his Catholic faith. He added that his wife and four other members of his family were subsequently received into the Church.

Crosby, with its synthesis of Lancashire recusancy and deep Liverpool Irish tradition, is a good place to end. Fr O'Leary's work at Jospice provides people with what Catholics used to call "a good death". It also illustrates how the baton of faith is passed on from one generation to the next and how the faithful adapt to whatever challenges the world may throw at them. A sponsored pilgrimage or a walk of witness are modern expressions of ancient customs.

A meditation

O English hearts, what heart can know
how spent with labours long ago
was England's church that bore you?
The paths you tread, in lane or street,
long since were trodden by the feet
of saints that went before you.
When priests like sudden angels came
to light in distant shires the flame
that faith's dull embers cherished,
when Mass and shrift were sought for still
in silent farm, on lonely hill,
ere ancient memories perished.

(Monsignor Ronald Knox)

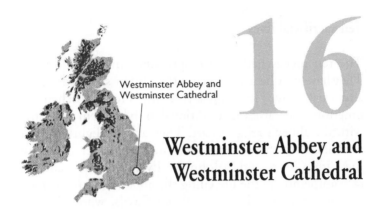

Westminster Abbey and
Westminster Cathedral

Westminster Abbey and Westminster Cathedral

WESTMINSTER Abbey is well known for its association with monarchs, great poets and lofty statesmen. In 1992, the abbey set up an organising committee to examine ways of commemorating the breadth and intensity of Christian sacrifice in the twentieth century. The outcome of their deliberations are the thought-provoking statues which should cause any pilgrim to stop, stand and ponder the lives of ten exceptional Christians.

On arriving at the west front of Westminster Abbey the pilgrim should look for the plinths now occupied by the modern martyrs. They sit in niches below the twin towers, which were a late addition to the abbey church and were designed by Christopher Wren, modified by Nicholas Hawksmoor and completed by his successor as architect, John James.

Dr George Carey, the Archbishop of Canterbury, in the presence of Her Majesty the Queen, and Cardinal Basil Hume, the late Archbishop of Westminster, unveiled statues of these ten modern martyrs. They help today's pilgrim to remember the words of Christ that "people will hate you because of me". More Christians perished in the twentieth century than in all the preceding centuries combined.

Ten sacrificial lives

The ten niches had been empty since the Middle Ages. They have now been conspicuously filled by statues designed and carved by Tim Crawley. Using French Richemont limestone the statues are traditional in style and in sympathy with the abbey's religious art. They appear slightly lighter in shade than the Abbey's walls and the higher statues of the Virgin Mary and St John the Evangelist. At a concert to commemorate the unveiling the abbey choir performed *O Vos Omnes* by the cellist Pablo Casals, whom Franco threatened with death. The choir's tenors exhorted the crowds: "Is it nothing to all ye that pass by?" Many were moved by Elizabeth Maconchy's setting of Dylan Thomas's "And Death Shall Have No Dominion", by the opening of Bernstein's *Chichester Psalms* and by the Latin of Penderecki's *Agnus Dei* and the German of Bach's *O Jesu Christ Meins Lebens Licht*. The concert's climax was the world premiere of John Hardy's powerful *De Profundis*, a setting of Scripture and martyrs' writings.

The modern occupants of the mediæval niches were selected for having "shown openness to death for the glory of Christ". Some are not martyrs in the traditional sense of having been killed simply because of their belief in Jesus. All died as a result of injustice, bigotry or oppression – such as Martin Luther King – but the prime motive in his assassination, for instance, was not his Christian faith.

It would be a pity, though, if the modern desire to be inclusive (and at times politically correct) should either belittle the remarkable people who have been chosen to occupy these plinths, or render one of our most ancient ways of recognising self-sacrifice a diminished currency.

Fedorovna, Masemola and Tapiedi

The Queen and Prince Philip took a particular interest in the unveiling of these plinths because, like others who had gathered for the 1998 ceremony, they had a relative among the honoured. Prince Philip read an extract from the Acts of the Apostles as a black cloth was lowered to uncover the carved statue of his great-aunt, Grand Duchess Elizabeth Feodorovna of Russia, grand-daughter of Queen Victoria and a saint in the Orthodox Church. Married to the fifth son of Tsar Alexander II, she gave away jewellery and sold her most luxurious belongings after Grand Duke Sergei was assassinated. She used the money to establish the Martha and Mary Home in Moscow and created the Sisters of Love and Charity. Their work of charity and prayer then flourished. After the Bolshevik revolution in 1917 she was imprisoned. In 1918, the night after the Tsar and his family were assassinated she, too, was shot dead by the Communists.

Among others who have been commended as exemplary men and women is Manche Masemola, a sixteen-year-old Anglican convert who was killed by her animist parents in Sekhukhuneland, Transvaal, South Africa, in 1928. They were frightened that she would leave them or refuse to marry. She was a member of the Pedi tribe and is buried alongside her sister on a remote hillside. Her younger sister died a few days after her. The burial site has become a place of pilgrimage for South African Christians.

Lucian Tapiedi of Papua New Guinea was killed during the Japanese invasion in 1942. Born in Taupota, Tapiedi's father had been a sorcerer but he became a Christian and a teacher. After the invasion the Japanese murdered many missionaries. Tapiedi helped a group trying to escape. They came to a village inhabited by the Orokaiva tribe, some of whom proved to be hostile. He died after he refused to abandon the missionaries with whom he worked. His killer, a tribesman, later converted to Christianity. His killer took the name Hivijapa Lucian and built a church dedicated to the memory of Tapiedi.

Bonhoeffer, John and King

In 1945 Dietrich Bonhoeffer, the German Lutheran pastor and theologian, was killed by the Nazis at Flossenburg. His godson sat alone in the centre of the nave of the abbey and played Sarabande's *Cello Suite* during the service of dedication. Bonhoeffer had run an illegal seminary at Finenwalde until it was shut by the SS in 1937, and he was arrested after he became involved in a failed putsch against Adolph Hitler in 1944. Bonhoeffer was part of the Confessing Church of Germany, which was founded in reaction to the pro-Nazi German Protestant Church.

Esther John, of Pakistan, was a Presbyterian evangelist thought to have been killed by a Muslim fanatic in 1960. She moved to Pakistan after India was partitioned and continued to develop her faith in secret. After seven years, she fled, terrified of being forced to marry a Muslim. She took the name of Esther John and started to evangelise the villages around Chichawatni, teaching local women to read. She often worked with them in the fields. In 1960 she was found murdered in her bed. Her killer was never found.

Martin Luther King, the Baptist pastor and civil rights leader, and holder of the 1967 Nobel Peace Prize, was assassinated in Memphis in 1968, shortly after he saw several laws protecting equal rights placed on the statute books. Dr King once said: "If physical death is the price I must pay to free my brothers and sisters from the permanent death of the spirit, then nothing could be more redemptive."

Zhiming, Luwum and Romero

Wang Zhiming was a Chinese pastor in the Yunnan region, killed during the Cultural Revolution in 1973, aged sixty-six. He defied Mao's orders to humiliate landlords or to denounce foreign powers. He continued holding secret services for nearly 3,000 Christians, whose church had been closed. Arrested by Red Guards, he was executed at a mass rally. In October 1980 the Chinese Communists "rehabilitated" him and offered his family compensation.

Janani Luwum of Uganda was the Anglican Archbishop murdered during the military dictatorship of Idi Amin, in 1977. After being summoned to Kampala to explain his criticisms of the violence being used by the security services, Archbishop Luwum said, "They are going to kill me. I am not afraid." His body was never found. His widow and daughter prayed together in the abbey before being taken to see the statue for the first time.

Two Catholics complete the company of ten. I was especially pleased to see the recognition of St Maximilian Kolbe, the Polish Franciscan killed by the Nazis in 1941. I wrote about Fr Kolbe at greater length in *Signs of Contradiction* (Hodder & Stoughton, 1996), He was arrested for fearlessly denouncing the Nazis, and while imprisoned at Auschwitz-Birkenau he stepped forward and took the place of one of the Jewish prisoners – Franciszek Galowniczek – who was about to be executed. In the concentration camp he gave his food to fellow prisoners and continued to celebrate Mass. He was killed by lethal injection and was canonised by Pope John Paul II. His cell has now become a shrine.

Oscar Romero was the Archbishop of El Salvador and was assassinated in 1980. He first declared his vocation for the priesthood when he was a boy of thirteen and living in a remote mountainous region of El Salvador. During the 1970s he became increasingly critical of the totalitarian regime which had taken control of his country, and in 1979 he presented the Pope with a dossier documenting human rights abuses. At the service of dedication his friend Julian Filochowski, the Director of the Catholic Aid agency CAFOD, read out Archbishop Romero's words, given in a taped interview two weeks before he was murdered while celebrating Mass in the chapel of the hospital where he lived. He said that martyrdom was a grace from God which he did not deserve:

> But if God accepts the sacrifice of my life, then may my blood be the seed of liberty and a sign that hope will soon become reality. Can you tell them if they succeed in killing me, that I pardon and bless those who do it. But I wish that they could realise that they are wasting their time. A bishop may die but the Church of God, which is the people, will never die.

Poets, kings and statesmen

The timelessness of the Christian experience is well summed up by the abbey church which the pilgrim enters. Since the days of William the Conqueror, all but two monarchs have been crowned here. Among the statesmen, both the Pitts, Disraeli, Gladstone and Palmerston are honoured here. Chaucer was the first poet to be buried in the abbey – in 1400 – leading to that part of the south transept becoming known as Poets' Corner. Some, like Tennyson, are buried here; others are commemorated. It was not until 1740 that Shakespeare was recognised, and William Blake had to wait until 1957, two hundred years after his birth. One of the more recent stones recalls the great Victorian Jesuit poet, Fr Gerard Manley Hopkins.

The abbey has also been at the heart of the great national dramas: victories and tragedies. The Tomb of the Unknown Warrior commemorates those who were slaughtered in World War I. The unknown warrior's body was brought from France in November 1920. Science, too, has its place: there is a monument to Newton, and the physicists Rutherford and Kelvin are commemorated.

Genesis and keeping Sunday special

The first church on this site was probably built on what was the island of Thorney. Serbert, King of the East Saxons, chose this site in the middle of the Thames. In the fourteenth century a tomb, said to contain Serbert's remains, was set up in the south ambulatory of the present church.

Legend has it that as the church neared completion, St Peter miraculously appeared and was ferried across to Thorney by some fishermen. In turn, they were struck with terror as the whole building was filled with light. The saint told them that he had consecrated the church and that they would be rewarded by a great catch of salmon. He concluded by telling them that they must not work again on a Sunday. St Peter might have had something to say about figures recently given to me in Parliament, which reveal that ten million people worked on a Sunday during the year 2000, with four-and-a-half million people working every Sunday.

The first known reference to a church here is a grant of land from Algeric, Bishop of Dorchester, in 693 and the name appears in another grant by Offa, King of the Mercians, to the monastery "in that terrible place of Westminster" (c.785).

The Benedictine foundation

The abbey has its origins with the arrival of Benedictine monks in around the year 960. They were settled there by St Dunstan. However, the abbey and collegiate church of Westminster owe their refoundation to St Edward the Confessor. Although none of the church which he built remains visible above ground level, the long vaulted Undercroft formed the ground floor of the Dormitory of the monks.

Edward built in Romanesque style and saw the abbey's completion in 1065. The church was consecrated on the feast of the Holy Innocents, just in time for the Norman Conquest. Edward died within months of the completion of the great building work and he is honoured in a shrine which lies at the heart of the abbey. The shrine includes the recesses where the sick knelt, hoping for a cure through the intercession of the saint. The shrine was made by the Roman Cosmati family (c.1269) and was once richly decorated. The restored wooden decoration at the top of the shrine is from the sixteenth century.

At Christmas 1066, a new king entered the abbey and William the Conqueror became the first Norman king of England.

The coronation chair of 1301, used by many of his descendants, is near the shrine close to the ambulatory, with the radiating chapels of St John the Baptist, St Paul, St Nicholas, and St Edmund and St Thomas.

Henry III's abbey church

Henry III commenced the demolition of the Norman church in 1245 and reconstructed the church in Early English style. Over the centuries which followed, the masons worked to that plan and the abbey church which is so familiar today was the result.

The western nave was the last part of the mediæval building to be completed, in 1403. One hundred years earlier, Henry VII's chapel was built on the site of the old Lady Chapel, and all the Tudors, with the exception of Henry VIII, lie within it. Elizabeth's coffin stands on that of her half-sister Mary's; as we noted in chapter 13, the inscription on the monument translates: "Consorts both in throne and grave, here we rest, two sisters, Elizabeth and Mary, in the hope of one resurrection." In a monument in the opposite aisle lies the body of Mary Queen of Scots, who was executed on Elizabeth's orders in 1587.

From Wren to Scott

That the abbey stands today is largely thanks to the painstaking restoration and maintenance which is a never-ending task. Sir Christopher Wren and the Catholic architect Sir Gilbert Scott (see chapter 4, "The Cathedrals") were two of the key influences in ensuring its survival. The present High Altar and reredos were erected in the nineteenth century to Sir Gilbert's design, and the mosaic of the Last Supper is by Salviati. These cycles of renewal are not a new experience.

In 1298 a ravaging fire had led to the abbey's cloisters being rebuilt, and the little cloister stands on the site of the monastic infirmary. This is a good place for the pilgrim to stop and pray and to try and recapture something of the Benedictine house of prayer which Henry VIII suppressed. Although the abbey was restored briefly during Mary's reign (1553–8), Elizabeth dissolved it once more. Westminster's last monk, Fra Buckley, lived on until 1610, but it would be over three hundred years before another Benedictine monk would lead worship on this hallowed ground.

In 1976, when Cardinal Basil Hume left his Ampleforth monastery to take up his post at Westminster Cathedral, the abbey invited him to bring members of his community and to sing the holy office. Once again, the abbey resonated with the liturgies used there for hundreds of years. The pilgrim's next destination is at the other end of Victoria Street, the Cardinal's cathedral church and his tomb, which have already become a place of modern pilgrimage.

Westminster Cathedral

On entering the cathedral's west door the pilgrim will see the mosaic of Christ seated and holding an open book displaying the words: "*Ego sum ostium; per me si quis introierit salvabitur*" ("I am the gate; if anyone enters by me, he shall be saved", John 10:9). Above the mosaic appear the words: "*Domine Jesu Rex et redemptor per sanguinem tuum salve nos*" ("Lord Jesus, King and Redeemer, save us by your blood").

In accordance with his own final wishes, Cardinal Hume is buried in the cathedral in the chapel of St Gregory and St Augustine. This lies to the right of the entrance. In addition to commemorating the sending of St Augustine to England by St Gregory in 597, the chapel is dedicated to the ancient bishops and saints of the north of England, to whom the Cardinal had a special devotion. St Gregory's words "*Non Angli sed angeli si Christiani*" ("They are not Angles but angels if they are Christians") are high above the entrance. St Gregory is also the patron saint of the Cathedral Choir School as well as being the patron of plainsong. The cathedral's former Master of Music, James O'Donnell, who did so much under Cardinal Hume's patronage to develop and entrench the cathedral's musical tradition, is now performing a similar role at the abbey.

Praying at Cardinal Hume's tomb

The Cardinal was laid to rest in a leaden inner coffin contained in a simple but solid oak outer case. In the chapel vaulting above the Cardinal's tomb, there are mosaics of Saints Oswald, Bede and Cuthbert. The link between St Gregory the Great and the Benedictine monks is illustrated by a mosaic of St Benedict on one of the panels. The Benedictine influence on the Christian buildings at both ends of Victoria Street is captured by this mosaic and in the life of Cardinal Hume.

Another English bishop, Richard Challoner, is buried nearby in the same chapel. He was the leading figure in the Catholic Church during the greater part of the eighteenth century, succeeding Dr Petre (who is buried in the ancient chapel at Stydd, chapter 15) as Vicar Apostolic in 1758. After years of ministering to the poor of central London he died, aged ninety, and was buried in the family crypt of Mr Bryant Barrett of Milton Manor. His coffin was exhumed and brought to Westminster Cathedral in 1946.

If the modern pilgrim has not yet understood that it is futile to begin a journey without a map or a compass this would be a good moment to acquire Cardinal Hume's 1984 publication *To Be a Pilgrim* (ST PAULS). His tomb is a good starting point for reading a text which is sub-titled *A Spiritual Notebook*. The Cardinal believed that the pilgrim on their spiritual journey needs to feed their intellect and their heart, but also needs to keep a record in a spiritual notebook of what interests and attracts them most.

The Beauty of God

As the pilgrim leaves Cardinal Hume's tomb it may be profitable to see this majestic building through the eye of a man who committed his life to Benedictine simplicity. Basil Hume believed that the beauty which the eye could behold and that which pleases the ear speaks of something other than itself. He believed that it speaks of God. Through noble buildings of distinction and through the beauty of music it is possible both to discern something of God and to communicate our praise for his goodness. "The cathedral," he said, "should be a chink in the cloud of unknowing enabling parishioners and visitors to glimpse something of divine beauty. It is a place where they meet Christ, and in and through him, gain strength and courage to take another step along the road to God" (*Westminster Cathedral: Building of Faith*, John Browne and Timothy Dean, Booth-Clibborn, 1995).

The Byzantine tradition

Westminster Cathedral is the master-work of John Francis Bentley (1839–1902), a Catholic convert, born in Doncaster in 1839, and one of seventeen children. Unique in its execution, it draws on the inspiration of Santa Sophia in

Constantinople and St Mark's in Venice and on the rich Byzantine tradition. The choice of the early Byzantine style enabled the exterior of the building to be constructed in an amazingly short space of time, especially when compared with the centuries which elapsed before the completion of its great mediæval counterparts. The interior remains incomplete. Dark and cavernous domes and soot-laden walls, which were to have been inlaid with shimmering gold and mosaics, may remind you either that our work is never finished, or that new generations must take up the challenge and press on with the work.

Cardinal Wiseman first expressed a desire, just before his death in 1865, that a cathedral might be built for his Metropolitan See. Cardinal Manning insisted that the first priority was the provision of religious education for the children of the Catholic poor, but having put the spiritual foundations in place it was he who purchased the first piece of land off Victoria Street in 1867, and as the years passed they acquired further parcels of land.

The Bentley commission

It was Manning's successor, Cardinal Vaughan, who, in 1894, appointed Bentley and commissioned the construction of the Cathedral of the Most Precious Blood. The full dedication of the cathedral – following the earliest Christian traditions – is to the Precious Blood of Jesus, to his mother, his foster father, St Joseph, St Peter his vicar, and to the secondary patrons, St Augustine and all the British saints, St Patrick and all the Irish saints.

The primary dedication, to the Precious Blood, is visually expressed by the great rood, or crucifix, which is suspended from the roof. On the reverse side of the cross Mary is depicted as the sorrowful mother with texts taken from the hymn *Stabat Mater*. In the narthex, close to the entrance, there are two central pillars of deep red Norwegian granite, symbolising the redeeming blood of Christ poured out for man's salvation. Close by, to the left, is a bronze enthroned statue of St Peter, close to the names of the popes and archbishops from the time of St Peter and St Augustine.

The papal pilgrim

At the foot of the steps of the sanctuary is a plaque commemorating the first visit to England of a successor of Peter. It bears the words "Behold the footsteps of the Supreme Pastor John Paul II who as a pilgrim to England, celebrated here his first Mass, 28th May 1982. May God be glorified in all things."

The nave stretches forward to the distant High Altar, which sits under a canopy or baldachino. Bentley was determined that the sanctuary of the cathedral should be the crowning glory of the building. Above the baldachino is a mosaic which shows Christ in majesty surrounded by the evangelists in symbolic form and contemplated by the apostles. Christ holds the chalice of the blood which saves us and there appear two verses from the *Te Deum*: "*Judex crederis esse venturus. Te ergo quaesumus tuis famulis subveni, quos pretioso sanguine redemisti*" ("We believe that you are the judge who will come. Therefore, we beseech you, come to the aid of your servants, whom you have redeemed by your precious blood"). At the Gospel side of the High Altar the archbishop's throne or cathedral, is situated. A gift from the Catholic bishops of England to Cardinal Vaughan, it is a replica of the throne in the basilica of St John Lateran in Rome.

On the piers of the nave are Eric Gill's Stations of the Cross. These were carved in low relief in Hopton-Wood stone. Gill was invited to carry out these designs six months after he was received into the Catholic Church, in 1913, and he undertook the work while the contemporary passion of the Via Dolorosa was being experienced by millions in the trenches of World War I. Gill said of his Stations:

> Beauty is absolute and is independent of our love. God is beautiful whether we love Him or not; but the taste of an apple is lovely only if we taste it and love the taste. Now a work of art to be such must have this absolute quality; for it is with the Absolute Beauty that the artist, as artist, is primarily concerned.

Gill did not want the pilgrim to "make the Stations". He said it would be deplorable if they were used as an excuse for idle sightseeing. Instead, the pilgrim might use them as an impassive reminder of Our Lord's Passion and use them like the beads on a rosary, quietly making their own meditation and saying their own prayers.

The Christian journey

Around the cathedral are side altars and chapels. Cardinal Vaughan asked the architect to physically portray the Christian journey, the pilgrimage from life to death. It starts with the baptistery and ends with the chapel of the Holy Souls.

In accordance with custom the baptistery is railed off and locked. Next to it is a small statue of St Christopher, given by the Catholic writer and Liberal MP Hilaire Belloc. It was presented as a petition seeking protection for troops embarking on hazardous journeys to the war front.

Between the chapel of St Gregory and St Augustine and the chapel of St Patrick is a mosaic dedicated to St Oliver Plunkett. The great Irish Archbishop of Armagh and Primate of All Ireland was the last of the Catholic martyrs to be dragged through the streets of London and executed at Tyburn. A vast crowd lined the route as he was taken to his place of execution on 11 July 1681.

The chapel of St Patrick and the saints of Ireland is

dominated by a statue of St Patrick placed here in 1961. The floor is mainly made of Irish marble and the design depicts the Celtic cross, with patterns from Clonmacnois. Around the walls of the chapel are badges of Irish regiments, mostly now disbanded. The book of remembrance commemorates the 500,000 Irish soldiers killed in World War I.

In the south aisle the pilgrim will find the chapel of St Andrew and the Scottish saints. The chapel houses a relic of St Andrew and contains stone quarried at Aberdeen and Peterhead. On the west wall, a beautiful mosaic depicts St Andrew the fisherman, and the windows use Scotland's colours, blue and white. On the east wall there are sheep reminding us of the flock which must be tended by an apostle of Christ. The ceiling vault was designed to shimmer like the scales of the fish. At the sides of the ceiling are the places associated with St Andrew – Bethsaida, Hagia Sophia, Milan, Amalfi and St Andrews in Scotland.

The missionary spirit

The chapel of St Paul commemorates the missionary spirit of the Church and its great apostle to the gentiles. On the west wall of the chapel St Paul's conversion on the road to Damascus is commemorated. Here is the inscription: "*Surge et ingredere civitatem, et ibi dicetur tibi quid te oporteat facere*" ("Get up and enter the city and you will be told what you are to do"). Cardinal Heenan, eighth Archbishop of Westminster and former Archbishop of Liverpool, who died in 1975, is buried at the foot of the twelfth station, opposite St Paul's Chapel.

Penance and pardon

Continuing east, the pilgrim now enters Mary's domain. Beginning just before the south transept and culminating in the Lady chapel, this is the area of the cathedral dedicated to the Virgin. Here, too, are the confessionals where many penitents, seeking reconciliation with God, receive healing in their lives.

The Lady Chapel

Here is an English mediæval image of Mary, recalling the traditional shrine at Westminster of Our Lady of the Pewe and depicting the Virgin as the seat of wisdom (see chapter 6). It stands below the thirteenth of Eric Gill's stations: "The body of Jesus is taken down from the cross and laid in his mother's bosom." In the Lady chapel we see Mary depicted with her divine Child and here the text reads "*Sub tuum praesidium confugimus sancta dei genitrix nostras deprecationes ne despicias in necessitatibus nostris*" ("We flee under your protection, Holy Mother of God. Do not reject our prayers in our hour of need"). The life of Mary forms a frieze around the whole chapel and here, too, are reminders of apparitions to St Simon Stock (see chapter 6) and to St Bernadette at Lourdes. Decorative canopies recall the fifteen mysteries of the Rosary.

Beneath the High Altar is the crypt chapel of St Peter. Cardinal Wiseman and Cardinal Manning are buried here. Nearby, in the main crypt, lie Cardinal Griffin (1943–56) and Cardinal Godfrey (1956–63).

The Blessed Sacrament Chapel

On the other side of the High Altar lies the chapel of the Blessed Sacrament, situated beyond the north transept. Votive candles flicker as private devotions and prayers are offered. The gates to the chapel depict the symbols Alpha and Omega, the first and last letters of the Greek alphabet. The 1962 mosaics are the work of Boris Anrep and reflect the unity and power of the Word of God. The nave and the vault symbolise the Old Testament and the apse celebrates the New Testament. Here is Abraham welcoming his three visitors and offering them food ,and here is Christ, the sacrificial Lamb of God. The Eucharist is here, in the form of bread and wine. Here, too, is the great high priest, Melchizedek.

Every morning, at half-hourly intervals, daily Mass is celebrated here and small knots of commuters, office workers and visitors pass in and out to make their devotions and to provide spiritual cohesion to their busy lives.

A pageant of chapels

At the north end of the aisle of the Blessed Sacrament is the little chapel of the Sacred Heart and St Michael the Archangel. St Michael slaying a dragon symbolises the spiritual battles which constantly beset the Kingdom of God.

Next is the chapel of St Thomas of Canterbury, recalling the great English martyr murdered in his cathedral for standing up for the rights of the Church against Henry II. Here Cardinal Vaughan, the cathedral's founder, asked to be buried. The crucifix in this chapel was the gift of Lady Alice Fitzwilliam and was crafted by the Bromsgrove Guild of Metal Workers. Cardinal Vaughan had a keen sense of history. He was unable to fulfil his wish that Benedictine monks come permanently to his new cathedral to celebrate the Divine Office and Liturgy. Perhaps it was fitting that one of his most notable twentieth-century successors should, however, be a Benedictine monk. That Westminster should once again have a Catholic cathedral church is Vaughan's lasting memorial.

Signs and symbols

Moving along the north transept, the pilgrim enters the chapel of St Joseph, Mary's husband. This patron of workers stood by Mary when she might easily have been rejected, having been found to be pregnant. Here in his chapel

Cardinal Hinsley was buried in 1943. The red hat which symbolises the rank of a cardinal is left to hang over his tomb, and as it decays it reminds each of us of our own mortality.

St George and the English Martyrs is the next chapel. St Thomas More and St John Fisher, the martyrs from the reign of Henry VIII, stand on either side of the cross. Executed in 1535, they were canonised in 1935. An inscription reads: "*Te martyrum candidatus laudat exercitus*" ("The white robed army of martyrs praises you"). In this chapel lie the remains of St John Southworth. Born in 1592 at Samlesbury Hall, near Preston in Lancashire, he studied at the English seminary at Douai in France (see chapter 15). In 1636 he and the remarkable Jesuit priest, Henry Morse, organised relief after the plague broke out among the poor of Westminster. Southworth became known as "the parish priest of Westminster." In 1636 he was imprisoned and on 28 June 1654, after several further spells in prison, was executed. At the gallows he said:

> Good people, I was born in Lancashire. This is the third time I have been apprehended and now being to die, I would gladly witness and profess openly my faith for which I suffer. Hither I was sent by my lawful superiors to teach the Catholic faith for which I suffer. Hither I was sent by my lawful superiors to teach Christ's faith, not to meddle with any temporal affairs. Christ sent his apostles, His apostles their successor, and their successor is me.

Then, looking at the crossbeam above his head, he stated: "This gallows I look on as His cross, which I gladly take to follow my dear Saviour. My faith is my crime, the performance of my duty the occasion of my condemnation."

The Spanish Ambassador purchased his body, apparently acting on behalf of the Duke of Norfolk. It was taken to the Continent, to Douai, and rediscovered by labourers building a new road in 1927. After a brief time at the convent at Tyburn his remains were placed in a glass coffin at Westminster Cathedral.

May we rest in peace

Finally, we come to the chapel of the Holy Souls. This solemnly reminds us that we, too, will die. Here is the clue to continuing life: the communion of the saints, whether, as Pope Paul VI put it, "they still make their pilgrim way on earth, whether their life over, they undergo purification or they enjoy the happiness of heaven". (*The Credo of the People of God*, 1968). The chapel takes us from Adam, our progenitor, to Christ, the Second Adam. Here is the Archangel Raphael, whose name means "God has healed". Here is Michael, holding the Devil in chains. Here are St Paul's words to the Corinthians (3:13-15) reminding us that the builder will be saved but only as through fire. And here, too, as we leave the pilgrim's way, are the often uttered words of the Catholic faithful in remembering their dead: "*Requiem aeternam dona eis domine et lux perpetua luceat eis*" ("Eternal rest give unto them, O Lord, and let perpetual light shine upon them").

Perhaps the pilgrim, surveying London from the top of the cathedral's tower, might consider the significance of this wonderful building. This was an extraordinary leap of faith by a community which, despite Newman and Manning, was still contemptuously dismissed as "the Italian Mission to the Irish." Yet, despite all the odds against them English Catholics were determined to create a building which expressed their enduring faith in God.

The Catholic spring blossoms into summer

When Cardinal Vaughan laid the foundation stone in 1895, he told Bentley not to design a Gothic cathedral.

His preference was for something Italianate. What he got was a design which Bentley said should not be "confined to Italy, England or any other nation", but rather should be absolutely primitive Christian–Byzantine, celebrating the universality of the Church. The design, which would enable the congregation to see and hear all the great liturgies and would not be seen to compete with the Gothic of Westminster Abbey, could be expedited without unnecessary delay. Cardinal Vaughan combined vision and a sense of what was achievable. Here would be the celebration of what Cardinal Manning called the Catholic spring.

Seven years (and twelve-and-a-half-million handmade bricks) later, in 1903, the fabric of the building was indeed complete, and the first major religious service was the funeral of Cardinal Vaughan, who, like John Bentley, died just before the completion of the main structure.

As a child brought to London to see the cathedral I remember the impact that the building had upon me. It was not until a redevelopment in 1976 led to the clearance of the buildings in front that the piazza was created and the full vista of this magnificent building could be appreciated by passers by. For my generation other obstacles impeding people's views of the Catholic Church in England have likewise been swept away. Primarily this was because of the ministry and example of Cardinal Basil Hume. In him, Manning's spring finally blossomed into summer, and through him the remaining impediments blocking people's view of the Catholic Church in England have been demolished. It took the return of a Benedictine monk to Westminster to achieve this. Let that pilgrim have the last word:

A meditation

Life is a pilgrimage

The greatest grace which God can give is the knowledge that He loves each one of us more than any lover ever loved his or her beloved. To realise that, and to allow it to sink deep into our hearts and our minds, can change our lives completely. Who can separate us from that love?

As we approach the last bit of the journey there are days when we fear that we face an unknown, unpredictable, uncertain future. That is a common experience. But do not worry; because the time comes when we no longer carry heavy bags and all those possessions. We shall travel through the cold, grey light of a bleak English morning into God's Spring and Summer; into His light and warmth.

"This day you will be with me in paradise" (Luke 23:43). This day will inevitably come for each one of us, we do not know when. But it most surely will come and what a joy it will be when we hear the words: "This day you will be with me in paradise." We must move in our spiritual lives from thinking of death as the great enemy and begin to think about "this day" as the one when we shall be going home, the one for which we were made and for which the whole of our lives is the preparation.

Life is indeed a pilgrimage as we walk each day closer to its end, which is the vision of God. We are made for that and life is a preparation for the moment when we move from this situation into eternal happiness. Joy and sorrow, agony and ecstasy, pain and well-being: they walk hand in hand up that hill which is called Calvary. But beyond it to a place where there is no more death, no sin, no pain, only empty tombs and life everlasting.

(Cardinal Basil Hume OSB, OM)

Appendix
Practical information

THIS is not meant to be a comprehensive list of places of accommodation but does provide some contact details of religious houses. Some take individuals, others take groups, others will be able to direct you to somewhere suitable. Some will also provide opportunities for guests to make a retreat. These are not hotels, and pilgrims should expect to give some practical help to the living communities in which they stay. In return, the pilgrim will usually receive excellent hospitality and resources for the next stage of their spiritual journey. Geoffrey Gerard in *Away From It All* (Lutterworth Press, 1992) provides the best guide available. Where a 'W' or 'M' appears alongside an entry it means that the facility is available to women or men only. Where an 'E' appears it indicates that the foundation is ecumenical; others are administered by Catholic Religious Orders.

The South West

Ammerdown Study Centre   E
   Radstock, Bath, Avon BA3 5SW
   01761 433709

Buckfast Abbey   M
   Buckfastleigh, Devon TQ11 OEE
   01364 645500

Emmaus House
   Clifton Hill, Bristol, Avon BS8 4PD
   0117 907 950

Lee Abbey Fellowship   E
   Lee Abbey, Lynton, Devon EX35 6JJ
   01598 752621

Trelowarren Fellowship E
  Mawgan in Meneage, Helston, Cornwall TR12 6A
  01326 221 366

The South

Convent of Poor Clares W
  Cross Bush, Arundel, West Sussex BN18 9PJ
  01903 882536

Park Place Pastoral Centre,
  Wickham, Fareham, Hampshire PO17 5HA
  01329 833043

Priory of Our Lady
  Sayes Common, Hassocks, West Sussex BN6 9HT
  01273 832901

Quarr Abbey M
  Ryde, Isle of Wight, PO33 4ES
  01983 882420

London and the Home Counties

All Saints Pastoral Centre
  London Colney, Herts AL2 1AF
  01727 822010

Brentwood Diocesan Pastoral Centre
  The Barn Hall, Boreham, Chelmsford,
  Essex CM3 3HT
  01245 451760

Cold Ash Centre
  The Ridge, Cold Ash, nr Newbury, Berkshire RG16 9HU
  06135 865353

Emmaus Retreat & Conference Centre
  Layhams Road, West Wickham, Kent BR4 9HH
  01208 777 2000

The Friars
  Aylesford, Maidstone, Kent ME20 7BX
  01622 717272

Minster Abbey
  nr Ramsgate, Kent CT12 4HF
  01843 821 254

St Augustine's Abbey
  Ramsgate, Kent CT11
  01843 593045 M

Turvey Abbey
  Turvey, Bedfordshire MK4 8DE
  0123 881 432

Campion House
  112 Thornbury Road, Isleworth,
  Middlesex TW7 4NN
  020 8560 1924

Convent of Marie Reparatrice
  115 Ridgway, Wimbledon, London SW19 4RB
  020 8946 1088

The Grail Centre
  125 Waxwell Lane, Pinner, Middlesex HA5 3ER
  020 8866 2195 and 020 8866 0505

Sacred Heart Priory
  38 Hyde Vale, Greenwich, London SE10 8QH
  020 8692 3382

San Damiano Convent, Franciscan Retreat Centre
  St Mary's Abbey, Mill Hill, London NW7 4HX
  020 8959 8331

Tyburn Convent   W
  8 Hyde Park Place, Bayswater Road,
  London W2 2LJ
  020 7723 7262

East Anglia and East Midlands

Hengrave Hall   **E**
   Mildenhall Road, Bury St Edmunds,
   Suffolk IP28 6LZ
   01284 701561

Massingham St Mary Retreat & Conference Centre
   Little Massingham, nr King's Lynn,
   Norfolk PE32 2JU
   01485 520245

The Old Stable House
   3 Sussex Lodge, Fordham Road, Newmarket,
   Suffolk CB8 7AF
   01638 667190

The Pickenham Centre   **E**
   Brecklands Green, North Pickenham,
   Swaffham, PE37 8LG
   01760 440 561

St Claret Retreat & Conference Centre
   The Towers, Buckden, Huntingdon,
   Cambridgeshire PE18 9TA
   01480 810344

Sue Ryder Retreat House   **E**
   The Martyr's House, Walsingham,
   Norfolk NR22 6AA
   01328 820622

West Midlands

Headley Lodge at Belmont Abbey
   Hereford HR2 9RZ
   01432 277475

Carmelite Priory
   nr Youlbury, Boar's Hill, Oxford OX1 5HB
   01865 730183

The Cherwell Centre
  16 Norham Gardens, Oxford OX2 6QB
  01865 552106

Hawkstone Hall
  Weston, Shrewsbury, Shropshire SY4 5LG
  01630 685242

Prinknash Abbey
  St Peter's Grange, Gloucester GL4 8EX
  01452 813592

Stanbrook Abbey
  St Mary's House, Jennett Tree Lane, Callow End,
  Worcester WR2 4TD
  01905 830307

St.Mary's Abbey
  Oulton, Stone, Staffordshire ST15 8UP
  01785 812498

St Raphael's Convent
  Brownshill, Stroud, Gloucestershire GL6 8AJ
  01453 882107

North East

Ampleforth Abbey
  The Grange, Ampleforth, York YO6 4EN
  01439 766000

The Briery Retreat House
  38 Victoria Avenue, Ilkley,
  West Yorkshire LS29 9BW
  01943 607287

Marygate House   E
  Holy Island, Berwick-upon-Tweed,
  Northumberland TD15 2SD
  01289 389246

Minsteracres Retreat Centre
  Minsteracres, Consett, Co. Durham DH8 9RT
  01434 673248

Myddleton Lodge Pastoral Centre
  Langbar Road, Ilkley, West Yorkshire LS29 OEB
  01943607887

St Bede's Pastoral Centre, 21 Blossom Street
  York YO2 2AQ
  01904 464900

North West

Cenacle Retreat & Conference Centre
  28 Alexandra Road, South Manchester M16 8HU
  0161 226 1241

Convent of Marie Repatrice
  183 Newton Drive, Blackpool, Lancashire FY3 8NU
  01253 391549

Loyola Hall
  Warrington Road, Rainhill, Prescot, Merseyside L35 6NZ
  0151 426 4137

St.Joseph's Retreat & Conference Centre
  Tilston Road, Malpas, Cheshire SY14 7DD
  01948 860416

Wistaston Hall
  89 Broughton Lane, Crewe,
  Cheshire CW2 8JS
  01270 663922

Hyning Monastery
  Carnforth
  01524732 684

Scotland

Holy Manna Retreat, Benedictine Monastery
  Mackerston Place, Largs KA30 8BY
  01475 687320

The House of Prayer
  8 Nile Grove, Edinburgh EH10 4RF
  0131 447 1772

The Iona Community
  Iona, Argyll PA76 6SN
  01681 700404   E

Kinharvie House
  New Abbey, Dumfries DG2 8DZ
  01387 850433

Mount Carmel Retreat Centre
  61 Hamilton Avenue, Pollokshields, Glasgow G41
  4HA
  0141 427 0794

Pluscarden Abbey
  Elgin, Moray, IV30 3UA
  01343 890257

Sancta Maria Abbey
  Nunraw, Haddington, East Lothian EH41 4LW
  0162 0830228

Wales

Caldey Abbey
  Isle of Caldey, Tenby, Dyfed SA70 7UH
  (*apply by letter only*)

The Franciscan Retreat Centre
  Pantasaph, Holywell, Clwyd CH8 8PE
  01352 711053

The Loreto Centre
Abbey Road, Llandudno, Gwynedd,
North Wales LL30 2EL
01492 878031

St Beuno's
Tremeirchion, St Asaph, Clwyd LL17 OAS
01745 583444

Ireland

The Irish Tourist Information Office in London can provide details of farmhouse and hotel accommodation in Ireland (08000397000); or reservations of registered accommodation can be made direct on a freephone number in Ireland (0080066866866) or there is a web site: www.ireland.travel.ie

Religious houses may usually be contacted by telephone.

Background information and select bibliography

Chapter 1: Glastonbury

Sacred Britain, Martin Palmer and Nigel Palmer, Piatkus, 1997.

Chapter 2: The Celtic sites: Iona, Lindisfarne and the northern saints

An Introduction to Celtic Christianity, James Mackey, T. & T. Clark, 1989.

Lindisfarne: The Cradle Island, Magnus Magnusson, Oriel Press, 1984.

Lindisfarne Landscapes, Sheila Mackay, St Andrew Press, 1996.

The Age of Bede, Bede – Life of Cuthbert, Life of Wilfred, Lives of the Abbots of Wearmouth and Jarrow, translated by J.F. Webb, Penguin, 1965.

The Lindisfarne Gospels, Janet Backhouse, Phaidon, 1981.

Chapter 3: The monasteries

Cistercian Way, Ian Brodie, Carnegie Press, 1989.

The Itineraries of John Leland, edited by Lucy Toulmin-Smith, 1907.

The Religious Orders of England, David Knowles, Cambridge University Press, 3 vols 1948-59.

Fools for God, Richard North, Collins, 1987.

Travellers in Britain, Richard Trench, Aurum Press, 1990.

Cathedrals and Abbeys of England, Very Revd Stephen Platten, Jarrold, 1999.

Abbeys, R Gilyard-Beer, London, 1971.

The Abbeys and Priories of Medieval England, C.P.S. Platt, Fordham, 1984.

The White Monks in Wales, J.M. Lewis and D.H. Williams, National Museum of Wales, Cardiff, 1976.

The Welsh Cistercians, D.H. Williams, Caldey Island, 1984.

Gregory's Angels, Dom Gordon Beattie, Gracewing, 1997.

Directory of Monastic Hospitality, The Economic Commission, 1991.

Fountains Abbey: details of activities and events, telephone 01765 608888.

Bolton Abbey: details of events, telephone 01756 710238.

Cartmell Priory: details of events, telephone 015395 36261.

Chapter 4: The cathedrals of England and Wales

Sacred Britain, Martin Palmer and Nigel Palmer, Piatkus, 1997.

Chapter 5: The holy wells

The Holy Wells of Wales, Francis Jones, University of Wales Press, 1992.

A Welsh Pilgrim's Manual, Brenda O'Malley, Gomer, 1989.

A Pilgrim's Manual – St David's, Brian O'Malley, Paulinus Press, 1991.

The Old Parish Churches of Mid Wales, Mike Salter, Folly Publishing, 1991.

Lives of the Welsh Saints, G.H. Doble, University of Wales Press, 1971.

A History and Guide to St Winifrid's Well, Revd Christopher David, 1971 (available at the Well bookshop).

The Story of St Winefride and Her Well and *St Winefride's Well*, two mediæval Welsh poems, translated by T.M. Charles-Edwards (available at the Well bookshop).

"The holy wells of County Kildare", Patricia Jackson, in *Journal of Kildare Archæological Society*, vol. 16.

"The holy wells of County Dublin", Caolmhin O'Danachair, in *Reportum Novarum*, Dublin Diocese.

The Holy Wells of Ireland, Patrick Logan, Colin Smythe,

1980 (reprinted 1992).

The Ancient Crosses and Holy Wells of Lancashire, Henry Taylor, 1906.

Chapters 6 and 7: The Marian shrines and Walsingham

Shrines of Our Lady in England and Wales, H.M. Gillett, Samuel Walker, 1957.

Our Lady's Dowry, Revd. T.E. Bridgett, Burns and Oates, 1875.

Walsingham: England's Nazareth, reprinted in 1990 by the Walsingham Guardians.

Chapter 8: Whitekirk and Haddington, St Andrews and other Scottish sites

The annual Haddington pilgrimage takes place on the second Saturday in May. The Pilgrimage Secretary is Mrs Irene Macrae (0131 663 3291). She can arrange speakers and videos about the pilgrimage. Mass may be said at any time, by arrangement with the parish priest at Haddington (01620 822138). Groups travel from the south of England by coach; details from 0181 647 5992. Train travel is possible as far as Dunbra, about ten miles from Haddington.

Chapters 9 and 10: Croagh Patrick, Tochar Padraig and following Patrick's path, and Knock

Tochar Padraig begins at Ballintubber Abbey, situated by Lough Cara off the Castlebar–Galway road.

Tochar Padraig – A Pilgrim's Progress, by Fr F. Fahey, takes you over a hundred stiles and twenty miles across country to Croagh Patrick, and is available at the abbey.

In the Steps of St Patrick, Brian de Breffny, Thames and Hudson, 1982.

The Mayo Guide, Bord Failte (the Irish Tourist Board), from the Western Regional Tourism Organisation, Westport (098-25711).

St Patrick's World, Liam De Paor, Four Courts Press, 1993.

Chapter 11: Lough Derg and some other Irish sites

Lough Derg and Patrick's Purgatory: contact the prior (00 353 72 61518). Cost is around £17 per person. Regular ferries travel from the UK to Ireland (Stenna Line 0990 707070). Michael Willis takes a group annually from Stirling: 29 Coney Park, Stirling FK7 9LU or m.willis@virgin.net.

Station Island, Seamus Heaney, Faber & Faber, 1984.

A Pilgrim's Handbook, Dublin Diocesan Jubilee Committee, Columba Press, 1999.

A Walking Tour of Dublin Churches, Vertitas Publications, 1988.

An Introduction to Celtic Christianity, James P. Mackey, T. & T. Clark.

Ancient Ireland: From Prehistory to the Middle Ages, Jacqueline O'Brien and Peter Harbison, Weldenfeld and Nicholson, 1966.

Celtic Fire: An Anthology of Celtic Christian Literature, Robert van de Weyer, Darton, Longman and Todd, 1990.

Celtic Miscellany, Kenneth Hurlstone Jackson, Penguin, 1951.

Glendalough and St Kevin, Lennox Barrow, Dundalgan Press, 1992.

Glendalough: A Celtic Pilgrimage, Michael Rodgers and Marcus Losack, Columba Press, 1996.

Guide to National Monuments of Ireland, Peter Harbison, Gill and Macmillan, 1975.

Irish Catholic Spirituality, John J. O'Riordain, Columba Press, 1998.

Irish Spirituality, edited by Michael Maher, Veritas Publications, 1981.

Places of Pilgrimage, Bernard Jackson, Geoffrey Chapman, 1989.

Pilgrimage in Ireland. The Monuments and the People, Peter Harbison, Barrie and Jenkins, 1991.

Sacred Places, Pilgrim Paths: An Anthology of Pilgrimage, Martin Robinson, HarperCollins, 1997.

Chapter 12: The Tower

The Tower of London: Notes for Catholics, J.J. Dwyer, Catholic Truth Society, c/o CTS Bookshop, 25 Ashley Place, London SW1P 1LT (Cathedral Plaza), 0171 7237262.

Tower Hill Underground Station is situated next to the Tower.

Chapters 13 and 14: Tyburn and The recusants

The Eighty-Five Martyrs, Roland Connelly, McCrimmons, 1987.

Lives of the English Martyrs, E.H. Burton and J.H. Pollen SJ, 1914.

Publications of the Catholic Record Society (available at the Catholic Central Library).

Catholicism in the Furness Peninsula, 1127–1997, Anne C. Parkinson, Centre for North West Regional Studies, University of Lancaster, 1998.

Harvington Hall is three miles south east of Kidderminster, half a mile east of the A450 Birmingham to Worcester Road and about half a mile north of the A448 from Kidderminster to Bromsgrove. Telephone 01562 777846, website www.harvingtonhall.org.uk.

Tyburn Convent and Archive, 8 Hyde Park Place, London W2 2LJ, telephone 0171 7237262.

Tyburn Virtual Tour: www.tyburnconvent.org.uk.

Guide to the Crypt of the Martyrs: available from Tyburn Convent.

They Died at Tyburn: available from Tyburn Convent.

The Forty-Four (martyrs of the English College, Rome): available from Tyburn Convent.

The Tyburner: magazine of the Tyburn nuns.

Chapter 15: Lancashire and Liverpool

Catholic Lancashire, from Reformation to Renewal, 1559–1991, J.A.Hilton, Phillimore, 1994.

Where Shall We Go in the Ribble Valley? Edward Popham,
Salford Catholic Truth Society, 1993.
The Maritime Museum, Albert Dock, Liverpool
(exhibitions on the Irish famine and slavery).

Chapter 16: Westminster Abbey and Westminster Cathedral

To Be A Pilgrim, Cardinal Basil Hume, ST PAULS, 1984.
Westminster Cathedral: Building of Faith, John Browne and
Timothy Dean, Booth-Clibborn Editors, 1995.

OTHER BOOKS AND RESOURCES

Ancient routes

The Road to Canterbury: A Modern Pilgrimage, Shirley Du
Boulay, HarperCollins, 1994.
Pilgrimage – an image of mediaeval religion, Jonathan
Sumption, Faber and Faber, 1975.
The Old Road, Hilaire Belloc: Constable, 1911.
The Pilgrims' Way from Winchester to Canterbury, Sean
Jennett, Cassell, 1971.
Exploring the Pilgrims' Way, Winchester to Canterbury, Alan
Charles, Countryside Books, 1990.
The Canterbury Pilgrimage, H. Snowden-Ward, A & C
Black, 1904.

Spiritual

The Imitation of Christ, Thomas à Kempis, Hodder &
Stoughton, 1979.
John Henry Newman: Prayers, Poems, Meditations, A.N.
Wilson, SPCK, 1989.
The Genesee Diary: Report from a Trappist Monastery, Henri
J.M. Nouwen, Doubleday, 1976.

The Way of a Pilgrim and *The Pilgrim Continues His Way*, translated from the Russian by Helen Bacovcin, Image Books, 1978

The Pilgrim's Progress, John Bunyan, Fount, 1979.

The Desert Journey, Carlo Carretto, Fount, 1992.

In Search of A Way: Two Journeys of Spiritual Discovery, Fr Gerard Hughes SJ, DLT, 1994.

To Be A Pilgrim, Cardinal Basil Hume, ST PAULS, 1984.

John of the Cross: selected writings, trans. Kieran Kavanaugh, SPCK 1987.

General

Sacred Places, Pilgrim Paths, An Anthology of Pilgrimage, Martin Robinson, Fount, 1998.

A Book of Feasts and Seasons, Joanna Bogle, Gracewing, 1986.

Old Catholic England, Fr Mark Elvins, Catholic Truth Society, London, 1978.

Travellers in Britain, Richard Trench, Aurum Press, 1990.

Forgotten Shrines, Dom Bede Camm OSB, Macdonald & Evans, 1910.

Shakespeare and the Jesuits, Professor Richard Wilson, http://www.lancs.ac.uk/users/english/jesuitp.htm

The Stripping of the Altars, Eamon Duffy, Yale University Press, 1992.

Customs and Traditions of England, Gary Hogg, David and Charles, 1979.

Pilgrim's England – a Personal Journey, William Purcell, Longman, 1981.

Pilgrimages, R. Barber, The Boydell Press, 1991.

The Path to Rome, Hilaire Belloc, G. Allen, London, 1902.

Miracles and Pilgrims: Popular Beliefs in Medieval England, Ronald C. Finucare, Dent, 1977.

In the Steps of the Pilgrims, S. Heath, Rich and Cowan, 1950

Places of Pilgrimage, B. Jackson, Geoffrey Chapman, 1989.

Other resources

Catholic Central Library: Lancing Street, London NW1 1ND.
Tel 020 7383 4333. Fax 020 7383 665.
email: librarian@catholic-library demon co.uk
website: www.catholic-library demon co.uk

Living Churchyards (Church and Conservation Project):
Arthur Rak Centre, National Agricultural Centre,
Stoneleigh Park Warwickshire CV8 2LZ.

Plants for a sacred garden or monastery garden: Veritas
Nursery, 22 The Avenue, Girvan, Ayrshire KA26, 9DS.
Tel/Fax 01465 713388.

Conservation Foundation, 1 Kensington Gore, London
SW7 2AR.

Sacred Land Project, ICOREC, Manchester Metropolitan
University, 799 Wilmslow Road, Manchester M20 2RR.

Christian Heritage Trails, Carlisle Diocesan Board of
Education, Carlisle, 1993.

Jubilee Office, Clonliffe College, Dublin 9.
e-mail: dublinjubilee2000@indigo.ie
website: www.dublin-jubilee.com

World Youth Day (young people's pilgrimages), Jubilee
Office, CYC, Arran Quay, Dublin 7. Tel 01 8725055.
e-mail: jubilee@cyc.ie
website: www.cyc.ie

Index